THE POLITICS
OF
PROGRAM
EVALUATION

SAGE YEARBOOKS IN POLITICS AND PUBLIC POLICY

Sponsored by the **Policy Studies Organization**
Series Editor: **STUART S. NAGEL,** *University of Illinois, Urbana*

INTERNATIONAL ADVISORY BOARD

BOOKS IN THIS SERIES

Volume 15. Sage Yearbooks in Politics and Public Policy

THE POLITICS
OF
PROGRAM
EVALUATION

DENNIS J. PALUMBO
Editor

SAGE PUBLICATIONS
The Publishers of Professional Social Science
Newbury Park   Beverly Hills   London   New Delhi

For information address:

SAGE Publications, Inc.
2111 West Hillcrest Drive
Newbury Park, California 91320

SAGE Publications Inc.
275 South Beverly Drive
Beverly Hills
California 90212

SAGE Publications Ltd.
28 Banner Street
London EC1Y 8QE
England

SAGE PUBLICATIONS India Pvt. Ltd.
M-32 Market
Greater Kailash I
New Delhi 110 048 India

Printed in the United States of America

Library of Congress Cataloging-in-Publication Data

The Politics of program evaluation.

(Sage yearbooks in politics and public policy; v. 15)
Includes bibliographies and index.
Contents: The political context of evaluation.
Introduction: politics and and evaluation / Dennis J.
Palumbo. Where politics and evaluation research meet /
Carol Weiss—[etc.]
   1. Policy sciences.   2. Evaluation research
(Social action programs)   I. *Palumbo, Dennis*
James, 1929—.   II. Series.
H97.P668   1986   361.6′1   86-13899
ISBN 0-8039-2736-3
ISBN 0-8039-2737-1 (pbk.)

CONTENTS

SERIES EDITOR'S INTRODUCTION

This is the fifteenth volume in the Sage Yearbooks in Politics and Public Policy series, published in cooperation with the Policy Studies Organization. It is the first volume in the series that deals explicitly with the role of politics and political science in public policy analysis. Other volumes in the series have dealt with the substance, process, and methodology of public analysis. This volume is thus overdue in a series that is closely associated with political science, although the series draws upon all the social sciences and other fields of knowledge as well.

Politics and political science enter into public policy analysis in various ways. One way is by virtue of the need of policy analysis to be sensitive to the problems of political feasibility. No matter how justifiable a public policy is in terms of its high benefits and low costs, it will not be adopted if it is not politically feasible because of the opposition of key interest groups. An example is the pollution tax, which has been widely advocated by economists as an ideal method for reducing pollution. The tax is levied in proportion to the amount of pollution generated by each business, thus theoretically providing firms with an incentive to reduce their pollution in order to lower their taxes. The money collected from the tax is used to build cleanup facilities such as water filtration plants and to do other things to lessen the adverse effects of pollution. The tax, however, is not politically feasible because it shifts the costs of pollution onto the responsible business firms and municipalities when they would prefer to have the costs covered by the general taxpayer or by those who would otherwise suffer the adverse effects. Marketable pollution rights developed by the Reagan administration are more politically feasible because they emphasize rights rather than penalties and because businesses can buy and sell them. They do, however, stimulate businesses to reduce their pollution levels so that they will not have to buy expensive rights from their competitors.

Another way in which politics and political science enter into public policy analysis is in the area of research utilization. If policy analysts want their research utilized, they should explicitly discuss how their research results can be made more acceptable to both liberals and conservatives. In the field of criminal justice nondiscretionary sentencing has been widely accepted partly because it appeals to liberals, who view it as a means of reducing discrimination. It also appeals to conservatives, who view it as a means for reducing leniency. More frequent pretrial release accompanied by screening, supervision, notification, and speedy trials has been accepted by liberals because the results involve a substantial increase in the percentage of defendants released prior to trial. Conservatives can also endorse such a system, since it tends to result in released defendants having briefer opportunities either to become nonshows or to commit crimes prior to trial, and it lessens the costs incurred by an unnecessarily large pretrial jail population.

Political institutions also play an important part in public policy analysis by providing structures relevant to the formulation of imaginative public policies designed to deal with social problems. Some political institutions provide multiple sources of ideas more than other political institutions. This may be true of (1) federalism, with multiple state or provincial governments to develop new ideas, (2) separation of powers, with executive, legislative, and judicial sources of ideas, (3) multiple political parties, factions, and interest groups, and (4) democracy, with its emphasis on consent by a majority of the public while allowing minority viewpoints to express themselves.

Along related lines are government structures relevant to the successful implementation of public policies. These may include having (1) a merit system for hiring and rewarding government personnel who implement government programs well, (2) an incentives system designed to encourage socially desired behavior on the part of those toward whom the government programs are directed, (3) systems for allowing flexible discretion while preventing abuses of it, and (4) a balance between public and private implementation of societal policies.

Related to policy implementation is the important political concept of administrative feasibility, as contrasted to political feasibility. Here the emphasis is on the extent to which public policies are capable of being successfully administered rather than just successfully adopted. No matter how popular the public policy might be in terms of easily obtaining legislative approval, the policy is a failure if it is not successfully administered, and it is an embarrassment to public policy analysis if that failure could have been anticipated and prevented. An example might be the highly popular program in the early 1970s of facilitating home ownership for the poor through low interest, long-term mortgages, and mortgage supplements. The program was supported by conservatives and liberals for giving poor people middle class values and better housing. The program was, however, a failure at least partly because it was largely administered by the private real estate market, rather than by government employees. The program was racked with scandal because entrepreneurs misinformed the poor about maintenance costs, foreclosed repeatedly on mortgages, and bribed assessors to recover even more than would otherwise be possible. On the other hand, public housing run by government employees has been a failure compared to the rent supplement program, which relies on the private marketplace.

In addition to talking about the role of politics and political institutions in public policy analysis, one should mention the related subject of the role of formal political science. All fields of political science are relevant to public policy analysis. One set of fields deals with government institutions. This includes (1) public law, which is concerned with reforming the judicial process and with substantive issues that relate to civil liberties, criminal justice, and the common law, (2) the legislative process, which is concerned with legislative reform and political feasibility, and (3) public administration, concerned with administrative reform and administrative feasibility.

Another set of political science fields deals with governmental levels. This includes (1) state and local government, which is concerned with policy problems that relate to education, crime, sanitation, and housing, (2) American national government, which is concerned with policy problems that relate to inflation/unemployment, energy, defense, telecommunications, and air pollution, (3) comparative government, which is partly concerned with comparing policy substance and process across a variety of countries, and (4) international relations, which focuses on facilitating international peace, trade, and cultural interaction.

Political science also includes a general concern for methodological and normative theory. On the methodological level, there is concern for how one establishes (1) relations between causal forces and the adoption of alternative public policies, (2) relations between public policies and societal effects, and (3) prescriptive conclusions as to which alternative policies to adopt. On the level of normative theory, political science is concerned with general concepts of (1) societal benefits and societal costs, (2) effectiveness, efficiency, and equity of public policies, (3) public participation, predictability, and procedural due process as public policy goals, and (4) liberal and conservative values.

Political factors like these are discussed in this book. The book is especially concerned with the politics of program evaluation in the context of the policy cycle of agenda setting, formulation, implementation, and termination, with evaluation at all stages. The book is also concerned with political factors in the research process that relate to evaluation and utilization. The chapters operate on various levels of generality, with a balance between broad principles and concrete examples. The chapters are written by leading scholars who bridge the fields of program evaluation and policy analysis, as well as the disciplines of social science and political science. This book, like the other Yearbooks in Politics and Public Policy, is also likely to be a substantial contribution to the literature of public policy studies.

—*Stuart S. Nagel*
Urbana, Illinois

PART I

THE POLITICAL CONTEXT

1

POLITICS AND EVALUATION

DENNIS J. PALUMBO
Arizona State University

Politics and evaluation are related in a number of ways. One is that evaluations, if they are used at all, become a part of the political decision process surrounding the program being evaluated. Evaluations consequently become participants in the political arena along with other political actors (Carol Weiss discusses this in Chapter 2.) A second way that politics and evaluation are related is that evaluations, by taking a position about how well a program is doing, are inherently and unavoidably political. Even though the study itself may be conducted in a nonpartisan and neutral manner, a finding that a program is working supports or can be used to support a program (or vice versa), and this is political. A third, negative, way that politics and evaluations are related is that an evaluation can be undertaken for the express purpose of supporting or building the image of a program. Many people interpret the phrase "political evaluation" using this last sense. It is not the meaning used in this book. We are interested in

Author's Note: *I am indebted to the contributors to this volume for the excellent comments they made on earlier drafts of this chapter. Their comments have greatly improved the chapter. Whatever errors or problems remain are, of course, solely my responsibility.*

the first two kinds of interrelation between politics and evaluation.

The fact that evaluations are inevitably political poses complex problems for evaluation researchers. Analysts and researchers are reluctant to become "poor politicians . . . abandoning the concern for error that made them methodologically rigorous and politically neutral" (Browne and Wildavsky, Chapter 5, this volume). At the same time, lack of attention to the political dimensions of policy analysis "contributes significantly to the use of evaluation as an ideological tool" (Fisher, 1980: 8). Evaluators must focus on and explicitly incorporate political dimensions in their studies in order to carve out a role in the policy decision process (Meltsner, 1972: 859). By concentrating on the technoeconomic aspects of an issue and leaving political considerations and questions of value to politicians, analysts "put themselves at a disadvantage in the contest for attention and influence, and their work loses the impact it might otherwise have" (Greenberger, 1983: 299). Evaluators, therefore, can have a greater impact on policies and programs if they incorporate political factors in their design and dissemination.

Whether or not evaluators should be concerned about politics and the politics of evaluation depends upon what position we take about the role that evaluations should play in policymaking. If evaluations are perceived to have a subordinate, and primarily technical, role (Rossi and Wright, 1985: 331), then there is little need for evaluators to be concerned about politics. They simply feed their technical information into the political process and it will be digested in whatever way the particular situation dictates: sometimes it will be used to bolster a good (or bad) program, sometimes it will be used to further the interests of a particular group or individual, sometimes it will be used to make improvements in programs, and sometimes it will be ignored. On the other hand, if evaluations are to play a major role in policymaking (Lasswell, 1951: 5, 8), then it is essential for evaluators to be concerned about the politics of evaluation; otherwise evaluations will not always be used in the positive sense of helping build or improve public policy, but will often be used in the negative sense of being tools of politicians and those committed to spreading ideological truth. Susan Tolchin in Chapter 9 of this book describes how the Reagan administration's OMB used cost-benefit analyses as a way of justifying the administration's desire to end regulation rather than make politically neutral decisions. Hoos (1972), Kramer (1975), Greenberger et al. (1983), and Katz (1984) also describe the political use of "scientific" research. Policy analysis is inevitably partisan, according to Lindblom and Cohen (1979) and Brewer and DeLeon (1983). Lindblom and Cohen (1979: 62) write:

> Even if the PSI [professional social inquiry] is itself as objective and disinterested as possible, these uses of it are partisan in that they serve the alliances and interests of persons who, playing roles in the interactive process, are necessarily partisan. With perhaps some rare and only imaginable exceptions, all participants in social interaction are partisans, even if not necessarily highly aggressive, irresponsible, narrow-minded, or bigoted. . . . More-over, although many policy analysts understand and accept the commonplace partisan use of their studies, they believe that they themselves speak for the "public interest" and do not understand the inevitably partisan character of their own work.

Martin Greenberger (1983: 256) agrees; he writes, "Analysis is inevitably subordinate to the very political process that provides it with raw material. It is itself a component of that process and can only work its influence through it."

This book shows how politics and evaluations are intertwined and the practical effect this has on evaluation research. The problem is a difficult one and we make no claim to have solved all of it. The chief difficulty is in being able to build political dimensions into the evaluation role without at the same time reducing evaluators to political supplicants or lackeys. It is not our purpose to counsel evaluators to become good or bad politicians. It is our purpose to advise them of the need to understand the political nature of evaluation, why and how politics enters into evaluation, and how they might incorporate politics into evaluations.

DEFINING EVALUATION AND POLITICS

If there are concepts that are more difficult to define than "evaluation" and "politics," I have not seen them. It is not possible to define evaluation or politics in a way that does not reflect a particular methodological or epistemological bias. There isn't one correct definition (just as there isn't one correct or true evaluation, as I shall argue below); there are many different definitions. Lincoln and Guba (1986: 8) cite four different definitions of evaluation. Each can be identified with a particular kind of evaluation. The four are as follows:

(1) Determining the congruence between performance and objectives. (This is the conventional summative or impact evaluation.)
(2) Obtaining information for judging decision alternatives. (This is the approach of operations research.)
(3) Comparing actual effects with demonstrated needs. (This is Scriven's goal-free evaluation.)
(4) Critically describing and appraising an evaluation through connoisseurship. (This is what art critics do.)

In addition there are utilization focused, stakeholder, theory-driven, responsive, and political evaluations. Lincoln and Guba (1986) themselves provide a four-part definition based on crossing the standard formative/summative dimensions with the concepts of merit and worth. For example, they identify a summative merit evaluation that is performed to certify the merit of a program against some set of standards after the program has been developed into its final form. In addition, they argue that evaluating is *not* research, but its own form of disciplined inquiry. According to them, evaluating has different purposes, objectives, audiences, and intended outcomes than research and thus the terms *evaluation* and *research* should not be used together. They write, "Systematic differences in intention or purpose of the activities signal profound differences in expected products, outcomes, and intended audiences. The distinctions drawn dramatize the need to view research, evaluation, and policy analysis as separate, discrete, and mutually exclusive activities. . . .

Correspondence occurs only to the extent that techniques used to arrive at data, and to draw conclusions from them, may occasionally overlap" (1986: 30). However, since academicians often engage in evaluating public policies and programs and claim that what they do is research (albeit "applied" research—see Chalip, 1985), I will use the terms together in this chapter. But I should warn the reader that the chapters that follow use the terms *evaluation, research,* and *analysis* in a variety of ways. Some (i.e., DeLeon) refer to *analysts,* meaning, I believe, academicians who do policy research (including political scientists, economists, psychologists and sociologists) as well as professional analysts who work for private or government agencies. Others (i.e., Patton, Chelimsky) refer to *program evaluators,* meaning, I believe, the professional program evaluator who works for a private firm or in a government agency.

Is evaluation a social science, an applied science, or a policy science? It isn't any of these. It isn't a social science in the traditional sense, although social scientists conduct evaluations. It isn't an applied science unless we can specify which science is being applied. And it isn't a policy science, at least not in the sense that Harold Lasswell (1951: 7) meant when he wrote:

> The policy approach is not to be confounded with the superficial ideal that social scientists ought to desert science and engage full time in practical politics. Nor should it be confused with the suggestion that social scientists ought to spend most of their time advising policymakers on immediate questions.

The policy sciences, Lasswell believed, ought to be directed toward the basic conflicts in our civilization, toward fundamental problems such as human interaction, economic cycles, and discrimination. Evaluation research obviously is somewhat different than this.

Rather than define evaluation, it is more useful to describe the several different types of evaluators as a way of distinguishing whom we are addressing in this book. There are almost as many different types of evaluators as there are definitions of evaluation.

One of the most rapidly increasing kinds are the "think tanks," such as the Brookings Institution, the American Enterprise Institute, and the Heritage Foundation. Conservatively oriented think tanks were multiplying at a more rapid rate in the 1980s than liberal think tanks. These evaluators of public policies and programs use a blend of political advocacy and public relations to promote their particular political persuasion. The mass media have evaluators of a second type, including reporters, television commentators, and syndicated columnists. Their evaluations, sometimes called "investigative reporting," are supposed to be more politically neutral than those of the think tanks. Politicians and candidates for office are a third type of evaluator. They constantly engage in evaluation, and their evaluations are strictly partisan and usually self-interested. University faculty, primarily in the social and behavioral sciences, are the fourth category of evaluator. They engage in evaluation in several ways. They not only train professional evaluators and analysts, but engage in evaluations themselves. The professional analysts or evaluators trained in universities may work in private research organizations such as Abt Associates or the Rand Corporation, or for governmental agencies such as the U.S. General Accounting Office, Congressional Research Office, or one of the many federal, state, or local government agencies. The goals of the professional evaluators and analysts working in governmental agencies or private firms are somewhat different from those of the academicians who trained them, so they are put into a fifth, separate category.

This book is meant primarily for the university-based evaluators and the professional evaluators they train who work in private research agencies or for government. Think-tank evaluators such as members of the Heritage Foundation, politicians who engage in highly political evaluations, and members of the news media will not get as much from the book as the others, although they also may find something of value in it.

Defining the term *politics* is also fraught with immense pitfalls. Common sense definitions of politics tend to be negative, portraying it as something that cigar-smoking males do behind

closed doors. The negative and narrow definition of politics often
spills over into the evaluation literature. For example, Abramson
and Banchick (1979) postulate that:

> A purely political evaluation is one which is undertaken for the
> sole purpose of justifying a previously arrived at position by
> government, administration, or program personnel, whereas the
> purely programmatic evaluation is undertaken solely for the
> purpose of determining appropriate program modifications.

Banner et al. (1975: 4) also feel that the effect of politics is
negative, since the politics of evaluation "may be viewed as a
phenomenon of major power and influence centers that manipulate 'objective' research to their own advantage." Frank Fisher
(1980: 7) notes that "all too often in the policy literature, politics
has been described in negative terms such as 'pressures and
expedient adjustments,' or 'haphazard acts—unresponsive to a
planned analysis of the needs of efficient decision design.'"

But the term *politics* has positive as well as negative connota-
tions. Carol Weiss in Chapter 2 of this book discusses three ways
in which politics and evaluation are related, and none of the three
is negative. According to Weiss,

(1) The programs being evaluated are political in that they have
    legislative sponsors and supporters, administrative careers
    attached to them, and the support of program staff, clients, and
    interest groups.
(2) Evaluation reports are fed into this political arena and become a
    part of the political decision process.
(3) Evaluation reports themselves unavoidably take a political
    position even if they claim to be objective.

Weiss places evaluation in a broad context, and I follow this
lead in this chapter and the rest of the book. *Politics* in this book
means more than narrow partisan politics among political
parties; it refers as well to the interactions of various actors within
and among bureaucracies, clients, interest groups, private organizations and legislatures as they relate to each other from

different positions of power, influence, and authority (Banner et al., 1975: 2).

Certain aspects of this definition should be stressed. One is that it refers to how administrators of programs interact with the people in their agency, with other agencies (both public and private) and with the clients and people affected by their program. If there is a single theme to this book it is that the politics of evaluation requires evaluators of any policy or program to recognize the existence of multiple decision makers and interests and incorporate them into the evaluation. In this regard, Cook (1985: 44) writes: "Indeed, in a democracy with pretensions to pluralism, formal policymakers should probably not be the only group whose information needs, and hence whose political interests, evaluators should meet. Every policy decision has the potential to impact on multiple stakeholder groups, and discussions with these groups often teach us that they want to learn different things." Of course, think tanks such as the Heritage Foundation do not worry about the needs of all stakeholders, because their goal is to promote one position rather than to satisfy the information needs of all groups. Professional evaluators whom we are addressing in this book cannot afford to do this. They will lose their credibility if they are openly partisan. I agree with the position of Carley (1980: 6-7), who writes:

> One could easily argue that most public sector decision-making is in the end the result of a political bargaining process. This being the case, rational analysis carried on in an ignorance of political reality may well end up so divorced from social reality as to be of little use to anyone. By the same token, however, vague and unsystematic "political" research *loaded with implicit causality and value judgments, and not subject to exposure or dissection*, is of no great value to policy making either. A *balanced perspective* helps policy makers and researchers select criteria for judging the relevance of analysis to a particular policy problem. It *does this by encouraging examination of the divergence between the problem as defined by the policy maker and as defined by the analysts, and by arguing that no analysis is understood until it is clear what, and whose, value judgments are part of the analysis—value judgments*

which must be considered an integral part of every analysis
[emphasis added].

The political dilemma facing evaluators is to steer a course between recognizing the political reality of evaluation and retaining the symbolism of neutrality. In the rest of this chapter I will discuss the various dimensions of this dilemma. Although I will try to present a balanced perspective, in some instances I will state the case for political evaluation a little strongly to boldly show what the position logically implies. The things I will say do not apply to and will not be eagerly accepted by all the types of evaluators mentioned above. Some evaluators—that is, professional evaluators working in profit-making research firms or in government agencies—may be more comfortable being technicians rather than agents of change, and all evaluators must assume the role of technician at least some of the time. I shall argue below that taking a stance as technician fills an important need for evaluators and thus cannot be avoided entirely, although it should be buttressed with nontechnical evaluation components. Public programs have political as well as substantive goals. Programs such as day care, head start, or compensatory education are meant to serve political ends as well as achieve specific programmatic objectives. The political ends involve more than serving interests or generating votes but include the extent to which the program promotes a more equitable and democratic society. It is the process by which these political ends are served that is the key to understanding the relationship between politics and evaluation. By narrowly focusing on program goals, evaluation has been naive about the political dynamics of programs. The neglect of this dimension makes it difficult to link the political dynamics of programs to the larger ideological, economic, and political context. In the course of this chapter I will discuss the politics of evaluation as it emanates from the conflicting imperatives of evaluators and administrators, what it means for methodological "purity," how it is related to goal setting in organizations, and how to incorporate politics into evaluations. The second chapter in this book focuses upon the general political context of evaluation. Part II of the book covers the politics of evaluation at different points in the policy cycle—design, implementation, and termination—beginning with Chelimsky's chapter on how to link program evaluation to user needs at these points in the policy cycle; and Part III of the book deals with the relationship between evaluation politics and research methods.

THE CONFLICTING IMPERATIVES
OF EVALUATORS AND ADMINISTRATORS

In a provocative article about the reemergence of institutional analysis in political science research, March and Olsen (1984: 734) state: "Most of the major actors in modern economic and political systems are formal organizations, and the institutions of law and bureaucracy occupy a dominant role in contemporary life." Each formal organization, such as a legislature, administrative agency, or university, has a different perspective about what is appropriate behavior and this is transmitted to the people who work in these organizations: "What is appropriate for a particular person in a particular situation is defined by the political and social system and transmitted through socialization" (1984: 741).

Appropriate behavior for evaluation researchers is quite different from what is appropriate for administrators, and this difference sets the stage for an important feature of the politics of evaluation research.[1] Rein (1983: 116) talks about the three conflicting imperatives of implementation (what is legally required, what is politically feasible, and what is administratively practical). Evaluators and administrators also operate by imperatives that often are in conflict. Evaluators are trapped by several opposing (but not irreconcilable) imperatives. One is to help administrators understand and improve their programs, another is to uncover the "facts" about the program even if they are negative, and a third is to increase knowledge about evaluation research and program administration. Balancing these imperatives is not easy. Often evaluators allow the second and third imperatives to predominate because there is more prestige and recognition in doing so. Unfortunately, the more they emphasize creating or adding to knowledge (i.e., reaching generalizations applicable to a wide number of circumstances), or "exposing" poorly run programs, the less helpful they are to administrators. Meltsner and Bellavita (1983: 18) succinctly describe the problem as follows:

> When managers say they need demographic and impact data, they mean specific information about particular populations in certain situations. Their information needs are grounded in idiosyncratic contexts that vary widely. Researchers and social scientists, who are interested in generalizations and causation, are not likely to be the ones to meet this need. It is a mistake to expect routine organizational informational needs to be a by-product of nonroutine researcher interests and tasks.

Hence, it is essential to balance the dual roles of developing new knowledge and solving practical problems. If one or the other dominates, the results will not be good for evaluation research nor for practitioners. One way out of this dilemma is suggested by Lincoln and Guba (1986), who say we should distinguish evaluation from research, since they each have different objectives, intended outcomes, and audiences; since developing new knowledge is *not* an objective of evaluation, the conflict disappears. But the conflict between helping the administrator and presenting the "facts" still remains. The facts, when made public, may set back the program and the policy under which it operates, particularly if there are some negative findings in the evaluation (as there often are).

Program opponents can use such negative findings to help defeat or cut back a program. R. Heiss, who directed the Denver Urban Observatory (one of a group of federally sponsored agencies in major cities aimed at analyzing and finding solutions for urban problems), writes (1974: 40): "The rational methodology of evaluation poses serious threats for the local governmental policy maker . . . Officeholders want to reduce conflict to keep things calm before elections while opponents need cannon fodder to gain headlines. An evaluation report produces just that kind of cannon fodder that political opponents can use." In my own experience evaluating community corrections programs, I was told by a state director of corrections, "I don't care how good your evaluation may be, in the current hostile political climate for community corrections, *any* evaluation would be harmful." Heiss describes how the opponent of the mayor of Denver used evaluations of programs conducted with the mayor's support in a successful campaign to unseat the major. He also quotes Governor Walker of Illinois as saying in a speech: "Very rarely does one see anything in the medium about program evaluation unless it has to do with a scandal" (1974: 40).

The imperatives under which administrators operate are quite different from those of researchers. The typical administrators are "trapped" by two opposing (but not irreconcilable) imperatives: on the one hand they are committed to the efficacy of a specific reform or program, yet they must also be program advocates and promoters. At the same time, the political structure in which they function will not allow even the slightest risk of failure. "For the administrator, avoiding political embarrassment rather than accomplishing program goals is the first priority" (Faux, 1971: 278). Because evaluations *may* turn up information that can embarrass an administrator, it is difficult to find an aggressive, effective administrator who puts a high priority on evaluation (Banner et al., 1975: 123). Administrators are not inclined to want their program evaluated by an outside third party because they have little to gain and much to lose from them. At the same time, they must use information because it is the symbol of good administration. Administrators will be willing to undergo an evaluation if they believe it will help them politically. But if evaluations cannot be turned to the advantage of program managers, then it is in their interests to suppress or simply ignore them. An example is the conflict between the Opportunity Funding Corporation (OFC), a Nixon administration program to help urban ghettos, and the Office of Economic Opportunity (OEO). The OFC was a nonprofit program funded by the OEO that was designed to test the ability of a variety of financial incentives such as loan guarantees and interest subsidies to attract private capital into central city ghettos. OEO wanted to evaluate the program, but OFC officials were opposed to having OEO do the evaluation. The OFC officials were convinced their approach would work if given a chance and suspicious that OEO was trying to eliminate the program. The OEO was ideologically opposed to OFC because the latter was a Nixon-supported approach that favored black capitalism as the best solution to the economic problems of the ghetto. OEO officials did not agree with this approach. Thus the OFC officials felt the evaluation was bound to be negative no matter how "scientific" it might be.

When evaluators speak truth to power, they should be aware (but often are not) that to an administrator information is an instrument of power. In a chapter about the importance of communicating effectively about performance, Bellavita (1986: 239) writes:

> The central implication of these research findings is that communi-
> cation in public policy is a political act that can influence the
> distribution of power and resources in society. The person sending
> a message is making a claim about what is real concerning a policy
> issue. When evaluators argue that a nutrition program reduces the
> number of low weight births . . . they are making an implicit claim
> that future policy actions should be influenced by this information.
> They are entering the political debate.

Lincoln and Guba (1986) agree:

> It may be taken as axiomatic that evaluations equitably carried
> out will inevitably upset the prevailing balance of power. Evalua-
> tion produces information and information is power.

Internal bureaucratic power as well as external power is involved. Numerous power struggles take place in bureaucracies. One is the struggle of managers to augment control over those lower down in the organization. Evaluations are used as a way of accomplishing this. In an empirical analysis of evaluation strategies in federal and local agencies, Steven Maynard-Moody

(1983: 384) found that of the many interest groups with a stake in program evaluation, "only federal agencies and top program management significantly influenced the design and interpretation of the evaluations. This finding supports the argument that evaluation program effectiveness is an aspect of the formal authority relationships in and surrounding social programs." Another way that administrators use analysis in power struggles is to delay or overturn a policy they oppose. Jenkins-Smith and Weimer (1985) describe how the Office of Management and Budget used analysis to delay for several years the implementation of the Strategic Petroleum Reserve. A third way is to make their boss look good. Michael Malbin (1980) describes how congressional staffers ignore or even suppress information that runs counter to arguments they wish to advance. Finally, information or evaluations will be used to legitimize a position already taken. James Katz (1984: 254) discusses how in emotional debates in the energy area, lines are drawn and no amount of analysis will change them except as support for positions already taken. The technical answer or truth—if it can be identified—does not matter.

How and why organizations use evaluations is part of how they use information in general. Information is a representation of social virtue to an administrator, for it enhances the perception that the administrator is competent and inspires confidence. Feldman and March (1981: 77) write: "There are no values closer to the core of Western ideology than these ideas of intelligent choice, and there is no institution prototypically committed to the systematic application of information to decisions than the modern bureaucratic organization." Because information has symbolic value, administrators will gather more information than they need; doing so symbolizes that the decision process is legitimate and the organization is well managed.

This information is used primarily in a symbolic fashion, and so are evaluations. If an evaluation is favorable, it will be used to promote an image of program success. If it is not favorable, it is much less likely to be used. There are numerous examples of this. One is an evaluation of the implementation of community corrections in three states by Palumbo et al. (1985). In 1985 the

Connecticut Department of Corrections published a small brochure that described an evaluation (done by an outside consultant)
of the impact of its transitional program for offenders being
released from prison. The brochure was entitled *Impact Positive!
An Evaluation of Community Services in Connecticut Corrections* (Connecticut Department of Corrections, no date). The
brochure describes the positive findings of the evaluation in
proud terms. A different evaluation of the implementation of the
program done by Palumbo et al. (1985) was also positive, but
found that the program was very centralized. Since this finding
might be construed as a criticism of the program, the director said
he would not disseminate this evaluation as widely as the previous
one unless this point was changed. He even argued that the
finding was incorrect. The questionnaire item related to centraliza-
tion asked how much access the respondent felt he or she had to
decisionmaking in the program. 75% of the 436 respondents said
"little or none," 19% said "a moderate amount," and only 7% said
"a great deal or a fairly large amount" (Palumbo et al., 1985: 14).
This latter was much lower than the percentage of respondents
who felt they had a great deal or fairly large amount of access in
two other states. The program director asked that this statement
be corrected, writing on the report:

> Connecticut is *not* overly centralized. Damn near every executive
> director (street-level implementors) will tell you so. Volunteers
> and line staffers won't though, but we don't care. Almost every
> executive will tell you they have excellent access to decision-
> making. Line staff and volunteers no, but that's ok.

He argued that for this question the appropriate sample was
executive directors of community agencies, not everyone, since
not everyone should have access to decisionmaking. In spite of
the fact that the evidence (i.e., 327 respondents out of 436)
indicated the department had a centralized decisionmaking
process, the administrator still believed the opposite, and wanted
this part of the evaluation changed. It was not a question of what
the correct "facts" were, but which "facts" to use.

Numerous other similar examples can be cited. Pauline

Ginsberg (1984: 69) writes that although mental health professionals and program evaluators seek objectivity through formal assessment instruments, more often than not these instruments are used to justify a decision that already has been made. The same conclusion was reached by Jay Belski (1985: 258) in regard to research about day care: "Scientific findings, it would seem, are of consequence when a prevailing ideology needs fuel for its arguments." And in the area of energy policy, James Katz (1984: 269) describes how various federal agencies such as the Congressional Budget Office and the General Accounting Office use analysis in a political manner. He argues, "In practice, it is exceedingly difficult to distinguish between policy-relevant analysis of information and policy advocacy, largely because choices about data interpretation are based on normative criteria."

In summary, the competing imperatives under which evaluators and administrators operate set the stage for evaluation politics. At one and the same time, they place evaluators and administrators in a hostile and symbiotic relationship. The relationship is hostile because academicians and practitioners have negative attitudes about each other. Crain and Carsrud (1985, p. 229) describe the conflict in the area of education as follows: "Not only do the academics look down their noses at school practitioners, but some practitioners consider academics to be time wasters at best and dangerous at worst." The relationship is symbiotic because academics need access to data that they cannot obtain without the help of practitioners, while practitioners need the credentials and legitimization that academicians can provide. Evaluators may want to be neutral and objective, but their results will be used politically, no matter how scientific they try to be. Moreover, as I shall now argue, they should not try to be neutral and objective for that is a misreading of the nature of science and research.

POLITICS AND EVALUATION METHODOLOGY

Rational values and scientific methods are important values for evaluation researchers as well as for administrators. Technical expertise in the form of sophisticated methods gives evaluation researchers a role to play in policymaking they would not likely have otherwise. It is crucial for evaluators to provide technical expertise to program managers because doing so legitimizes the evaluator's role in the policymaking process at the same time that it provides information that administrators need. If evaluators did not have technical expertise, they would not have a role in policymaking greater than that of ordinary citizens.

However, there is considerable misunderstanding about what technical expertise and science imply for evaluation methods. Does being scientific mean being objective? Does being scientific mean that the results are definitive and true? The answer to both questions is *no*. Donald Campbell writes that, in fact, scientists are passionate believers in their theories and carry this into their research. Campbell (1984: 35) says:

> The objectivity of science does not come from turning over the running experiments to people who could not care less about the outcome, nor from having a separate staff to read the meters. It comes from a social process that can be called competitive cross-validation, and from the fact that there are many independent decision makers who are capable of rerunning an experiment at least in a theoretically essential form. If evaluation researchers present their findings as if they were definitive achievements and deserving to override ordinary wisdom when they disagree, then they can be socially destructive. We can be engaged in a political misuse of the authority of science.

Similarly, Chalip (1985) writes, "Objective knowledge is consequent on dispute and triangulation by a many-valued community of fallible social scientists . . . not from consensual value neutralism." Also, Nelkin (1980) found that the introduction of expertise and scientific knowledge reduces public choice and threatens democratic values. A narrow focus on issues raised by analysts can induce bitter controversies and evoke hostilities (Rainwater and Yancey, 1967; Beals, 1969).

A second misreading of science is the belief that science has nothing to say about values. This view has been soundly rejected in recent years. Campbell (1984: 27) writes: "Today the tide has completely turned among the theorists of science in philosophy, sociology, and elsewhere. Logical positivism is almost universally rejected." The prevailing view today is that science is not value free: the values of researchers are part and parcel of their research. Researchers are both an "eye" that observes and an "I" that is involved in what is being observed. The two cannot be separated. Ingram and Scaff (Chapter 4) show that disciplinary paradigms are not neutral—they support particular values and ideologies. For example, public choice theory is based on the assumption of individualistic rationality that prefers market solutions over planned ones; cost-benefit analysis elevates efficiency as the sole value; and summative evaluations are biased in favor of rationalistic, top-down administrative structures.

These discoveries have left methodology somewhat in disarray. There is no clear-cut theoretical or philosophical foundation underlying current policy analysis (Kelly, 1986). What seems to be developing in place of logical positivism is the notion of multiple realities (Cook, 1985). According to this position, it is mistaken to say there is a single, correct description of objects in the external world (including social programs). We create reality just as we create institutions and agencies (Miller, 1984). Although the "external" world is complex and cannot exhaustively be described (or created at will), there are correct and incorrect descriptions. According to Scriven (1984) there is a correct but not a unique description of external reality. To the value-neutral researcher, seeing is believing, but to the value-committed researcher, believing is seeing (Rein, 1983). The poet Archibald MacLeish has said that we have lost or are losing our human ability to *feel* facts. Knowledge without feeling can lead only to public irresponsibility and indifference. Of course, evaluation researchers should not be so committed that they produce or create whatever data they need to support their own or the program administrator's preconceived values. This would constitute political evaluation in its most negative sense. But at the same time, values in general and political values in particular are an inescapable component of research. Barry and Rae (1975: 340) reflect this fact in their definition of evaluation: "Evaluating is assigning value to things—roughly speaking, determining whether they are good or bad. We shall take political evaluation to consist in the first instance in assigning value to alternative policies, laws, or general decisions binding on a collectivity."

What does "assigning value to alternative policies" entail? It involves a judgment about the goals themselves rather than just about the means of achieving them. For example, assume the program being evaluated is a community corrections program that has the following four goals: (1) committing nonviolent felony offenders to state prison for shorter terms, (2) cutting the costs of corrections, (3) rehabilitating offenders, and (4) decentralizing corrections decisionmaking to the community level. Evaluating the program in a political sense requires determining not only whether these goals are being achieved but also whether the goals themselves are good or bad. In other words, is a policy of reducing the incarceration of nonviolent felony offenders better than a policy of incarcerating the same offenders for longer terms?

I cannot go into the details of whether this goal is good or bad; the point is that a good evaluation cannot avoid this question. It is not sufficient simply to determine whether the goals are being met, for several reasons. One is that not everyone will agree that these are the main goals of community corrections or what priority should be given to each. Conservatives may emphasize one goal (for example, cutting costs) and liberals another (for example, rehabilitation). Second, focusing on efficiency criteria alone ignores the important questions underlying the program. As Fisher (1980: 23) writes, "Applicable only to means, the criterion of efficiency is inappropriate for dealing with the most important questions that plague decision makers—questions concerning which goals or ends to pursue." Third, an emphasis on efficiency has consequences for the policy that often go unnoticed by the evaluation researcher. For example, it is possible, even likely, that private, profit-making firms can build and operate prisons more efficiently than public agencies. But this may well have the consequence of supporting and furthering retribution policy in corrections and setting back rehabilitation even further than it already has been (Palumbo, 1985). An evaluation of prisons that focuses only on efficiency would miss these policy consequences. Unexamined technicalism in evaluation research is worse than no evaluation at all, because it fails to address the crucial issues involved in policymaking. Most social crises involve more than matters of inefficient programs; they involve basic value conflicts (Fisher, 1980: xiv). However difficult it is for evaluation researchers to accept, the fact is that there isn't a "true" or "scientifically correct" answer to value questions. Consider the abortion controversy. This question will never be "settled"; there always will be changes and shifts in abortion policy as political forces battle and the power of various groups waxes and wanes. Although most other policy issues are not as emotionally powerful as abortion policy, the same kind of political process operates in them as well. Likewise, there is no single, true set of facts; the facts one looks for are determined by the epistemological and political values that guide the inquiry.

The question of how evaluators can address the basic value conflicts in public policy is not an easy one to answer. Logical positivism does not help, because it argues that science has nothing to say about values. Some evaluators still accept this position. Some researchers would go as far as to argue that the emotionally charged and difficult issues underlying policies and programs cannot be resolved by analysis (Katz, 1984: 234). Banfield has called policy analysis "metaphysical madness." After examining a number of studies of the energy crisis during the 1970s, Martin Greenberger (1983: 271) concluded: "Facts *alone* cannot resolve a controversy rooted in subjective values and ideological positions. Indeed facts can exacerbate the controversy." Rossi and Wright (1985: 330), after examining gun control legislation, write, "Very often . . . 'facts' are off on the periphery of a debate whose main themes center on value issues. The opponents and advocates of gun control are often debating world views, ideologies, and ways of life. On these usually far more important points, social science at its best is mute." Rita Kelly (Chapter 10) addresses this question and proposes an approach for solving at least part of the problem. Guba and Lincoln (1981;

Lincoln and Guba, 1985, 1986) have proposed naturalistic methods as a way of solving the value conflict problem. In Chapter 7 of this book they discuss full collaboration with all program stakeholders (agents, beneficiaries, and victims) as a way of resolving the inherent value conflicts. By *full collaboration* they mean that "stakeholding audiences should be given the opportunity to provide inputs at *every stage* of the evaluation: the charge, the goal, the design, the data collection and analysis methods, and the interpretation." Naturalistic methods are a much better approach to solving the problem of value conflicts because they address the question and show how evaluators can speak to value conflicts; logical positivism simply abrogates responsibility in this area by saying that science has nothing to contribute to value conflicts. The latter position removes evaluation from playing a role in the most important realm of policymaking—that is, in the politics of program formulation and implementation.

In summary, value-neutral research is not possible nor desirable. Values inevitably are a part of any evaluation. This means that evaluations will not result in a "correct" finding; they will take a political position about the desirability of various goals, whether *directly,* by judging that the goals are worthwhile, or *indirectly,* by concluding that the goals are being achieved efficiently. Evaluation, therefore, becomes a part of the goal-setting process in organizations (i.e., legislatures, administrative agencies, nonprofit private groups, profit-making organizations), a process that is unquestionably political.

ORGANIZATIONAL GOALS AND EVALUATION

Organizations are more than mere instruments for achieving goals; they are dynamic social systems consisting of diverse groups that have competing interests and unequal shares of power. Politics are as much a part of every organization's daily life as they are of the wider society in which the organizations are located. And politics are involved in determining which goals are to be given priority by the organization. Finding that objectives are or are not being met has political consequences, because such a finding may give support to the "ins" in an agency and keep them in power.

Organizational goals are not imposed on the organization from the outside (although outside forces help shape organizational goals). Nor can goals be objectively identified by researchers searching legal documents or formal organizational statements. Such a view totally ignores the reality of organizational processes and the existence of informal groups within as well as outside the organization. In Allison's (1971) bureaucratic politics model, goals are *resultants* rather than choices (see also Brewer and deLeon, 1983). They *emerge* from games among players who perceive quite different faces of an issue and who differ markedly in the actions they prefer (Bardach, 1977). Thus where you stand on any given issue depends upon what position you occupy in an organization and what information you have. Upper-level administrators will have a quite different view of what goals should be given priority than will street-level bureaucrats (Palumbo et al., 1985). This, of course, has important repercussions on evaluation since it affects those who should participate in designing and carrying out the evaluation. Michael Patton deals with this issue in Chapter 4.

Organizational goals are the desired end-state of an organization, specifying what values are to be attained by selected activities of the organization (Dornbush and Scott, 1975: 68-69). But who determines what the goals of an organization will be? An organization is not a collective actor that in some metaphysical manner arrives at a definition of its goals and then mobilizes energies to attain them. Nor are goals the sum total of the goals of its individual members. Either extreme is an incorrect view of goal setting in an organization. The determination of goals is a political exercise.

Not all members of an organization participate equally in the goal-setting process, which often results in conflict. "When the interests of these various individuals and groups [in an organization] diverge," Cyert and March (1963: 70) write, "coalitions are formed and bargains struck the resulting agreements defining the desired end states." Goals are primarily inspirational devices for an agency (Scriven, 1984: 57), they also reflect who wields power in an organization.

There are at least four interests involved in setting the goals of an organization: the overseers, the administrators, program advocates, and clients (Rein, 1983: 115; Patton, 1978). (These are not necessarily the ones who *should* be involved.) Each of these interests also contain subgroups. Administrators can be divided into upper- and street-level groups, as well as into specific divisions or bureaus. An example is the large number of different groups that are involved in setting goals in a community corrections program. They include legislators, judges, prosecutors, sheriffs, guards, probation officers, psychologists, counselors, mental health professionals, central office staff, and program directors. Each will see the program differently and push for different goals. Legislators in the role of overseers will emphasize costs; they want to see that their money is being spent for what was intended. Judges, prosecutors, and sheriffs emphasize safety and security; they want to be sure that offenders, while in the program, do not commit serious crimes that may receive wide publicity. Probation officers also have an interest in public safety goals but, along with counselors, they also stress rehabilitation and treatment. Local county commissions emphasize the opportunity for local control and the opportunity to get state money. Program directors want goals that may be measurable and achievable, such as reducing the number of individuals being incarcerated in state prisons. This latter also helps fulfill the reform goals of not putting nonviolent felony offenders in prison. Similarly, Cook (1985: 36) describes the various groups involved in the health system. They included "not only federal agencies and congressional committees and their staffs, but also hospital administrators and the professional associations representing them; physicians and nurses and the associations representing them; insurance companies; hospital patients; and health policy researchers. These groups have different interests concerning health matters and different information needs about particular health problems."

The politics involved pertain not only to the groups that support a particular set of goals, but also to bureaucratic fighting among administrative agencies. Consider, as an example, arms-control policymaking. Bureaucratic infighting between the State and Defense Departments and the National Security Council has been common. Under the Reagan administration, the infighting is over the extent to which administrators support the president's hard-line stand toward the Soviets. Those in the Special Arms Control Policy Group who do not support the Strategic Defense Initiative (SDI) goals are considered outcasts. Walter Pincus (1985: 6) writes: "Given the sanctity of SDI, it may be understandable that one senior Defense Department official likens himself and his Pentagon colleagues to 'Horatius at the bridge,' battling others who want to 'sell out' Reagan's dream." One's position on goals is thus an important aspect of bureaucratic politics.

Politics do not stop when implementation begins; goals are redefined during implementation largely as a result of political forces. In the bottom-up view of implementation it is those at the bottom—the street-level bureaucrats—who are the principal policymakers, because they have more knowledge of what works and the discretion to make decisions about how to implement a program (Lipsky, 1980; Elmore, 1982). This is not to say that they always make good policy any more than those at the top do. Nor is it correct to say that the street-level bureaucrats are the sole influence on policy. The main point is that evaluators need to understand and take cognizance of the reality of implementation politics.

Finally, the clients, audience, and "victims" (see Guba and Lincoln, Chapter 7) of a program should be but usually are not a part of the goal setting process. It is difficult but not impossible to get the elderly in nursing homes, the mentally ill in hospitals, medical patients, the poor on welfare, students, or offenders to participate in defining program goals. The problem is that in some instances these groups are not considered to have a legitimate role to play in the program. They are the ones the program is supposed to do something *to* or *for*, but they are not supposed to have a role to play in evaluating or influencing the program. Should nonviolent felony offenders be involved in determining if incarceration in prison should be used instead of community correction alternatives? Should the poor receiving welfare help decide if workfare is a good approach to the welfare problem? How they perceive the program and what they believe are its benefits/drawbacks, indeed would be useful in an evaluation. Even program opponents should be involved, because they very likely will have important political views that should be considered.

Of course, policymaking isn't strictly and only political. Administrators are concerned about achieving goals, and they would like to do this efficiently. Thus I am not arguing that goals are infinitely elastic and changeable nor that efficiency is not a concern of program administrators (top or street level). The message is rather straightforward and clear: Public agencies try to achieve policy goals as efficiently as they can, and politics is a part of this. Goals are subjected to a trial by fire during implementation that eliminates those that are politically objectionable and practically unachievable. Of course, mistakes are made and programs fail either because they are ill-conceived or poorly implemented (Linder and Peters, forthcoming). Evaluation, political or otherwise, needs to point out these failures. So I am not saying that political evaluation should always come up with positive results. Loyalty and support are key virtues in political influence. But evaluators are not political in the sense of being part of a particular political regime. They are political in the sense that their evaluations become part of the political process, as Carol Weiss so aptly points out in Chapter 2 of this book. In this political role (which is but one of their several roles), they have a special function. This function is to focus on and make all participants aware of the broader public interest involved in public policies and programs. How they might do this is the topic of the last section of this introduction.

INCORPORATING POLITICS IN EVALUATIONS

Most evaluation researchers who are trained to be competent methodologists may feel uncomfortable in a political role. But policy evaluation does not require that evaluation researchers be politicians; it requires only that they understand and incorporate political dimensions into their research. It is the practitioner, not the evaluator, who is responsible for solving, or at least ameliorating, social problems. It is the practitioner who is a part of the politics of program formulation and implementation. The role of the evaluator is to assist the practitioner by providing valid, useful, and relevant information, which, of course, means political data as well as summative and formative. "Serving political objectives is a legitimate and natural use for analysis in a democratic society" (Greenberger, 1983: 309). Crain and Carsrud (1985: 229) make the same point very crisply: "The policymaker has the responsibility for taking value positions and certainly cannot surrender that to the scientist. Social scientists interested in influencing social policy must compromise their own values. Scientists may resent having to do so, but the alternative is to retreat into a position of morally superior impotence."

The first and most important task in political evaluation is to talk with all relevant stakeholders (i.e., administrators, target groups, clients, legislators, interest groups and community representatives), to determine what they believe are the aims of the program. What are the political consequences of following one as opposed to another set of goals is a standard question that practitioners will be interested in; who will support and who oppose particular goals can be determined through discussion with all of the stakeholders. By doing this, an evaluator can help determine how well the *political goals* of a program are being met. Since the stakeholders will have interests they want to promote, an evaluation will be relevant to the extent that it addresses and incorporates these interests in its design and analysis. Greenberger (1983: 20) describes what he calls "public analysis" in these terms: "We would have public analysis delineate the points of view of each of the parties in dispute, define the problem according to these points of view, collect technical facts bearing on this problem, explore the attributes of those most affected by it, and then integrate the definitions, technical facts, and attitudes into alternatives for decision makers to consider. Analysts would thereby be supplying the political dimensions now missing in much policy analysis."

The evaluator is similar to a political adviser insofar as the evaluation includes information about how much support a program has and who supports and opposes it. Administrators will know some of this, but providing systematic information will be helpful. Thus survey or interview questions about how much commitment and support various groups have for a program should be a part of almost all evaluations. But such political data are not the only political data that would be helpful to administrators. Information about the reasons for opposing a program and strategies for more effectively communicating program information to all groups also should be included (Bellavita, 1986). In doing this, the evaluator cannot avoid taking sides. Lincoln and Guba (1986) write: "Good evaluations . . . cannot end with a simple report of conclusions and recommendations but in the delineation of value judgment options that must be further explored before any action alternative can be specified. Thus the evaluator becomes less technician than change agent; less objective scientist than active collaborator." Of course, evaluators should not simply be advocates or collaborators of the program *managers* only, but of the program and policy itself, and of the clients and consumers of the program (Scriven, 1984). For example, evaluators may be the only way that the poor, students, offenders, welfare recipients, or mentally ill can influence policy. These "stakeholders" often are not included in the formulation and implementation of an evaluation. It is in this way that evaluators can represent the public interest rather than specific power holder interests. The evaluator thus is an advocate for what a fair and equitable program would accomplish in solving the social problem at which it is addressed.

Another way that evaluators can incorporate politics into their work is by recognizing the different kinds of information needs of different points in the policy cycle (Chelimsky, Chapter 3, this volume). Understanding the dynamics of the policy cycle can improve an evaluator's knowledge of the political process into which the evaluation is fed. The policy cycle consists of agenda setting (or getting a problem onto the public policy agenda), problem definition, policy design, program implementation, policy or program impact, and termination. Figure 1.1 displays

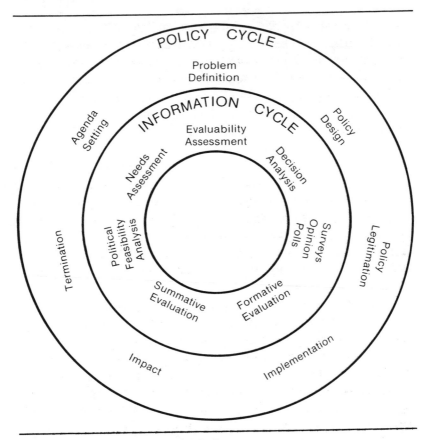

Figure 1.1 Evaluation and the Policy Cycle

these stages in the policy cycle and the different types of analyses that are needed at each stage.

At the *agenda setting* stage the principal question is whether or not the social problem should become a concern of the government (or of the organization). Some political scientists (Cobb and Elder, 1983) believe that this is the most important stage in policymaking, for if a matter is kept off the agenda, nothing will be done about it, and what is *not* done may well be more important than what *is* done. Community and organizational power brokers are the key to deciding what will become part of the agenda. Information for agenda setting can be gotten through *needs assessment.*From a purely rational perspective, a needs assessment would produce information "from the communities regarding their diffuse and interrelated needs"(Neuber, 1980: 15). Needs assessment is a way of enhancing two-way communication between the community and service providers.

The next step in the policy cycle is *defining the problem*. This is a key step, since the way the problem is defined greatly influences the design and implementation of a program. As initially posed, a problem usually is vaguely or ambiguously stated. The analyst cannot redefine a problem by him or herself, but must include the views of all stakeholders. *Evaluability assessment* is one method of doing this. As originally developed, evaluability assessment was a way to document and clarify program intent from the point of view of key actors in and around the program; "It explores program reality in order to clarify the plausibility of program objectives and the feasibility of performance measurement" (Wholey, 1983: 36).

Policy design, the next stage in the cycle, involves identifying alternative means of achieving program ends with the purpose of selecting the most cost-effective alternative. It is prospective in that it attempts to estimate the effects of a program *before* it is implemented. *Decision analysis* is the principal mode of analysis at this stage. Its aim is "understanding the efficiency implication of alternative intervention strategies" (Catterall, 1985: 1). The next stage—*legitimizing a policy or program*—is a purely political act. It puts the formal stamp of public approval on a program. The enactment of a law therefore should be done after sufficient public hearings and assessments of the degree to which the public supports a program. Public opinion survey information is important at this stage.

Policies next are translated into programs that are *implemented*. How well they are implemented is the concern of *formative evaluation*; this involves an analysis of the extent to which a program is implemented and the conditions that promote successful implementation. Once a program has been sufficiently implemented, its *impact* can be assessed. *Summative evaluation*, which is the method for determining what impact the program has, should be done after a program is fully implemented under favorable conditions. Finally, a program may be *terminated* or modified, and this tends to be a strictly political decision (deLeon, 1983). *Political feasibility* rather than summative evaluation usually is the determining factor at this stage (DeLeon, Chapter 6, this volume).

Of course, nor all of these stages happen in precise sequential order, the stages can be defined in various ways, and there is considerable overlapping among them. For example, an impact evaluation of a previously implemented program might be useful during the design of a new program (Chelimsky, Chapter 3). The key point is that the policy cycle is a long and complicated process in which politics, knowledge, and information enter and leave in convoluted and complex ways. Program evaluation in its original summative sense does not get involved until a policy has been formulated *and* implemented. By then it is difficult to have much impact on a policy, because policies take on lives of their own once they are implemented; they will have accumulated a number of beneficiaries and interest groups that will not want to see the policy or program changed no matter how well or poorly it is meeting its stated or intended objectives. Fine tuning and minor adjustments are about all that generally is possible after a policy has entered the implementation phase. Greater impact is possible if information is introduced during the agenda-setting, problem-definition, and policy-design stages, when an approach to a social problem is first being fashioned. Evaluators are not often involved during these crucial policy shaping stages of the cycle, which is one of the principal disadvantages of traditional evaluation research. However, there are ways of overcoming this disadvantage. Chelimsky (Chapter 3) discusses how to link program evaluation to user needs. She identifies the three broad program purposes that evaluation may serve (i.e., policy formulation, policy execution, and accountability) and the type of evaluations that may meet the user's needs in each category. The types of information users identified by Chelimsky are not the same as the stakeholders identified above. But, as she says, it "is important for an evaluator to be able to recognize and identify the dimensions of each evaluation user's information need and, as a result, to make conscious decisions in the design phase about what information will or will not be obtained and available to that user." St. Pierre (1985: 207) also has found that evaluations of compensatory education programs were successful because the evaluators spent a great deal of effort in specifying the questions of greatest concern and most use to the principal user of the evaluation, which he identified as the U.S. Congress.

In Chapter 6, DeLeon discusses policy termination as a political phenomenon and argues that termination is the most problematic of political activities. Thus termination should not often be a goal of evaluation (Palumbo and Nachmias, 1984). Because evaluators are most often involved during the implementation stage, it is crucial for them to understand the politics of implementation. In addition to the discussion of aspects of implementation politics above, Brown and Wildavsky answer the question "What should evaluation mean to implementation?" in Chapter 5.

Political evaluation in the sense that I am using it here can have beneficial consequences for policymaking. The participants in the policy process need information specialized to their respective roles in the process. Evaluations can become an effective counter in the policy negotiations that take place (Lindblom and Cohen, 1979: 64), and they can put breaks on unjustifiably costly programs (Jenkins-Smith and Weiner, 1985). By determining how much support exists for various policy options, political evaluation can promote agreement on decisions. Truth is better established through a dialectic process than by one definitive study (Cook, 1985). Analyzing the interests of the participants may be as important as analyzing the issues (Schelling, in Greenberger, 1983: 300). Building this kind of information into the evaluation would improve it, make it politically more relevant, and thereby increase its usefulness (Greenberger: 300).

Of course, there are dangers in political evaluation. One is that the powerful may benefit more than others, since they are most likely to control the conditions under which evaluations are done. Given the very high costs of evaluating social programs (Ferber and Hirsch, 1982), only those who can come up with big sums of money may control the outcome. In addition, low-quality research may displace better research if the goal simply is to persuade others of the legitimacy of a program; poor-quality research may do this as well as or even better than scientifically sound research. The American Tobacco Institute's research campaign on tobacco and health is a case in point (Fritschler, 1983). Greenberger and his colleagues (1983: 283) found that the highest-quality analyses concerning the energy crisis received the least attention and exerted the least immediate influence in policy. They found that the factors that were most strongly related to use were the timing of the research and how it accords or clashes with the beliefs of those in power.

CONCLUSION

Politics and evaluation are intricately intertwined. University researchers and professional evaluators cannot engage in openly political evaluations because to do so would abrogate the role they want to play in policymaking. Their original hope was to be able to provide factual information and scientific methods to help program administrators improve the performance of their agencies. This role is quite different than that of the think tanks, mass media representatives, and politicians. It also is a much-needed role in policymaking, but one that is in danger of diminishing as public officials become more cynical about the need for facts and information that has not been ideologically sifted. The effectiveness of evaluation depends upon incorporating political reality into evaluation. This book takes some first steps in the direction of helping evaluators do so.

NOTE

1. A related but not identical argument is made by Dunn (1980) and Caplan (1979) in the two-community theory. In my argument there are not only two competing belief systems of researchers and policymakers, but also conflicts within each world view.

REFERENCES

Abramson, T. and Gail Banchick (1979) "Determinants of the Evaluator's Role: Political and Programmatic Motives," in T. Bramson et al. (eds.) Handbook of Vocational Education. Newbury Park, CA: Sage.
Allison, Graham (1971) Essence of Decision. Boston: Little, Brown.

Banner, David K., Samuel Doctors, and Andrew Gordon (1975) The Politics of Local Program Evaluation. Cambridge, MA: Ballinger.

Bardach, Eugene (1977) The Implementation Game. Cambridge: MIT Press.

Barry, Brian and Douglas Rae (1975) "Political Evaluation," in F. I. Greenstein and N. Polsby (eds.) Handbook of Political Science, vol. 1. Reading, MA: Addison-Wesley.

Beals, R. L. (1969) Politics of Research: An Inquiry into the Ethics and Responsibilities of Social Scientists. Chicago: Aldine.

Bellavita, Christopher (1986) "Communicating Effectively About Performance as a Purposive Activity," in J. Wholey et al. (eds.) Performance and Credibility. Developing Excellence in Public and Nonprofit Organizations. Lexington, MA: Lexington Books.

Belski, Jay (1985) "The Science and Politics of Day Care," in R. Lance Shotland and Melvin M. Mark (eds.) Social Science and Public Policy. Newbury Park, CA: Sage.

Brewer, G. and Peter DeLeon (1983) The Foundations of Policy Analysis. Homewood, IL: Dorsey Press.

Campbell, Donald (1984) "Can We Be Scientific in Applied Social Science?" in Ross Conner and Associates (eds.) Evaluation Studies Review Annual, vol. 9. Newbury Park, CA: Sage.

Caplan, Nathan (1979) "The Two-Communities Theory and Knowledge Utilization." American Behavioral Scientist 22: 459-470.

Carley, Michael (1980) Rational Techniques in Policy Analysis. London: Heineman.

Catterall, James S. [ed.] (1985) Economic Evaluation of Public Programs. San Francisco: Jossey-Bass.

Chalip, Laurence (1985) "Policy Research as Social Science: Outflanking the Value Dilemma." Policy Studies Review 5, 2: 287-308.

Cobb, Roger W. and Charles D. Elder (1983) Participation in American Politics: The Dynamics of Agenda Building. Baltimore: Johns Hopkins University Press.

Cohen, D. K. and C. E. Lindblom (1979) "Solving Problems of Bureaucracy: Limits on Social Science." American Behavioral Scientist 22: 547-560.

Connecticut Department of Correction (no date) Impact Positive! An Evaluation of Community Services in Connecticut. Hartford: Author. (Available from Connecticut Department of Correction, 340 Capitol Avenue, CT 06108.)

Cook, Thomas P. "Post Positivist Critical Multiplism," in R. Lance Shotland and Melvin M. Mark (eds.) Social Science and Social Policy. Newbury Park, CA: Sage.

Crain, Robert L. and Karen B. Carsrud (1985) "The Role of the Social Sciences in School Desegregation Policy," in R. Lance Shotland and Melvin M. Mark (eds.) Social Science and Social Policy. Newbury Park, CA: Sage.

Cronbach, L. J. (1980) Toward Reform of Program Evaluation. San Francisco: Jossey-Bass.

Cyert, R. M. and J. C. March (1963) A Behavioral Theory of the Firm. Englewood Cliffs, NJ: Prentice-Hall.

DeLeon, Peter. (1983) "Policy Evaluation and Program Termination." Policy Studies Review 2, 4: 631-648.

Dornbush, Sanford M. and W. Richard Scott (1975) Evaluation and the Exercise of Authority. San Francisco: Jossey-Bass.

Dunn, William E. (1980) "The Two-Communities Metaphor and Models of Knowledge Use: An Exploratory Case Survey." Knowledge: Creation, Diffusion, Utilization 1: 515-536.

Elmore, Richard (1982) "Backward Mapping: Implementation Research and Policy

Decision," in Walter Williams (ed.) Studying Implementation. Chatam, NJ: Chatam House.

Evans, John W. and Walter Williams (1969) "The Politics of Evaluation: The Case of Head Start." Annals of the American Academy of Political and Social Science (September).

Faux, Geoffrey (1971) "Politics and Bureaucracy in Community Controlled Economic Development." Law and Contemporary Problems (Spring).

Feldman, Martha S., and James G. March (1981) "Information in Organizations as Signal and Symbol." Administrative Science Quarterly 26: 171-86.

Ferber, R., and Werner Z. Hirsch (1982) Social Experimentation and Economic Policy. Cambridge, MA: Cambridge University Press.

Fisher, Frank (1980) Politics, Values, and Public Policy, The Problem of Methodology. Boulder, CO: Westview.

Fritschler, A. Lee (1983) Smoking and Politics: Policymaking in the Federal Bureaucracy (3rd ed.) Englewood Cliffs, NJ: Prentice-Hall.

Giancomenico, Majone (1977) "On the Notion of Political Feasibility," in Stuart Nagel (ed.) Policy Studies Review Annual. Newbury Park, CA: Sage.

Ginsberg, Pauline (1984) "Dysfunctional Potential of Performance Measurement," in C. Windle (ed.) National Institute of Mental Health, Series BN No. 5, Program Performance Measurements: Demands, Technology, and Dangers. DHHS Pub No. (ADM) 84-1357. Washington, DC: Government Printing Office.

Greenberger, Martin et al. (1983) Caught Unawares: The Energy Decade in Retrospect. New York: Ballinger.

Guba, Egon and Yvonna Lincoln (1981) Effective Evaluation. San Francisco: Jossey-Bass.

Heiss, F. William (1974) "The Politics of Local Government Policy Evaluation: Some Observations." Urban Analysis 5: 37-45.

Hoos, Ida (1972) "Systems Techniques for Managing Society: A Critique." Public Administration Review 32 (March-April).

Horowitz, Irving L. and J. E. Katz (1975) Social Science and Public Policy in the U.S. New York: Praeger.

Jenkins-Smith, Hank C. and David L. Weimer (1985) "Analyses as Retrograde Action: The Case of Strategic Petroleum Reserves." Public Administration Review 45 (July-August): 485-495.

Katz, James E. (1984) Congress and National Energy Policy. New Brunswick, NJ: Transaction.

Kelly, Rita Mae (1986) "Trends in the Logic of Policy Inquiry: A Comparison of Approaches and a Commentary." Policy Studies Review 5 (February): 520-528.

Kramer, Fred (1975) "Policy Analysis as Ideology." Public Administration Review 35 (September-October).

Lasswell, H. D. (1951) "The Policy Orientation," pp. 3-15 in D. Lerner and H. D. Lasswell (eds.) The Policy Sciences. Stanford, CA: Stanford University Press.

Lerner, Daniel and Harold Lasswell [eds.] (1951) The Policy Sciences. Stanford, CA: Stanford University Press.

Lincoln, Yvonna S. and Egon Guba (1985) Naturalistic Inquiry. Newbury Park, CA: Sage.

Lincoln, Yvonna S. and Egon Guba (1986) "Research, Evaluation, and Policy Analysis: Heuristics for Disciplined Inquiry." Policy Studies Review 5 (February): 546-565.

Lindblom, Charles E., and D. K. Cohen (1979) Usable Knowledge: Social Science and

Social Problem Solving. New Haven, CT: Yale University Press.

Lipsky, Michael (1980) Street Level Bureaucracy. New York: Russell Sage.

Malbin, Michael (1980) Unelected Representatives. New York: Basic Books.

March, James G. and Johan P. Olsen (1984) "The New Institutionalism: Organizational Factors in Political Life." American Political Science Review 78, 3: 734-749.

Maynard-Moody, Stephen (1983) "Program Evaluation and Administrative Control." Policy Studies Review 2 (February): 371-391.

Meltsner, Arnold (1972) "Political Feasibility and Policy Analysis." Public Administration Review 32 (November-December).

Meltsner, Arnold and Christopher Bellavita (1983) The Policy Organization. Newbury Park, CA: Sage.

Miller, Trudi (1984) "Conclusion: A Design Social Perspective," pp. 251-268 in Trudi Miller (ed.) Public Sector Performance: A Conceptual Turning Point. Baltimore, MD: Johns Hopkins University Press.

Nelkin, D. (1980) "Scientific Knowledge, Public Policy, and Democracy: A Review Essay." Knowledge: Creation, Diffusion, Utilization 1: 106-122.

Neuber, Keith A. and Associates (1980) Needs Assessment: A Model for Community Planning. Newbury Park, CA: Sage.

Palumbo, Dennis (1986) "Privatization and Corrections Policy." Policy Studies Review, 5(3), 598-606.

Palumbo, Dennis, Michael Musheno, and Steven Maynard-Moody (1985) An Evaluation of the Implementation of Community Corrections in Oregon, Colorado and Connecticut. Final report prepared for Grant 82-15-CV-KO15, National Institute of Justice, June.

Palumbo, D. and D. Nachmias (1984) "The Preconditions for Successful Evaluation. Is There an Ideal Type?" in Evaluation Studies Reviews Annual, vol. 9. Ross Conner and Associates (eds.) Newbury Park, CA: Sage.

Patton, Michael Q. (1978) Utilization-Focused Evaluation. Newbury Park, CA: Sage.

Pincus, Walter (1985) "A Tough Arms Control Team." Washington Post National Weekly Edition (October 7): 6.

Rainwater, L. and W. L. Yancey (1967) The Moynihan Report and the Politics of Controversy. Cambridge: MIT Press.

Rein, Martin (1983) From Policy to Practice. New York: M. E. Sharpe.

Rivlin, A. M. (1973) "The Forensic Use of Social Science." Harvard Educational Review 43: 61-75.

Rossi, Peter and James D. Wright (1985) "Social Science Research and the Politics of Gun Control," in R. Lance Shotland and Melvin M. Mark (eds.) Social Science and Public Policy. Newbury Park, CA: Sage.

St. Pierre, Robert (1985) "Are the Social Sciences Able to Answer Questions About Compensatory Education Program?" in R. Lance Shotland and Melvin M. Mark (eds.) Social Science and Public Policy. Newbury Park, CA: Sage.

Scriven, Michael (1984) "Evaluation Ideologies," in Ross Conner and Associates (eds.) Evaluation Studies Review Annual, vol. 9. Newbury Park, CA: Sage.

Tolchin, Susan and Martin Tolchin (1983) Dismantling America: The Rush to Deregulate. Boston: Houghton Mifflin.

Wholey, Joseph S. (1983) Evaluation and Effective Public Management. Boston: Little, Brown.

Zuniga, R. (1975) "The Experimenting Society and Radical Social Reform: The Role of the Social Scientist in Chile's Unidad Popular Experience." American Psychologist 30: 99-115.

2

WHERE POLITICS AND
EVALUATION RESEARCH MEET

CAROL H. WEISS
Harvard University

Evaluation research is a rational enterprise. It examines the effects of politics and programs on their targets—whether individuals, groups, institutions, or communities—in terms of the goals they are meant to achieve. By objective and systematic methods, evaluation research assesses the extent to which goals are realized and looks at the factors that are associated with successful or unsuccessful outcomes. The assumption is that by providing "the facts," evaluation assists decision makers to make wise choices among future courses of action. Careful and unbiased data on the consequences of programs should improve decision making.

But evaluation is a rational enterprise that takes place in a political context. Political considerations intrude in three major ways, and the evaluator who fails to recognize their presence is in for a series of shocks and frustrations:

First, the policies and programs with which evaluation deals are the creatures of political decisions. They were proposed,

---

Author's Note: *This article is based on a paper presented at the annual meeting of the American Psychological Association, Montreal, August 30, 1973.*

47

defined, debated, enacted, and funded through political processes, and in implementation they remain subject to pressures—both supportive and hostile—that arise out of the play of politics.

Second, because evaluation is undertaken in order to feed into decision making, its reports enter the political arena. There, evaluative evidence of program outcomes has to compete for attention with other factors that carry weight in the political process.

Third, and perhaps least recognized, evaluation itself has a political stance. By its very nature it makes implicit political statements about such issues as the problematic nature of some programs and the unchallengeability of others, the legitimacy of program goals and program strategies, the utility of strategies of incremental reform, and even the appropriate role of the social scientist in policy and program formation.

Knowing that political constraints and resistances exist is not a reason for abandoning evaluation research; rather it is a precondition for usable evaluation research. Only when the evaluator has insight into the interests and motivations of other actors in the system, into the roles that the evaluator is consciously or inadvertently playing, the obstacles and opportunities that impinge upon the evaluative effort, and the limitations and possibilities for putting the results of evaluation to work—only with sensitivity to the politics of evaluation research—can the evaluator be as creative and strategically useful as possible.

PROGRAMS ARE POLITICAL CREATURES

Evaluation research assesses the effects of social programs, which in recent years have increasingly been governmental programs and larger in scale and scope than the programs studied in earlier decades. There have been important evaluations of job training programs, compensatory education, mental health centers, community health services, Head Start and Follow Through, community action, law enforcement, corrections, and other government interventions. Although there have been occasional studies of long-established traditional services, most evaluation efforts have been addressed to new programs; it is the program into which new money is being poured that tends to raise the most immediate questions about viability and continuation.

The programs with which the evaluator deals are not neutral, antiseptic, laboratory-type entities. They emerged from the rough and tumble of political support, opposition, and bargaining. Attached to them are the reputations of legislative sponsors, the careers of administrators, the jobs of program staff, and the expectations of clients. The support of these groups coalesces around the program, but the counterpressures that were activated during its development remain active and the program remains vulnerable to interference from legislatures, bureaucracies, interest groups, professional guilds, and the media. It is affected as well by interagency and intra-agency jockeying for advantage and influence.

The politics of program survival is an ancient and important art. Much of the literature on bureaucracy stresses the investment that individuals within an organization have in maintaining the organization's existence, influence, and empire. As Morton Halperin (1971) succinctly states:

> Organizational interests, then, are for many participants a dominant factor in determining the face of the issue which they see and the stand which they take. . . . Organizations with missions strive to maintain or to improve their (1) autonomy, (2) organizational morale, (3) organizational "essence," and (4) roles and missions. Organizations with high-cost capabilities are also concerned with maintaining or increasing (5) budgets.

It is not only around evaluation that social scientists bemoan the political factors that distort what they see as rational behavior. Economist Julius Margolis (1971) recently noted:

> You may go through a scientific analysis to answer the question of where the airport should be located, but an altogether different decision may finally emerge from the bureaucracy.

Bureaucrats—or, in our terms, program administrators and operators—are not irrational; they have a different model of rationality in mind. They are concerned not just with today's progress in achieving program goals, but with building long-term support for the program. This may require attention to factors and to people that can be helpful in later events and future contests. Administrators also have to build and maintain the organization—recruit staff with needed qualifications, train them to the appropriate functions, arrange effective interstaff relations and communications, keep people happy and working enthusiastically, and expand the influence and mission of the agency. There are budgetary interests, too, such as the need to maintain, increase, or maximize appropriations for agency functioning. Clients have to be attracted, a favorable public image developed, and a complex system managed and operated. Accomplishing the goals for which the program was set up is not unimportant, but it is not the only, the largest, or, usually, the most immediate of the concerns on the administrator's docket.

Particularly when an organization is newly formed to run new programs, its viability may be uncertain. If the organization is dealing with marginal clienteles, it can fall heir to the marginal repute of its clients, and it is likely to have relatively low public acceptance. Organizational vulnerability can become the dominant factor in determining what actions to take, and the need to build and maintain support can overwhelm the imperatives to achieve program goals.

In sum, social programs are the creatures of legislative politics and of bureaucratic politics. The model of the system that is most salient to program managers—and the components of the system with which they are concerned—are bound to be different from the model of the social scientist/evaluator. A program manager's view is probably no less rational. In fact, evidence suggests that programs can and do survive evaluations that show dismal failure to achieve goals. These programs, however, are less likely to survive a hostile congressional committee, newspaper exposes, or withdrawal of the support of professional groups.

There have been occasional references in evaluation literature to the need to recognize organizational "system" objectives as well as program goals (as in work by Schulberg and Baker, 1968), but the notion has never caught on. So evaluators continue to regard these concerns of program staff as diversions from their true mission, and give them no points on the scorecard for effectiveness in the politics of organizational survival.

The disparity in viewpoint between evaluation researchers and program managers has consequences for the kind of study that is done, how well it is done, and the reception it gets when it is completed. Obviously the political sensitivities of program managers can dim their receptivity to any evaluation at all, and when a study *is* undertaken, can limit a program manager's cooperation on decisive issues of research design and data collection. Again, at the completion of the study the program manager's political perspective will lessen the likelihood that he will view evaluative findings as conclusive or the need to act on them as imperative. Even rigorously documented evidence of outcomes may not outweigh all other interests and concerns.

More subtly, some political fallout shapes the very definition of an evaluation study. As an example, let us look at the specification of program goals that become the evaluator's criteria for effectiveness. Because of the political processes of persuasion and negotiation that are required to get a program enacted, inflated promises are made in the guise of program goals. Public housing will not just provide decent living space; it will improve health, enhance marital stability, reduce crime, and lead to improved school performance.

Furthermore, the goals often lack the clarity and intellectual coherence that evaluation criteria should have. Rather than being clear, specific, and measurable, they are diffuse and sometimes inherently incompatible. Again it is the need to develop coalition support that leaves its mark. Holders of diverse values and different interests have to be won over, and in the process a host of realistic and unrealistic goal commitments are made.

Given the consequent grandiosity and diffuseness of program goals, there tends to be little agreement, even within the program, on which goals are real—real in the sense that effort is actually going into attaining them—and which are window-dressing. With this ambiguity, actors at different levels in the system perceive and interpret goals in different ways. What the Congress writes into legislation as program objectives is not necessarily what the secretary's office or the director of the national program see as their mission, nor what the state or local project managers or the operating staff actually try to accomplish.

Evaluators are faced with the task of sifting the real from the unreal, the important from the unimportant, perhaps even uncovering the covert goals that genuinely set the direction of the program (but are unlikely to surface in open discussion), and discovering priorities among goals. Unless they are astute enough to direct their research toward authentic goals, they wind up evaluating the program against meaningless criteria. Unless they are skillful enough to devise measures that provide valid indicators of success in this complex web of expectations, they run the risk of having their report disowned and disregarded. It is not uncommon for evaluation reports to meet the disclaimer: "But that's not what we were trying to do."

While the evaluation study is in progress, political pressures can alter or undermine it. Let us look at one final example of how organizational politics can affect the shape of evaluation research. Programs do not always keep to their original course; over time, often a short span of time, they can shift in activities, in overall strategy, and even in the objectives they seek to attain. They are responding to a host of factors: budget cutting or budget expansion, changes in administration or in top officials, veering of the ideological winds, changes in congressional support, public appraisal, initiation of rival agencies and rival programs, pervasive client dissatisfaction, or critical media coverage.

Whereas evaluators want to study the effects of a stable and specifiable stimulus, program managers have much less interest in the integrity of the study than in assuring that the program makes the best possible adaptation to conditions. This leaves evaluators in a predicament: They are measuring outcomes of a "program" that has little coherence. What are the inputs? To what are the outcomes attributable? If the program succeeds, what activities should be replicated? If the program fails, what features were at fault? Unless programs under study are sheltered from the extremes of political turbulence, evaluation research produces outcome data that are almost impossible to interpret. On the other hand, to expect programs to remain unchanging laboratory treatments is to ignore the political imperatives. In this regard, as in others, programs have a logic and a rationality of their own.

THE POLITICS OF HIGHER-ECHELON DECISION MAKING

Much evaluation research is sponsored not by individual projects or by managers of federal programs but by those at superordinate levels, such as a director of an agency or a secretary or assistant secretary of a federal department, and the reports often go to cognizant officials in the Office of Management and Budget (OMB), to the White House, and to members of congressional committees. If the organizations that run programs have a vested interest in their protection, these higher-level decision makers can view the conclusions of evaluation research with a more open mind. They are likely to be less concerned with issues or organizational survival or expansion and more concerned with ensuring that the public policies are worth what they cost and produce the desired effects. Of course, some legislators and cabinet or subcabinet officials are members of the alliance that supports particular programs. But it is generally true that the further removed the decision makers are from direct responsibility for running the program, the more dispassionately they consider the evidence.

This, of course, does not mean that policymakers venerate outcome data or regard it as the decisive input for decision. They are members of a policymaking system that has its own values and its own rules. Their model of the system, its boundaries and pivotal components, goes far beyond concern with program effectiveness. Their decisions are rooted in all the complexities of the democratic decisionmaking process: the allocation of power and authority, the development of coalitions, and the trade-offs with interest groups, professional guilds, and salient publics. How well a program is doing may be less important than the position of the congressional committee chairman, the political clout of its supporters, or other demands on the budget. A considerable amount of ineffectiveness may be tolerated if a program fits well with prevailing values, if it satisfies voters, or if it pays off political debts.

What evaluation research can do is clarify what the political trade-offs involve. It should show how much is being given up to satisfy political demands and what kinds of program effects decision makers are settling for or forgoing when they adopt a position. It will not be the sole basis for a decision, and legitimately so. Other information and other values inevitably enter a democratic policy process. But evidence of effectiveness should be introduced to indicate the consequences that various decisions entail.

As a matter of record, relatively few evaluation studies have had a noticeable effect on the making and remaking of public policy. There are some striking exceptions, and in any case, our time frame may be too short. Perhaps it takes five or ten years or more before decision makers respond to the accumulation of consistent evidence. There may need to be a sharp change in administration or a decisive shift in expectations. But to date, as Peter Rossi (1969) has pointed out, devastating evidence of program failure has left some policies and programs unscathed, and positive evidence has not shielded others from dissolution. Clearly, other factors weigh heavily in the politics of the decision process.

Perhaps one of the reasons that evaluations are so readily disregarded is that they address only official goals. If an evaluator also assessed a program's effectiveness in meeting political goals—such as showing that the administration is "doing something," or that the program is placating interest groups or enhancing the influence of a particular department—he might learn more about the measures of success that decision makers value. He might learn why some programs survive despite abysmal outcomes, why some that look fine on indicators of goal achievement go down the drain, and which factors have the most influence on the making and persistence of policy. Just as economic cost-benefit analysis added the vital dimension of cost to analysis of outcomes, *political-benefit* analysis might help to resolve questions about political benefits and forgone opportunities.

It is true that many public officials in the Congress and the executive branch sincerely believe that policy choices should consistently be based on what works and what doesn't. It is also true that like all the other actors in the drama, policymakers respond to the imperatives of their own institutions. One seemingly peripheral but consequential factor is the time horizon of the policy process. Presidents, governors, and legislators have a relatively short time perspective. They want to make a record before the next election. Appointed officials in the top positions of government agencies tend to serve for even shorter periods. The average tenure of officials in federal departments is a little over two years, as shown in a Brookings Institution study conducted by David Stanley, Dean Mann, and Jameson Doig (1967). The emphasis therefore tends to be on takeoffs, not on landings. It is often more important to a politically astute official to launch a program with great fanfare to show how much he is doing than to worry about how effectively the program serves people's needs. The annual cycle of the budget process also has the effect of foreshortening the time perspective. When decisions on funding level have to be made within twelve months, there is little time to gather evidence (competent evidence, at least) on program outcomes or to consider whatever information has been gathered.

What does it take to get the results of evaluation research a hearing? In a discussion of policy analysis (of which evaluation research is one phase), Charles Lindblom (1968) states that differences in values and value priorities constitute an inevitable limitation on the use of objective rational analysis. As I have already noted, maximizing program effectiveness is only one of many values that enter decisions. Therefore, Lindblom explains, the way that analysis is used is not as a substitute for politics but as a "tactic in the play of power":

> It does not avoid fighting over policy; it is a method of fighting. . . .
> And it does not run afoul of disagreements on goals or values . . .

because it accepts as generally valid the values of the policy-maker to whom it is addressed.

It does appear that evaluation research is most likely to affect decisions when the researcher accepts the values, assumptions, and objectives of the decision maker. This means, obviously, that decision makers heed and use results that come out the way they want them to. But it suggests more than the rationalization or predetermined positions. There is a further, important implication that those who value the *criteria* that evaluation research uses, those who are concerned with the achievement of official program goals, will pay attention as well. The key factor is that they accept the assumptions built into the study. Whether or not the outcome results agree with their own wishes, they are likely to give the evidence a hearing. But evaluation results are not likely to be persuasive to those for whom other values have higher priority. If a decision maker thinks it is important for job trainees to get and hold on to skilled jobs, he will take negative evaluation findings seriously, but if he is satisfied that job training programs seem to keep the ghettos quiet, then job outcome data mean much less.

THE POLITICS IMPLICIT
IN EVALUATION RESEARCH

The third element of politics in the evaluation context is the stance of evaluation itself. Social scientists tend to see evaluation research, like all research, as objective, unbiased, and non-political, as a corrective for the special pleading and selfish interests of program operators and policymakers alike. Evaluation produces hard evidence of actual outcomes. But it incorporates as well a series of assumptions, and many researchers are unaware of the political nature of the assumptions they make and the role they play.

First, evaluation research asks the question, How effective is the program in meeting its goals? Thus it accepts the desirability of achieving these goals. By testing the effectiveness of the program against the goal criteria, it not only accepts the rightness of the goals, it also tends to accept the premises underlying the program. There is an implicit assumption that this type of program strategy is a reasonable way to deal with the problem, that there is justification for the social diagnosis and prescription that the program represents. Further, evaluation research assumes that the program has a realistic chance of reaching the goals—or else the study would be a frittering away of time, energy, and talent.

For many programs, social science knowledge and theory would suggest that the goals are not well reasoned, that the problem diagnosis, the selection of the point of intervention, and the type of intervention are inappropriate, and that chances of success are slight. But when a social scientist agrees to evaluate a program, he or she gives an aura of legitimacy to the enterprise.

Furthermore, as Roland Warren (1973) has noted, the evaluator who limits a study to the effects of the experimental variables— those few factors that the program manipulates—conveys the message that other elements in the situations are either unimportant or that they are fixed and unchangeable. The intervention strategy is viewed as the key element, and all other conditions that may give rise to, sustain, or alter the problem are brushed aside. In particular, most evaluations—by accepting a program emphasis on services—tend to ignore the social and institutional structures within which the problems of the target groups are generated and sustained. Although evaluation studies can examine the effects of nonprogram variables, they generally concentrate on identifying changes in those persons who receive program services compared to those who do not, and they hold constant (by randomization or other techniques) critical structural variables in the lives of that particular population.

Warren suggests that there is an unhappy convergence between the preferred methodology of evaluation research—the controlled experiment—and the preferred method of operation of most single-focus agencies. Agencies tend to deal in piecemeal programs, addressing a single problem with limited intervention. He writes:

> For various reasons of practice and practicality they confine themselves to a very limited, relatively identifiable type of intervention, while other things in the life situation of the target population are . . . left unaltered. . . . The more piecemeal, the fewer the experimental variables involved, the more applicable is the [experimental] research design.

Methodologically, of course, experimental designs can be applied to highly complex programs (which are what factorial designs are about), but in practice there does seem to be an affinity between the experiment and the limited focus program. And if there is anything that we should have learned from the history of social reform, it is that fragmented program approaches make very little headway in solving serious social problems. An hour of counseling per week, or the introduction of parapro-fessional aides, or citizen representation on the board of directors—efforts like these cannot possibly have significant consequences in alleviating major ills.

Another political statement is implicit in the selection of some programs to undergo evaluation, while others go unexamined. The unanalyzed program is safe and undisturbed, while the evaluated program is subjected to scrutiny. What criteria are used in selecting programs to evaluate? Obviously, it is the new and (perhaps) innovative program that is put on trial while the hardy perennials go on, whether or not they are accomplishing their goals, through the sheer weight of tradition.

Other criteria for selecting programs for evaluations are even more overtly political. Thus in a discussion of program analysis, Charles Schultze (1968) makes two recommendations: (1) Program analysts should give more consideration to programs that do not directly affect the structure of institutional and political power than to programs that fundamentally affect income distribution or impinge on the power structure, and (2) analysts can be more useful by studying new and expanding programs than by studying long-existing programs with well-organized constituencies.

There are persuasive reasons for such prescriptions. Evaluators, like all other analysts who ignore the political constraints of special interests, institutional power, and protective layers of alliances may confront the decision maker with troublesome information. If time after time they bring in news that calls for difficult political choices, if they too often put the decision maker in a position that is politically unviable, evaluators may discredit evaluation research as a useful tool. Nevertheless, there are serious political implications in restricting evaluation to the unprotected program and the program that is marginal to the distribution of economic and political power.

The structure of the evaluation research enterprise also has political overtones. To begin with, evaluation is generally commissioned by the agency responsible for the program, not by the recipients of its efforts. This is so obvious and taken for granted that its implications are easily overlooked. Some of its consequences, however, are that the officials' goal statements form the basis for study and if recipients have different needs or different ends in mind, these do not surface. Another probability is that the evaluator interprets his data in light of the contingencies open to the agency. The agency is the client, and the evaluator tries to gear his recommendations to accord with realistic practicalities. Furthermore, he reports study findings to decision makers and managers, usually not to program participants; if the findings are negative, officials may not completely bury the report (although sometimes they try), but they can at least release it with their own interpretations: "We need more money," "We need more time," or "The evaluation was too crude to measure the important changes that took place."

To the extent that administrators' interpretations shape the understanding of a study's import, they constrain the decisions likely to be made about that program in the future and even to influence the demands of the target groups. An evaluation report showing that Program A is doing little good, if interpreted from the perspective of the participants in the program, might well lead to very different recommendations from those developed by an agency-oriented evaluator or a program official.

Most of these political implications of evaluation research have an "establishment" orientation. They accept the world as it is: as it is defined in agency structure, in official diagnoses of social problems, and in the types of ameliorative activities that are run. But the basic proclivity of evaluation research is reformist. Its whole thrust is to improve the way that society copes with social problems. At the same time that evaluation research accepts program assumptions, it also subjects them to scrutiny; its aim is to locate discrepancies between intent and actual outcome.

In addition to this reformist thrust, Harold Orlans (1973) has indicated that social science evaluators tend to be more liberal in orientation than many of the agencies they study. And their perspectives inevitably affect their research. As social scientists increasingly recognize, no study collects neutral "facts": All research entails value decisions and to some degree reflects the researcher's selections, assumptions, and interpretations. This liberal bias of much evaluation research can threaten its credibility to officialdom. Thus Laurence Lynn, Jr. (1973), a federal assistant secretary, writes:

> The choices of conceptual frameworks, assumptions, output measures, variables, hypotheses, and data provide wide latitude for judgment, and values of the researcher often guide the decisions to at least some degree. Evaluation is much more of an art than a science, and the artist's soul may be as influential as his mind. To the extent that this is true, the evaluator becomes another special interest or advocate rather than a purveyor of objectively developed evidence and insights, and *the credibility of his work can be challenged.*

In this statement there seems to be an assumption that such a thing as "objectively developed evidence" exists and that assumptions and values are foreign intrusions. But the message that comes through is that "objectively developed evidence" is that which develops only out of government-sanctioned assumptions and values. Certainly evaluators funded by government have an obligation to start with the official framework, but they should be able to look at other variables and other outcomes, wanted and unwanted, in addition to those set by official policy.

The intrinsically reformist orientation of evaluation research is apparent in its product. Evaluation conclusions are the identification of some greater or lesser shortfall between goals and outcomes, and the usual recommendations will call for modifications in program operation. The assumptions here are (1) that reforms in current policies and programs will serve to improve government performance without drastic restructuring and (2) that decision makers will heed the evidence and respond to improving programming. It is worthwhile examining both these assumptions, particularly when we take note of one major piece of intelligence: Evaluation research discloses that most programs dealing with social problems fail to accomplish their goals. The finding of little impact is pervasive over a wide band of program fields and program strategies. True, much of the evaluation research has been methodologically deficient and needs upgrading. (There is an extensive literature on methodological shortcomings. Donald Campbell, 1970, and Selma Mushkin, 1973, are among those who have written cogent critiques.) But there is little evidence that methodologically sounder studies find more positive outcomes. Numbers of excellent studies have been carried out, and they generally report findings at least as negative as do the poor ones. Moreover, the pattern of null results is dolefully consistent. So despite the conceptual and methodological shortcomings of many of the studies, the cumulative evidence has to be taken seriously.

What does the evaluation researcher recommend when he finds that the program is ineffective? For a time, it may be a reasonable response to call attention to possible variations that may increase success—higher levels of funding, more skilled management, better trained staff, better coordination with other services, more intensive treatment, and so on. If these recommendations are ignored, if the political response is to persist with the same low-cost, low-trouble program, there is not much more that the social scientist can learn by evaluating participant outcomes. If program changes are made, then further evaluation research is in order. But there comes a time when scores or even hundreds of variants of a program have been run, for example, in compensatory education or rehabilitation of criminal offenders, and none of them has shown much success. If it was not evident before, it should be clear by then that tinkering with the same approaches in different combination is unlikely to pay off.

There needs to be serious reexamination of the basic problem, how it is defined, what social phenomena nurture and sustain it, how it is related to other social conditions and social processes, and the total configuration of forces that have overwhelmed past program efforts. Fragmented, one-service-at-a-time programs, dissociated from people's total patterns of living, may have to be abandoned, and as Daniel Moynihan (1970) has suggested, integrated policies that reach deeper into the social fabric will have to be developed. What this suggests is that in fields where the whole array of past program approaches has proved bankrupt, the assumption is no longer tenable that evaluation research of one program at a time can draw useful implications for action or that piecemeal modifications will improve effectiveness.

As for the other major premise on which the utility of evaluation research is based—that policymakers will heed research results and respond by improving programming—there is not much positive evidence either. I have noted that the politics of program survival and the politics of higher policymaking accord evaluative evidence relatively minor weight in the decisional calculus. It is when evaluation results confirm what decision makers already believe or disclose what they are predisposed to accept that evaluation is most apt to get serious attention. Thus, for example, the Nixon administration was willing to listen to the negative findings about the Johnson Great Society programs. As Allen Schick (1971) has noted, evaluation research is comfortably compatible with a government perspective of disillusionment with major program initiatives—with stock-taking and retrenchment. As a consequence, the fiscal year 1973 budget submitted to Congress proposed to cut out or cut back programs that weren't working. The evaluation researcher—now that somebody was paying attention to findings—was cast in the role of political hatchet man.

Because evaluation researchers tend to be liberal, reformist, humanitarian, and advocates of the underdog, it is exceedingly uncomfortable to have evaluation findings used to justify an end of spending on domestic social programs. On the other hand, it is extremely difficult for evaluators to advocate continuation of programs that they have found had no apparent results. The political dilemma is real and painful. It has led some social scientists to justify continued spending on avowedly ineffective programs to preserve the illusion that something is being done. Others have called for continued spending, whatever the outcome, so not to lose the momentum of social progress. Others justify the programs with explanations that they regarded as specious when used by program staff: the programs serve other purposes, the evaluations aren't very good, the programs need more money, they need more time. My own bent is to find some truth in each of these justifications, but they tend to be declarations based on social ideology and faith. Evaluators can maintain them only so long without providing evidence that these factors are responsible for the poor showing or that the programs are achieving other valued ends.

What would be a responsible position for evaluation research? It seems to me that there are a few steps that can be taken. One reform in evaluation research would be to put program goals in sensible perspective. Among the many reasons for the negative pall of evaluation results is that studies have accepted bloated promises and political rhetoric as authentic program goals. Whatever eager sponsors may say, day-care centers will not end welfare dependency, and neighborhood government will not create widespread feelings of citizen efficacy. Programs should have more modest expectations (helping people to cope is not an unimportant contribution), and they should be evaluated against more reasonable goals. Furthermore, evaluations that average the effects of numbers of local projects and come up with summary "pass/fail" measures are not likely to be optimally useful. More learning will come from specifying the conditions that are associated with better or poorer outcomes—conditions of program operation as well as conditions in the larger social context.

A further step along this course would be to evaluate a particularly strong version of the program before, or along with, the evaluation of the ordinary levels at which it functions. This would tend to show whether the program *at its best* can achieve the desired results, whether accomplishments diminish as resource level or skills decline, and how intensive an effort it takes for a program to work. If the full-strength "model" program has little effect, then it is fruitless to tinker with modest, low-budget versions of it.

More fundamentally, however, it seems to me that now in some fields there is a limit to how much more evaluation research can accomplish. In areas where numbers of good studies have been done and have found negative results, there seems little point in devoting significant effort to evaluations of minor program variants. Evaluation research is not likely to tell much more. There is apparently something wrong with many of our social policies and much social programming. We do not know *how* to solve some of the major problems facing the society. Nor do we apply the knowledge that we have. We mount limited-focus programs to cope with broad-gauge problems. We devote limited resources to long-standing and stubborn problems. Above all, we concentrate attention on changing the attitudes and behavior of target groups without concomitant attention to the institutional structures and social arrangements that tend to keep them "target groups."

For the social scientist who wants to contribute to the improvement of social programming, there may be more effective routes at this point than through evaluation research. There may be greater potential in doing research on the processes that give rise to social problems, the institutional structures that contribute to their origin and persistence, the social arrangements that overwhelm efforts to eradicate them, and the points at which they are vulnerable to societal intervention. Pivotal contributions are needed in understanding the dynamics of such processes and in applying the knowledge, theory, and experience that exist to the formulation of policy. I suspect that in many areas this effort will lead us to think in new categories and suggest different orders or intervention. As we gain deeper awareness of the complexities and interrelationships that maintain problem behavior, perhaps we can develop coherent, integrated, mutually supportive sets of activities, incentives, regulations, and rewards that represent a concerted attack and begin to deserve the title of "policy."

How receptive will established institutions be to new ways of looking at problems and to the new courses of action that derive from them? I suggested earlier that decision makers tend to use research only when its results match their preconceptions and its assumptions accord with their values. There will certainly be resistance to analysis that suggests changes in power relations and in institutional policy and practice. But legislatures and agencies are not monoliths, and there may well be some supporters, too. As time goes on, if confirming evidence piles up year after year on the failures of old approaches and if mounting data suggest new modes of intervention, this will percolate through the concerned publics. When the political climate veers toward the search for new initiatives, or if sudden crises arise and there is a scramble for effective policy mechanisms, some empirically grounded guidelines will be available.

Of course, there remains a vital role for evaluation research. It is important to focus attention on the consequences of programs, old and new, to keep uncovering their shortcomings so that the message gets through, and to locate those programs that do have positive effects and can be extended and expanded.

It is important to improve the craft of evaluation so that we have greater confidence in its results. To have immediate and direct influence on decisions, there is a vital place for "inside evaluation" that is consonant with decision makers' goals and values—and perhaps stretches their sights a bit. There is also a place for independent evaluation based on different assumptions with wider perspectives, and for the structures to sustain it. One of the more interesting roles for evaluation is as "social experimentation" on proposed new program ventures—to test controlled small-scale prototypes before major programs are launched and thereby gain good measures of their consequences.

Nevertheless, given the record of largely ineffective social programming, I think the time has come to put more of our research talents into even earlier phases of the policy process, into work that contributes to the development of ideas and prototypes.

I believe that we need more research on the social processes and institutional structures that sustain the problems of society and closer social science involvement in the application of that research. I have hope that this can contribute to understanding which factors have to be altered if change is to occur and, in time, to more effective program and policy formation.

POSTSCRIPT

This essay on evaluation research in the political context was written in 1973. I presented it at the annual meeting of the American Psychological Association in August 1973, and it was published in *Evaluation* magazine later that year (vol. 1, no. 3). Now that I reread it after all these years, I find that I still agree with almost everything I wrote then. I still see programs as political entities. I know even more about the political nature of the response to evaluation results, because I have spent eight years studying how policymakers and program planners use evaluation and other kinds of social science research. I am still convinced that evaluation itself has a political stance and sends out political messages.

If I were to be writing the essay now, perhaps I might make a small change. I think that I would tone down the paragraphs near the end that call for greater support for basic social science as a foundation for social policy. The notion, I think, is right, but I no longer have the same ringing fervor that basic research on institutional structures and institutional arrangements is a practicable means for fashioning wise social policy. Experience in the 1970s and early 1980s has tempered my optimism that the route from basic social science to policy change is readily navigable: that basic social scientists will do work that addresses central social issues, that the work they do will converge rather than splinter and complexify, and that people in policymaking positions will learn about and heed basic research results. The same problems that plague evaluation research as an instrument for policy action apply to basic research—and with even greater force. Whatever the values of social science for understanding institutional structures and processes, and I believe there are many, social science is not an easy or efficient route to social reform. It has effects, but the effects are likely to be slow and erratic.

As a counterbalance, I am somewhat more impressed with the findings that evaluation studies have provided. Perhaps they have not led to massive breakthroughs and revolutionary insights, but they have increased our understanding of how programs operate, what effects they have, and what the consequences are of different program strategies. In many agencies and in many countries, policymakers, program managers, and planners have paid attention. Incremental improvements have been made, and cumulative increments are not such small potatoes after all.

When I began thinking about the politics of evaluation, I could not find anything in the literature on the subject. I am sure that other people were aware of the political aspects of evaluation, but they did not seem to be discussing them in public. In fact, the first essay that I wrote on the subject, "The Politicization of Evaluation" (*Journal of Social Issues*, 1970) came to be written precisely because the subject seemed to be taboo. I had attended a conference on evaluation at the American Academy of Arts and Sciences in 1969, and for two days a group of evaluation bigwigs talked about every evaluation topic under the sun. Except politics. They talked about the pros and cons of experimental design and cost-benefit analysis, the perils of measurement, the need for qualitative descriptions of program process, necessary training for evaluators, and many other fascinating topics, but not a word about the political aspects of the evaluation enterprise. As I recall, I made a timid but totally unsuccessful effort to introduce the subject. Following the meeting, I went home and wrote the article about "politicization." It seemed too important a set of issues to leave to staff gossip and midnight struggles with one's soul. I thought that it was vital to make the subject visible and discussable within the profession.

In the 1970 article I wrote:

Evaluation has always had explicitly political overtones. It is designed to yield conclusions about the worth of programs and, in so doing, is intended to affect the allocation of resources. . . . Not so long ago, innovative social action programming and its accompanying evaluation were small-scale enterprises. The greatest effect that evaluation could have would be to encourage further street work with gang youth (by the sponsoring agency and maybe one or two agencies like it) or discouraging individual counseling sessions for clinic patients. The effects tended to be localized, since programs and their evaluations were bounded. . . . The big change is that both programming and evaluation are now national in scope.

Now, of course, the politics of evaluation is a familiar enough subject to have inspired many articles and several books, including this one. It is good to see the range of discussion and the quality of attention that the authors here devote to it. In contrarian fashion, I now have an impulse to counter some of the more extreme statements that have been made. Some people now see politics rampant in every decision of evaluation methodology and presentation, as if evaluators were much the same as program advocates and policy lobbyists in their approach to the public arena. True, evaluation is political in important ways, but it is not an advocacy game. Evaluators still abide by the rules of their disciplines: They believe in careful research design and appropriate comparisons; they believe in collecting fair and comparable data from program participants and nonparticipants; they believe in scrupulous analysis of their data; they strive to present the data fully and fairly, without camouflaging findings that they personally regret or blowing out of proportion findings that they happen to like. Evaluators have points of view, certainly. They choose to look at certain kinds of programs and work for certain categories of program stakeholders, and their implicit values color methodological choices. But they are not on the scene to espouse a political position; they were invited in to the policy arena because they have technical expertise that will help to reveal one or more of the several realities that surround the program. They are there to help clarify the questions that people in various positions are asking and even to provide some answers. While they cannot avoid getting involved in the political issues that surround every program—for example, which questions get priority—their professional identities require that once embarked on a study they conduct the study with all the objectivity that the methods of social science allow.

If I do not want to change much of what I wrote earlier about the politics of evaluation, there is certainly much to add. It is enlightening to see the wealth of issues that the other contributors to this volume have put on the collective table.

REFERENCES

Campbell, Donald T. and Albert Erlebacher (1970) "How Regression Artifacts in Quasi-Experimental Evaluations Can Mistakenly Make Compensatory Education Look Harmful," in J. Hellmuth (ed.) Compensatory Education: A National Debate, vol. 3. New York: Brunner/Mazel.

Caplan, Nathan and Stephen D. Nelson (1973) "On Being Useful: The Nature and Consequences of Psychological Research on Social Problems." American Psychologist 28, 3: 199-211.

Halperin, Morton H. (1971) Why Bureaucrats Play Games. Reprint 199. Washington, DC: Brookings Institution.

Hatry, Harry P., Richard E. Winnie, and Donald M. Fisk (1973) Practical Program Evaluation for State and Local Government Officials. Washington, DC: Urban Institute.

Lindblom, Charles E. (1968) The Policy-Making Process. Englewood Cliffs, NJ: Prentice-Hall.

Lynn, Laurence E., Jr., (1973) "A Federal Evaluation Office?" Evaluation 1, 2: 56-59, 92, 96.

Margolis, Julius (1971) "Evaluative Criteria in Social Policy," pp. 25-31 in T. R. Dye (ed.) The Measurement of Policy Impact. Tallahassee: Florida State University.

Moynihan, Daniel P. (1970) "Policy vs. Program in the 70s." Public Interest 20: 90-100

Mushkin, Selma J. (1973) "Evaluations: Use with Caution." Evaluation 1, 2: 30-35.

Orlans, Harold (1973) Contracting for Knowledge. San Francisco: Jossey-Bass.

Rossi, Peter (1969) "Practice, Method, and Theory in Evaluating Social-Action Programs," pp. 217-34 in J. L. Sundquist (ed.) On Fighting Poverty: Perspectives from Experience. New York: Basic Books.

Schick, Allen (1971) "From Analysis to Evaluation." Annals of the American Academy of Political and Social Science 394: 57-71

Schulberg, Herbert C. and Frank Baker (1968) "Program Evaluation Models and the Implementation of Research Findings." American J. of Public Health 58, 7: 1248-55.

Schultze, Charles L. (1968) The Politics and Economics of Public Spending. Washington, DC: Brookings Institution.

Stanley, David T., Dean E. Mann, and Jameson W. Doig (1967) Men Who Govern: A Biographical Profile of Federal Political Executives. Washington, DC: Brookings Institution.

Ward, David A. and Gene G. Kassebaum (1972) "On Biting the Hand That Feeds: Some
    Implications of Sociological Evaluations of Correctional Effectiveness," in Carol H.
    Weiss (ed.) Evaluating Action Programs: Readings in Social Action and Education.
    Boston: Allyn & Bacon: 300-310.
Warren, Roland (1973) "The Social Context of Program Evaluation Research." presented
    Ohio State University Symposium on Evaluation in Human Service Programs, June.
Weiss, Carol H. (1970) "The Politicization of Evaluation Research." J. of Social Issues 26,
    4:57-68.
Weiss, Carol H. (1972) Evaluation Research Methods of Assessing Program Effectiveness.
    Englewood Cliffs, NJ: Prentice-Hall.
Weiss, Carol H. (1973) "The Politics of Impact Measurement." Policy Studies J. 1, 3:
    179-83.

PART II

THE POLICY CYCLE

3

LINKING PROGRAM EVALUATION
TO USER NEEDS

E L E A N O R   C H E L I M S K Y

U.S. General Accounting Office

THE EVALUATION/USE LINKAGE

If program evaluation, like basic research, existed only to improve knowledge in a particular area, its success could be measured exclusively in terms of the degree to which it had advanced understanding in that area. But although one purpose of program evaluation is indeed to contribute to such knowledge and understanding, another equally important purpose is to be useful in bringing information to bear on political decisions of many different types. While there is nothing new in this statement, it does mean that measuring the success of a program evaluation must include judgments not only about the degree of increase or improvement in knowledge achieved by the evaluation, but also about the degree to which the evaluation was valuable to a particular sponsor, user or audience in meeting specific information needs. Since it is obvious that all types of knowledge-producing evaluations may not be relevant to all audiences, this raises the question of how program evaluation can best be linked to the differing information needs of its various users.

Author's Note: *The views and opinions expressed by the author are her own and should not be construed to be the policy or position of the General Accounting Office.*

But to raise this question is simultaneously to raise a subset of component questions. For example, what kinds of information needs can an evaluation be expected to supply? And how do these needs differ for various users, or target audiences? Who are the typical users of the evaluation and what kinds of relationships, if any, exist among them? Should an evaluator, in designing a study, seek to bring information to one user only, or can many users be targeted by the same evaluation? How do new programs differ from existing programs, and controversial programs from accepted programs, in their evaluative information needs? Are all types of evaluations likely to be useful at different times to different audiences, or are some information needs unique to particular functions, particular audiences, particular times, so that certain types of evaluations will be predictably more relevant to some users than to others? In sum, given a variety of demands—that is, information needs stemming from a variety of users performing a variety of public functions—and given also a variety in supply—that is, the different program evaluation types available to meet those different needs—how are demand and supply currently linked? How should they be linked? And, most importantly, how can that linkage be improved?

This article proposes to examine the linkage between program evaluation and its users at the federal level. I think this is important to do correctly, because there seems to be developing a perhaps unnecessarily narrow view among evaluators of the kinds of questions an evaluation can and should answer, and as a result of that view, a perhaps unnecessarily rapid jumping to conclusions—again, among evaluators—about how to improve evaluation use. For example, all evaluations are not required to address cause-and-effect questions, all don't need to solve policy problems, all are not asked to change the world. It is the users of evaluation who ask the evaluative questions. But it is not always clear that those users feel the evaluations they eventually receive have answered the questions they asked.

So it seems lawful to take another look at that linkage, and to do so I will try to explore the relationship between different types of functions and users, different types of information needs, different times in the life of a public program, and different types of evaluation studies. I will focus not upon the qualities and failures of the evaluation types or upon the merits of the information needs, but upon the evaluation/use linkage itself, by looking both at the demand for evaluative information and at the supply of program evaluation types available to meet that demand. My purpose here is not only to improve the targeting of program evaluations upon general information needs, but also to improve the targeting of specific *types* of evaluations upon specific *types* of information needs, and, as a result, to improve the usefulness of evaluation findings for policy or program management decision making.

WHAT ARE THE PURPOSES
THAT EVALUATION MAY SERVE?

Program evaluations serve general audiences (such as the public or the media, which are the ultimate users of many evaluations) and individual public decision makers with particular information needs. These decision makers may be in the executive or legislative branches of government, they may play management or policy roles with respect to public programs, and they may need information from evaluation for the following three very broad kinds of purposes:

- for policy formulation—that is, for example, to assess and/or justify the need for a new program;
- for policy execution—that is, for example, to ensure that a program is implemented in the most cost/effective way; and
- for accountability in public decision making—that is, for example, to determine the effectiveness of an operating program and the need for its continuation, modification, or termination.

The purpose of *policy formulation*, which applies essentially to new programs, requires information from evaluation in at least three major areas: (1) Information on the problem or threat addressed by the program (e.g., How big is it? What is its frequency and direction? How is it changing? Do we really need a new program or new legislation to address it? If we do, how likely is the program to be successful?); (2) Information on the results of past programs or related efforts that attempted to deal with the problem or threat (e.g., Were those programs feasible? Did they succeed? What problems did they encounter?); and (3) Information allowing the selection of one alternative program over another (e.g., What are the likely comparable costs and benefits of going one way versus another? What kinds of growth rates were experienced by the different programs in the past?).

The purpose of *policy execution*, on the other hand, applies either to new or to existing programs and asks different evaluative questions from those of policy formulation. Here users will want to have: (1) Information on program implementation (such as the degree to which the program is operational, how similar it is across sites, whether it conforms to the policies and expectations formulated, how much it costs, how stakeholders feel about it, whether there are major problems of service delivery or of error, fraud, abuse, etc.); (2) Information on program management (such as the degree of control over expenditures, the qualifications and credentials of personnel, the allocation of resources, the use of program information in decision making, etc.); and (3) Ongoing information on the current state of the problem addressed by the program (e.g., Is the problem growing? Is it diminishing? Is it diminishing enough so the program is no longer needed? Is it changing in terms of its significant characteristics so that the program also needs to be changed?).

Finally, the purpose of *accountability*, which applies to both new and existing programs, requires information from evaluation that again differs markedly from the other two policy purposes. Here evaluations must emphasize: (1) Information on program outcomes (i.e., What happened as a result of designing the program and implementing it?); (2) Information on whether the program achieved its goals; and (3) Information on the effects (unexpected as well as expected) of the program.

These different types of information needs that are related to the three kinds of general policy purposes have implications, of course, for the types of evaluations that are most likely to satisfy the particular information need. (This point will be discussed later in some detail.) But those information needs must also be understood in relation to the functions and roles of the evaluation users. Where they sit not only determines where they stand but also influences the evaluative questions they ask.

WHAT ARE THE TYPICAL FUNCTIONS OR ROLES OF EVALUATION USERS AND HOW DO THEY DIFFER?

Who, then, are the typical governmental users of evaluative information developed for the three policy purposes, how do their functions or roles differ, and to whom do they report? Among the types of executive and legislative branch decision makers who need and use evaluative information to serve one or more of these purposes are the following six:

In the executive branch

- program managers,
- agency heads and top policymakers in an individual agency or department, and
- central government budget and policy authorities.

In the legislative branch

- four legislative agencies; that is, the Congressional Research Service (CRS), the General Accounting Office (GAO), the Office of Technology Assessment (OTA), and the Congressional Budget Office (CBO),
- congressional authorization, appropriations, and budget committees, and
- oversight committees.

Executive branch *program managers* seek evaluative information to plan, implement, manage, and eventually modify their programs so as to make them as cost/effective as possible. Their personal accountability for this work is usually to the head of their branch or agency, or to one of the agency's top policymakers. Thus the program manager must consider, along with his or her own needs, the views and needs of his or her boss in developing an evaluative approach.

The functions and roles of agency heads and other top policymakers require somewhat different types of evaluative information than do those of program managers. For example, a departmental secretary is less interested than a program manager in detailed program information, but will instead need data to determine and/or justify the need for a new program, to assess the effectiveness of an operating program, or to review the need to continue or modify a program. This is because an agency's top managers are likely to have to report on these matters not only to the administration (i.e., to the Office of Management and Budget—OMB—as well as to the policymaking Executive Office of the President) but also to the Congress (through its authorization, appropriations, budget, and oversight committees).

With regard to staff from OMB and the Executive Office, these decision makers—in their central budget and policy functions—may also look to evaluation to inform them about the effectiveness of a program or to help in the decision to continue, cut or otherwise change it. Their accountability is to the president.

In the legislative branch, congressional authorization, appropriations, and budget committees use evaluation findings essentially as contributing information to program funding or refunding decisions. Congressional oversight committees, on the other hand, rely on evaluation not only to supply findings about agency programs but also to bring information about how agencies are performing their various functions (such as personnel and resource management, for example) or how agencies have organized themselves to conduct research or to ensure internal controls. Although all four of these types of congressional committees may use executive agency produced evaluation findings in their negotiation and decision-making processes, they also rely on evaluation findings from independent sources such as universities, consulting firms and other groups. They may use those findings directly, through the work of congressional staff, or indirectly, through the proxy of one or another of the legislative agencies. CRS may, for example, report findings to congressional sponsors from a wide variety of evaluations in an "issues" article for legislative use. The GAO, which has a congressional mandate to perform program evaluations, may either report its own findings to the Congress, or analyze evaluation findings from many different sources to inform the Congress, or critique methodological or other technical aspects of existing evaluations when findings conflict (or appear to conflict). OTA may use evaluation findings as a foundation from which to forecast technological impacts, and CBO may use them as part of the empirical base on which to construct the likely outcomes of alternative economic policies. The accountability of the legislative agencies is to the Congress; the Congress's accountability, like that of the president, is, of course, to the public via regular general elections.

The six different types of evaluation users, then, have some purposes in common and some that are uniquely their own. As a result, there are some areas of evaluative information need that they share and some that are distinct. Only a program manager or the GAO, for example, may need to receive fine-grained information on implementation and operational issues specific to one or two local sites in a large national program. Yet, even though there may not be many audiences for this information, it may be crucial to the needs of those two users. On the other hand, evaluation findings on

- the effectiveness of a program,
- client satisfaction or frustration with program services,
- the views of program stakeholders,
- trends in the problem(s) addressed by the program, or
- changes in the dimensions or focus of the program

are likely to be helpful to all users, and may interest general audiences as well.

However, the degree of detail needed by users from evaluative information that all of them may want, will differ depending upon the user's specific function, purpose, and particular accountability. A member of Congress, for example, may need to be aware only of the major findings of a program evaluation, whereas an agency head—who may be called upon by OMB, the president, or the Congress to defend the program or explain the findings—will require a much more detailed knowledge of the information produced. This means that although the basic information produced by an evaluation may be useful to several different audiences, different versions of that information, presenting different levels of detail, may be needed.

The question of the appropriateness of a particular evaluation to the needs of multiple users is one that evaluators ought to consider very carefully. Evaluations are so few in number, and the idea of serving several users with the same evaluation is so attractive that a danger exists of introducing information distortion inadvertently. Explicit statements by the evaluators about the objectives and limitations of the evaluation are needed to ensure than an evaluation performed, say for the head of an agency to learn the opinions of practitioners or stakeholders about a program, is not interpreted by a secondary user—the press, for example—as an evaluation of program effectiveness.

Further, the ability to serve multiple users is always constrained by the need for an evaluator to answer the precise questions posed by the primary user, and the need for the conclusiveness of the answers given to match that user's particular information need. For example, it is reasonable to undertake an expensive, large-scale effectiveness evaluation when the primary user must have the most conclusive information possible. But if an evaluation user wants to develop some general information in an area where little currently exists, then less conclusive—and less costly—information may be both appropriate and desirable.

Finally, it is important to point out an essential difference in purpose between evaluative information designed for executive branch and legislative branch users. While both branches may need evaluative evidence on, say, the need for a program as part of their policy-formulating role (that is, their planning of authorizing functions), and while they may both need evidence of efficiency or effectiveness to support their accountability role in their administrative and legislative oversight processes, it is the administration alone that is charged with program implementation and the administration, therefore, which has the greater need for the policy execution type of evaluation information. As a result, executive branch managers and—to a lesser degree—agency heads, may often (and quite properly) be virtually the sole users of certain types of detailed evaluative information that supports decisionmaking about program operations.

This suggests that, as a general rule, evaluators, in thinking about the eventual use of their evaluations, can expect their work on program effectiveness and on the feasibility and logic of proposed new programs to be more valuable to a greater variety of secondary users than their work on program operations.

HOW DO EVALUATIVE INFORMATION NEEDS DIFFER FOR NEW PROGRAMS VERSUS OLD ONES? FOR ACCEPTED PROGRAMS VERSUS CONTROVERSIAL ONES?

Information needs not only differ for different users, they also differ between new and existing programs. A new program has a need for planning information not presented by an established program. But an established program needs effectiveness information and other information on a periodic basis that can only be obtained when a program has been fully operational for some time.

Information needs are also affected by a program's dimensions, life cycle, and by the circumstances surrounding it. In a new program, for example, it makes a difference, with regard to the evidence required to justify its need, if the program is large or small, expensive or modest, controversial or consensual, presenting many unknowns or instead, clearly feasible. A large and expensive program needs stronger evaluative justification than does a small, modest one, because of accountability to the taxpayer. This is often important for defense programs (like the MX missile and B1 bomber, for example) that cost a great deal and whose logic and assumptions are typically subject to extensive debate, first within the administration, and then, by the Congress, and in the press.

Even when new programs are small, however, they need to have a very sound basis and rationale if they are controversial. A recent example was the Reagan administration's proposal to end the moratorium on the production of nerve gas and to begin augmenting the existing stockpile of unitary weapons with new "binary" weapons. The appropriations requested were not large, as defense programs go. However, emotions surrounding the issue of chemical warfare run high, the moratorium had existed for many years, the administration's case for ending the moratorium and starting production on binary weapons was not supported by strong evidence and the Congress rejected production of any new chemical weapons.

Proposed programs whose scientific or technological feasibility is still unclear also need to have sound logic and convincing presumptions of effectiveness behind them. When feasibility programs are real, they are sure to surface in the debate on funding, and should therefore be persuasively addressed in the program rationale. Yet it sometimes happens that an agency may believe a new research program is needed, and that its feasibility problems cannot be resolved without federal funds. Under those circumstances, the temptation can be very great to minimize the feasibility problems so as to obtain appropriations for the program. While this strategy may work over the short term (and in fact it has worked *very often* and *very well* over the short term for the Department of Defense) it tends to mislead policymakers, to create overoptimistic expectations for the program and to give credence to a highly simplistic and really quite mythical view of the research process. In particular, by minimizing technical problems, the implication is that of a low-risk, routine, regular process in which

> (i) research regularly uncovers new ideas that (ii) are then fed into the hands of development engineers who (iii) neatly establish the technical and economic feasibility of a new gadget or technology that (iv) can then be introduced smoothly into efficient production, and thus (v) the research-to-production process effortlessly solves some problem or meets some national need [Nichols, 1971, apropos of various DOD presentations to the Congress].

Of course, the long-term effect of this oversimplification of the research process—which in its true nature is iterative and nonlinear, irregular, idiosyncratic, and highly uncertain—will be the quasi-certitude of negative evaluation findings if the program's evaluation should mistakenly structure its criteria for success on the agenda's rhetoric. This is because the presence of significant technical unknowns in a program means that events are unpredictable and that major problems may arise in development or testing that could cost a lot of money and take a long time to solve.

The point here is that oversimplifying and overpromising about what evidence is available to rationalize funding for a new program can misfire badly. One result just discussed is that evaluation findings for the program may be meaningless if the program's objectives were overstated and unachievable from the start. Another result is that efforts to deal with the evaluation failures (for example by modifying objectives or continuing to test and retest) can cause a further stretching out of what may already have been a long development cycle. A third—and perhaps the most important—result is that the credibility of the overpromisers inevitably suffers over the long term as, one after the other, the negative evaluation findings come in on programs about which so very much had been promised.

All of this underscores the truly critical need for evaluative information—and for an evaluative mechanism capable of intervening—in the policy-formulation process that generates new programs. This is especially important for new programs that are controversial and for those that present significant scientific or technical unknowns.

HOW DO THE PURPOSES AND ROLES
OF EVALUATION USERS
SHAPE THEIR INFORMATION NEEDS?

Given six (illustrative and nonexhaustive) types of evaluation users with differing functions and roles, and given also general information needs vis-à-vis public programs, what can now be said about their *specific* information needs? To begin with, are these quite distinct from each other, or are there areas of commonality? Table 3.1 lists examples of specific evaluative

TABLE 3.1
Evaluation Users' Information Needs

TYPE OF PROGRAM	(1) USER: Executive Branch Program Manager FUNCTION: Policy Execution: Program Planning, Implementation, and Effectiveness ACCOUNTABILITY: To Agency Head or Top Agency Policymakers	(2) USER: Executive Branch Agency Head/Top Agency Policymaker FUNCTION: Policy Formulation and Execution: Administrative Program Oversight ACCOUNTABILITY: To Central Budgetary and Policy Authorities, to the President, and to the Congress
NEW PROGRAM PROPOSAL	INFORMATION NEEDS Program Planning For Example: -Monitoring and analysis of the problem/threat -Effectiveness of past efforts to solve the problem, or related problem, or threat -Comparative costs and benefits of alternative program options -Logic of relationship between problem/threat and program assumptions -Determination of likely feasibility, costs, acceptability, and effectiveness vis-à-vis problem Assurance of Future Information For Example: -Pilot test -Evaluation design -Internal controls -Audit plan -Data system design to monitor problem/program	INFORMATION NEEDS Program Decisions For Example: -Results of program manager's analysis -Critique of program planning effort -Comparative costs, benefits, and budgetary impact vis-à-vis other agency programs and general administration policy -Constituency, stakeholder, and legislative acceptability of program -Continued monitoring of problem/threat Evaluation Decisions For Example: -Kinds of future information to be developed -In-house, grant, or contract evaluation approval
NEWLY IMPLEMENTED OR EXISTING PROGRAM	INFORMATION NEEDS Program Implementation For Example: -Costs -Extent operational -Size of population being served compared to expectations -Practitioner satisfaction -Client satisfaction -Degree of error, fraud, abuse -Relationship of program as implemented to legislative and administration intent -Results of problem/threat monitoring Program Effectiveness For Example: -Outcomes of the program -Impact made by the program on the problem/threat -Expected/unexpected effects Program Decisions For Example: -Modification -Reevaluation	INFORMATION NEEDS Program Decisions For Example: -Monitoring of costs, stakeholder satisfaction, levels of error, fraud or abuse -Assessment of program effectiveness findings -Determination of continuing need for program or program components -Analysis of program's budgetary impact on agency -Monitoring of problem/threat -Program continuation or modification decisions Evaluation Decisions For Example: -Assessment of information gaps -Agenda for development of missing or inadequate information

TABLE 3.1 Continued

TYPE OF PROGRAM	(3) USER: Executive Branch Central Budgetary and Policy Authorities FUNCTION: Policy Formulation and Oversight of Policy and Program Execution ACCOUNTABILITY: To the President	(4) USER: Legislative Branch Agencies (CRS, GAO, OTA, and CBO) FUNCTION: Policy Formulation and Oversight: Budget, Analysis, Audit, and Evaluation Support to the Congress ACCOUNTABILITY: To the Congress
NEW PROGRAM PROPOSAL	INFORMATION NEEDS Program Decisions For Example: -Results of program manager's analysis -Strength of administration, constituency, legislative support for program -Comparative costs and benefits across agencies and programs vis-à-vis administration policy goals and budget constraints -Examination of degree of duplication, overlap, goal conflicts, etc., between proposed new program and existing programs Evaluation Decisions For Example: -Review of agency head decisions -Modification to kinds of information being developed	INFORMATION NEEDS Review of Program Planning For Example: -Examination of evidence presented in support of program -Verification of alternatives to program considered -Assessment of program logic related to problem or threat -Reanalysis of likely feasibility, costs, benefits, and budgetary impact of program -Examination of controls against error, fraud and abuse -Review of evaluation and data system design Recommendations For Example: -Other options -Evaluation/audit language
NEWLY IMPLEMENTED OR EXISTING PROGRAM	INFORMATION NEEDS Program Decisions For Example: -Assessment of evaluation/audit findings -Assessment of agency head's budgetary and policy decisions vis-à-vis the program -Determination of strength of program success as related to administrations' new goals/priorities/problems -Reexamination of political constituency needs Evaluation Decisions For Example: -Review of agency head decisions on information gaps -Modifications to agency evaluation agenda	INFORMATION NEEDS Program Review For Example: -Methodological review of implementation findings -Methodological review of effectiveness findings -Re-analysis of costs and benefits -Review of program management -Original review of program implementation or effectiveness -Analysis of agency decisions -Analysis of present and future budgetary impacts -Analysis of current trends in the problem/threat addressed by the program Recommendations For Example: -Further analysis of program effects -Program modification -Evaluation, audit or, other modification

(continued)

TABLE 3.1 Continued

(5)	(6)
USER: Legislative Branch Authorization, Appropriations, and Budget Committees FUNCTION: Policy Formulation and Oversight: Enactment of Priority Programs Within Budget Constraints ACCOUNTABILITY: To the Public	USER: Legislative Branch Oversight Committees FUNCTION: Legislative Oversight of Executive Branch Programs and Management ACCOUNTABILITY: To the Public
INFORMATION NEEDS Program Decisions For Example: -Results of executive branch analyses (program proposal and rationale) -Results of analyses by legislative branch agencies -Review by committee staff -Hearings/debate -Assessment by committees of strength of constituency/congressional support for program versus committee priorities and budget constraints Evaluation Decisions For Example: -Audit/evaluation language -Modifications to program or evaluation plans -Data collection	**INFORMATION NEEDS** Program Decisions For Example: -Assessment of oversight needs for the program -Review of legislative agencies analyses of likely program feasibility, cost and effectiveness -Review of plans for controls, audit, evaluation, and management Evaluation Decisions For Example: -Audit/evaluation language -Modifications to program, evaluation, or management plans -Data collection
INFORMATION NEEDS Program Decisions For Example: -Results of executive branch evaluations and audits -Results of legislative branch methodological reviews of findings -Review by committee staff -Assessment by committee of continued need and support for program in view of budget constraints and status of problem/threat -Determination of program modifications Evaluation Decisions For Example: -Mandate to evaluate or audit aspects of the program -Changes in program regulations such as data collection requirements, etc.	**INFORMATION NEEDS** Program Decisions For Example: -Analysis of the results of all evaluations, audits, and analyses performed by the executive branch -Results of legislative agencies reanalysis or evaluations -Assessment of match between implemented program and legislative intent -Examination of agency management of program and of control systems -Determination of program/agency modifications Evaluation Decisions For Example: -Mandate to evaluate or audit program -Mandate to review agency evaluation process -Mandate to review management process

information needs each user might be expected to have, based on purpose and function and on whether or not the program is an existing or a new one.

Each of the examples of information need shown in the table has been related directly to the functions or roles of a particular user. Thus the likely relevance to other users of each piece of evaluative information in support of a specific information need can be tracked across the columns of the table. For example, it is clear from Table 3.1 that evaluative information that can be used to monitor and analyze the problem or threat addressed by an existing program is not only useful to the program manager, but also to the agency head, to legislative agencies and to congressional committees of both types. In the same way, for a new program, the program manager's analytical justification of that program will be examined over and over by a bevy of other evaluation users. On the other hand, the information need for comparative evaluation of competing programs in terms of administration policy goals is more likely to be restricted in some measure to OMB and to the White House.

Looking across the columns of Table 3.1, an important distinction to be made among the six user groups is that although all groups may need evaluative information in support of their functions, not all are responsible for producing them. In fact, if evaluation producers are distinguished from evaluation reviewers and users, then the six groups of evaluation users can be narrowed to four, because two groups—the program managers and legislative agency staff—are responsible for developing a large part of the evaluative information required. The evaluating work done or monitored by these producers (who are, of course, often users as well) is then available for reanalysis and reuse by policymakers in both executive and legislative branches.

Again, looking across the columns of Table 3.1 and bearing in mind the three policy purposes discussed earlier—policy formulation, policy execution, and accountability—five basic program activities, performed in varying degrees across the spectrum of evaluation users, can be derived:

(1) planning and rationalizing a program and its evaluation,
(2) implementing and managing a program,
(3) justifying the effectiveness of program implementation and management,
(4) demonstrating the effectiveness of a program, and
(5) measuring ongoing problem or program progress.

All of these activities call for specific types of evaluative information that, of course, needs to be produced before it can be used or reviewed. But which users of evaluation are also producers, and how does the answer to that question affect the linkages between evaluation and use?

WHAT IS THE DISTRIBUTION OF PRODUCERS, REVIEWERS, AND USERS OF EVALUATION IN TERMS OF THE FIVE PROGRAM ACTIVITIES?

Table 3.2 examines the five activities derived from Table 3.1 (listed above), in terms of the roles of four groups of evaluation users in producing, reviewing, and using the evaluative information generated in support of the activities. For the five activities requiring evaluative information, the table shows considerable congruence with regard to the use—if not the production—of the evaluative information by the four groups. For example, knowledge needed by all reviewers and users of a new program proposal (included in Table 3.2, first column on the left) necessarily involves several types of evaluative information, some of whose dimensions were already outlined in Table 3.1. Program managers, executive branch agency heads, and central authorities, as well as legislative agencies and committees, all need to see evidence of the problem or threat that a proposed new program is designed to solve or meet, and evidence that the program is likely to solve that problem or meet that threat. Such evidence can come from evaluations that (1) develop basic data on what is known about the problem being addressed by the new program or about programs of the past that addressed the problem; (2) identify knowledge gaps—that is, recognize what is *not* known about the

TABLE 3.2
Producers, Reviewers, and Users of Evaluative Information

Type of User	Five Types of Activities Generating Evaluative Information Needs				
	Planning and Rationalizing a Program and its Evaluation	Implementing and Managing a Program	Justifying the Effectiveness of Program Implementation and Management	Demonstrating the Effectiveness of a Program	Measuring Ongoing Problem/Program Progress
Program Manager	Producer/User	Producer/User	Producer/User	Producer/User	Producer/User
Agency Head/ Central Agencies	Reviewer/User	Reviewer/User	Reviewer/User	Reviewer/User	Reviewer/User
Legislative Agencies	Reviewer/User	Reviewer/User	Producer/Reviewer/ User	Producer/Reviewer/ User	Producer/Reviewer/ User
Congressional Committees	Reviewer/User	Reviewer/User	Reviewer/User	Reviewer/User	Reviewer/User

problem and about programs of the past that addressed it—in order to estimate as well as possible the likelihood of program success; (3) establish the relative merits of past positions—especially conflicting positions—taken by proponents, opponents, theorists, practitioners, and analysts with regard to the program or policy; and (4) assess the prior findings of studies designed to determine the effects of implementing alternative policies or programs.

In a similar way, for an implemented or existing program, the same reviewers and users will require some level of information on the operational realities of the program, on its effectiveness, and on its present and future budgetary impacts.

On the other hand, it is important to note that although the generic needs may be the same, the *specific* information need of each user and the level of analysis requirement may be different. For example, both the administration and the Congress may need evaluative information on program effectiveness. But while the administration's need could perhaps be satisfied in some areas by evaluation studies that are not generalizable to the nation as a whole, generalizable information might be precisely what a congressional authorizing committee would feel it must have.

Similarly, a unit of analysis requirement at the state level that might yield sufficient information for an agency head's or congressional committee's problem-measuring (or monitoring) activity might not be sufficiently sensitive for a program manager's or legislative agency's analytical needs. In the legislative oversight of a criminal justice program, for example, state-level data on crime rates might be sufficient for a congressional committee. But to be useful to program managers needing to understand program activity results and implement changes in the program on a site-by-site basis, these data would have to be broken down much further (by type of crime and offender, by season, by time of day, and by location, for example). In order to understand why proactive patrol by police may have been unsuccessful in, say, shopping malls and to locate it in places where it is likely to be successful in reducing crime, program managers must have information about the places and times that constitute targets of opportunity for particular types of crimes and criminals.

These differences in specific information need and in unit of analysis requirement have crucial implications for the evaluations that need to be done to satisfy each user and for the degree to which a single evaluation can serve multiple users. In each case, therefore, it is important for an evaluator to be able to recognize and identify the dimensions of each evaluation user's information need and, as a result, to make conscious decisions in the design phase about what information will or will not be obtained and available to that user.

On the other hand, it seems logical that at least evaluations should be able to address the information needs of many users. For example, a study of the effectiveness of past efforts to solve a problem that a producer (i.e., program manager or legislative agency) would prepare to justify a proposed new program could be useful to all evaluation reviewers and users without any change in the content of the analysis.

What, then, does this tell us about the types of evaluation that can support the specific activities and information needs of evaluation users? Put another way, how can the evaluations that are now regularly performed be linked to these activities and needs? What indicators show their relevance to the specific requirements of individual evaluation users? What gaps exist?

HOW ARE SPECIFIC TYPES OF EVALUATION STUDIES LINKED TO SPECIFIC PROGRAM AND POLICY INFORMATION NEEDS?

The Evaluation Research Society (ERS Standards Committee, 1981) has identified six types of routinely conducted evaluation studies. These are discussed below:

(1) Front-end analysis. This is the evaluative work that answers questions of the sort described earlier under the policy-formulation purpose. It is typically done before deciding to move ahead with a new program.

(2) Evaluability assessment. This examines the logic of a program's assumptions and activities in terms of its objectives,

describes the characteristics of program implementation, determines the feasibility and usefulness of performing an evaluation of the program's effectiveness, and, if the latter determination is positive, lays the groundwork for such an evaluation. In that sense, an evaluability assessment may be the first phase of a larger evaluation effort. It can serve both policy-formulation and policy-execution purposes.

(3) Process evaluation. This is a form of evaluation that either stands alone or is developed in combination with another type of evaluation. As a stand-alone, it typically falls under the policy-execution purpose: to analyze the processes of program implementation—management strategies, operations, costs, interactions among clients and practitioners, error rates, and so on—in order to improve them. In combination with another evaluation type (most often an effectiveness evaluation), it can serve the accountability purpose as well, with objectives that may include (a) helping to determine the design of the effectiveness evaluation or (b) helping to explain its findings. In the first case, the process evaluation will precede the effectiveness evaluation, in the second, the two will be conducted more or less simultaneously.

(4) Effectiveness or impact evaluation. This type of evaluation seeks to find out how well a program is working and thus primarily serves the accountability purpose. However, until superseded by later studies its findings continue to be useful for both the policy-formulation and -execution purposes of subsequent programs (or succeeding phases of the same program). To serve these purposes, the evaluation must be able to show that any changes observed are in fact results of the program, rather than of other factors or forces. This means that the design for this kind of evaluation needs to include a basis for comparison that permits an understanding of what would have been observed in the absence of the program.

(5) Program and problem monitoring. This type of evaluation tracks progress (long term or short term) in areas such as changes in the problem addressed by the program, program compliance with policy, service delivery, and numbers of clients. Administrative data systems that can form the bases for quasi-experimental

designs of the interrupted time-series variety often develop around the program and problem monitoring effort. As a result, this type of evaluation can serve the three purposes of evaluation: policy formulation, execution, and accountability.

(6) Metaevaluation or evaluation synthesis. This form of evaluation uses existing evaluations to determine what has been learned about a program. Depending on the availability of evaluations and other empirical work, this type of evaluation can address many different evaluation questions, including those about the effectiveness of the program and about the extent of existing knowledge in a given program or problem area. As such, like monitoring, it can serve all three evaluation purposes.

To this list may be added a seventh type of evaluation, the *case study*. This evaluation strategy is less well defined than the ones identified earlier. For the purposes of this chapter, it can be called "an analytic description of an event, a process, an institution or a program" (Hoaglin et al., 1982). A case study may use one of the six forms given by the ERS standards, but it always has the special characteristics of yielding rich, in-depth information about an *individual instance* of a program or process. The evaluative case study can be used as a stand-alone (e.g., to invalidate a conventionally accepted hypothesis), in combination with another evaluation (e.g., to examine how findings from individual cases may relate to national findings); or cumulatively (e.g., to build up evidence piece by piece when a program is so complex or large-scale that evaluation of the whole is infeasible or must be delayed).

When these seven types of program evaluation studies are linked with the five types of activities generating the evaluative information needs, a general idea is provided of the number and kinds of purposes that currently practiced program evaluations can serve for the evaluation users identified earlier. Table 3.3 indicates some of the primary linkages (that is, secondary linkages, such as the reuse of an individual effectiveness evaluation in policy formulation, have been omitted for clarity).

Several things are immediately obvious in examining Table 3.3. First, program and problem monitoring data are useful for

TABLE 3.3

Primary Linkages of Program Evaluation Types with Evaluative Information Needs of User Groups

Type of Activity Generating Evaluative Information Need	Seven Types of Program Evaluations						
	Front end Analysis	Evaluability Assessment	Process Evaluation	Effectiveness or Impact Evaluation	Program and Problem Monitoring	Metaevaluation or Evaluation Synthesis	Case Study Evaluation
Planning and Rationalizing a Program and Its Evaluation	X				X	X	
Implementing and Managing a Program		X	X		X		X
Justifying the Effectiveness of Program Implementation and Management			X	X	X	X	X
Demonstrating the Effectiveness of a Program	O	O	O	X	X	X	X
Measuring Ongoing Problem/Program Progress	X			X	X		

NOTE: X = fulfills the information need standing alone; O = fulfills the information need supplemented by other evaluation work.

every one of the five types of activities. This is because such data are marvelously versatile. They can help establish the range and frequency of a problem (before it has even been decided to propose a program); they can inform on progress in implementing and managing the program; they can be used—in conjunction with other efforts—to determine the effectiveness of both the program as a whole (longitudinal administrative data can be critical here) and its implementation or management; finally, they are the instrument of choice for maintaining a minimum level of awareness of ongoing progress in either the program itself or the problem it is intended to address.

A second obvious point from the table is that establishing the effectiveness of a program can involve all seven types of evaluation, some of them used in conjunction with each other. This may result from three factors: the difficulty of demonstrating program effectiveness, the usefulness of employing several different methods in the same evaluation to better assure that demonstration, and the great interest of evaluators in performing them. This is an important point, because effectiveness evaluations are typically the longest, most arduous, and most costly to perform. If program evaluations are to be linked to specific user needs, then the time, costs, and character of the information produced are highly relevant factors. On the other hand, it is also the case that process evaluations, monitoring, front-end evaluations, and evaluability assessments, used alone, cannot normally supply evidence of effectiveness adequate for, say, the legislative oversight function.

In terms of the three policy purposes discussed earlier, although seven types of evaluation primarily serve the needs of accountability (as reflected in the demonstration of implementation, management or program effectiveness), and four types serve policy execution (implementing and managing a program), only three serve the needs of policy formulation (i.e., planning and rationalizing a program) in the executive branch. This is especially striking in that policy execution (i.e., implementing and managing a program) is the activity of only one type of executive branch evaluation user (see Table 3.2), that is, the program manager, while that of policy formulation is common to all three executive branch users. This is not to say that front-end analysis, problem monitoring, and metaevaluation are not powerful tools in support of policy formulation. But given the nearly exclusive production role of program managers in the executive branch, it is not apparent how and where these policy formulation evaluations—which could help in major ways to assist the decision making of agency heads, central budgetary and policy authorities, and especially, the Congress—can be or are being developed. This is particularly important today for the legislative acceptability of new defense initiatives, one of the few areas in which the current administration has chosen to introduce new programs.

With regard to legislative users, the lack of evaluations supporting policy formulation in the executive branch puts the onus on those other evaluation producers, the legislative agencies, to fill the void. Unfortunately, the oversight needs for evaluative information are so overwhelming, and the legislative agencies have been so understaffed for the work they need to accomplish, that legislative information requirements to support either congressional or administration proposals for new programs (How needed are they? What is known about past efforts to address them? Are they feasible? Will they bring the expected results? How should they best be structured?) may well be one of the most significant areas needing reinforced attention by program evaluators. Meeting these requirements takes on added difficulty because of the size and complexity of the new defense proposals. As these begin to account for an increasing proportion of the national budget and as scientists and engineers continue to develop increasingly sophisticated technology, it is clear that explanations, justifications, and supporting data for the new programs become more and more important. Yet these latter have not only been in short supply; they have also been presented in terms of highly optimistic and even misleading rationales.

Another reason that evaluators should pay more attention to front-end analysis and to the needs of policy formulation in both branches of government is that the benefits of early problem identification considerably outweigh their cost, especially from the taxpayer's point of view. While establishing program effects is a very important function for evaluation in support of oversight, it is also costly and often unsuccessful because the program is so far along and its advocates are so well entrenched. This is all the more reason for evaluators to try harder to ensure the presence of sound information early on in the executive and legislative branch debates about new programs.

SUMMARY AND CONCLUSIONS

This chapter has sought to establish a framework by which to link types of evaluation with managers' and policymakers' information needs. The reasons I felt it is important to do this are three:

(1) Stating the importance of user-focused evaluation is not enough. What has to be done is to actually design the evaluation around the user's specific information needs.
(2) It is through the evaluation user (or sponsor) that the evaluation does or does not become a part of the political process. This is to say that all evaluations are not necessarily political in themselves. But if they should enter the political arena, via the user, then credibility (i.e, objectivity and methodological quality) is the sine qua non for their success.
(3) In my view it is at least as important for the use of evaluations that they be better directed to user needs as it is for evaluators to be more understanding of the ways of politics. Even the most profound understanding will not keep a piece of analysis from being buffeted about by political storms. But proper direction of the study to the needed policy purpose, and appropriate labeling of what the study is and what it is not, can go a long way toward improving the appropriateness of evaluation use without inevitably embroiling the evaluator in politics.

This is why I have looked at evaluation politics, rather than institutional politics, to see if comparing what users get from evaluation with what they need from it because of their political functions and roles can illuminate recent problems in the area of evaluation use.

This involved, first, characterizing strategic (rather than effective) demand and supply. I tried to do this by identifying three broad policy or program purposes that evaluations may serve (that is, policy formulation, policy execution, and accountability); pinpointing six illustrative types of evaluation user groups that generate evaluative requirements; and then describing those evaluative information needs with respect to new as well as operational programs. This gives a crude sense of the strategic demand for evaluation in public policy and decision making at the federal level (see Table 3.1). In addition, since each example of information need is directly related to the political function or role of a particular user, the likely relevance to other uses of each piece of evaluative information can be tracked.

Next, I derived from Table 3.1 five categories of activities generating evaluative information needs that could be linked to current practice in program evaluation. The six user groups were reduced to four on the basis of their producer or user role in evaluation, and then the activity categories requiring information support were examined in terms both of their distribution across groups and the role of the groups with regard to production, review, or use of the evaluative information (see Table 3.2).

The results suggested that many users can benefit from information needed for all the five activities. However, the type of need and the appropriate unit of analysis may be different.

Seven frequently performed types of program evaluation were then identified and linked with the five activities driving evaluative information needs, to get more precise indicators with regard to multiple use of the same evaluation (see Table 3.3). First, program and problem monitoring information appears to be useful for every one of the five types of activities. Second, establishing program effectiveness can involve all seven types of evaluation.

Other points are as follows:

- It is important that the evaluator be familiar with the characteristics (e.g., cost, time to produce, quality of information) of as many types of evaluation as possible when designing efforts to establish program effectiveness.

• Evaluation production is currently better targeted to accountability and policy execution than to policy formulation.
• Evaluators need to devote more effort to working in the policy formulation area, particularly in analyzing the justifications for new programs and policies.

Evaluation to support policy formulation is especially important when programs are controversial or involve major technical uncertainty.

Several problems need to be overcome if proposed new programs are to receive better evaluative scrutiny early enough to be useful. First, there is currently little *effective* demand for such scrutiny, and there are few effective producers of the needed information. Second, time frames for this kind of information are typically short, and evaluators will need to adjust to that constraint. Finally, there seems to be no institutional executive branch mechanism for producing this information, and an appropriate locus for the activity would need to be found.

As things stand, it appears that legislative agencies will be asked to devote more and more of their resources to policy-formulation work. If this should continue, the balance of analytical power—as between the executive and legislative branches of government—could eventually be transformed, much as it was in the sixties, when the executive branch outstripped the analytical capabilities of the Congress. This time, however, the preponderance of analytical capability could be on the legislative side unless there were a concomitant—devoutly to be wished—development of a similar resource in the executive branch.

REFERENCES

ERS Standards Committee (1981) "Evaluation Research Society Standards for Program Evaluation," in Peter H. Rossi (ed.) New Directions for Program Evaluation: Standards for Evaluation Practice. San Francisco: Jossey-Bass.
Hoaglin, David C., Richard J. Light, Buckman McPeek, Frederick Mosteller, and

Michael A. Stoto (1982) Data for Decisions. Cambridge, MA: Abt.

Nichols, Rodney (1971) "Mission-Oriented R&D." Science 172 (April): 29-36.

4

EVALUATION'S POLITICAL INHERENCY: PRACTICAL IMPLICATIONS FOR DESIGN AND USE

MICHAEL QUINN PATTON
University of Minnesota

A theory of evaluation must be as much a theory of political interaction as it is a theory of how to determine facts [Cronbach, 1980:3].

A METAPHORIC CONTEXT: BRIDGE TO STAKEHOLDERS

The setting is a meeting of the National Agriculture Planning Committee in the small Caribbean island of Dominica. The participants include agricultural officials, farmers, extension staff, and private sector interests (people who would be recognized by evaluators as "stakeholders" in the inevitable and necessary jargon of our emergent profession). Prior to the formal start of this session, which begins characteristically late, but will be devoted to the question of how to evaluate the effectiveness of agricultural extension once it finally gets underway, the participants are, again characteristically, lamenting the state of the world, to wit: a lack of funds for this or that critical project; inane government policies (especially of the United States variety); the imminent collapse of the world economy; the weather; and other matters of importance over which they comfortably have little or no control.

The chair finally calls the session to order. As the longtime Director of Extension he is much experienced in participants' lamentations: despairing over impossibilities; blaming everyone and everything out of sight; and resignation to the ultimate omnipresence of Murphy's Law (though they might not put it quite like that).

He is an avid tournament bridge player, and has just returned from an international competition in which the Dominica team did as well as one would expect from a country with a maximum pool of 80,000 players if every man, woman and child caught the bridge disease. He begins the evaluation session with an astute observation based only partly on his card playing expertise: "As we begin this evaluation, let us keep in mind that:

'LIFE CONSISTS NOT IN HOLDING GOOD CARDS, BUT IN PLAYING THOSE WE DO HOLD WELL'."

* * * * *

Now consider another scene, a session at the joint meeting of the new American Evaluation Association and the Canadian Evaluation Society in Toronto, October, 1985. The participants are evaluators from many different disciplines and program areas. What they seem to share, in this session on increasing evaluation use, are lamentations on the suffering of underappreciated evaluators who must put up with all sorts and varieties of stakeholders—incompetent bureaucrats, self-serving politicians, autocratic administrators, methodologically ignorant program staff, and uncooperative clients who can't seem to fill out even a simple questionnaire correctly. There is despair over misuse of evaluations and evaluators; blame for everything and everyone out of sight; and deep appreciation for Hennes's Law: "Evaluators do IT under difficult circumstances."

What is lacking in this second setting is someone to rise to the occasion and point out:

EVALUATION CONSISTS NOT IN BEING DEALT GOOD STAKEHOLDERS, BUT IN PLAYING WELL THOSE WE ARE DEALT.

* * * * *

Mr. Michael Rayner, Comptroller General of Canada, is something of an expert in dealing with political stakeholders. Following his keynote address to the 1985 professional evaluation meetings in Toronto, Mr. Rayner was asked how he dealt with Parliamentary politicians who distorted or refused to act on evaluation recommendations and legislative audit findings. He responded: "It's not a perfect world." He went on to describe both victories and defeats in getting evaluation taken seriously, but the gist of his response remained, "It's an imperfect world."

For many evaluators, schooled in the pristine purity of scientific truth, a perfect world would be one where objective facts reign supreme as the basis for all decision making. Ignorance, vested interests, stakeholder idiosyncrasies, and political compromises would be banned from the evaluation researcher's idyllic Camelot. Forget the unendingly boring nature of this vision. Examine not the fitness of scientists to play the role of truth-rendering philosopher kings. Consider only this: such a world cannot and will not ever exist.

Every chapter of this book makes it clear that it's not a perfect world, and part of the imperfection is the intrinsically political nature of human beings and human social institutions. Evaluation is inherently political, and cannot be otherwise. The evidence and supporting arguments for this assertion are presented throughout this book, as well as in a chapter on "The Power of Evaluation" in *Utilization-Focused Evaluation* (Patton, 1986). Having thus asserted evaluation's political inherency, the issue becomes what to do about it. What are the practical implications for evaluation design and use of evaluation's political inherency? That is the subject of this chapter. Carrying forward the playing card metaphor that opened this chapter, evaluators operating in an inherently political world might do worse than to heed the wisdom of the Gambler as sung by Kenny Rogers: you have to know when to hold them and when to fold them.

The evaluation gamble in an imperfect world is that data can make a difference; that some scientific logic and attention to empirical reality is better than none; and that some stakeholder grounding in and concern for empirically derived judgments is better than a world of pure, unadulterated politics based entirely on might. This chapter explores how to make the power of evaluation felt in an imperfectly political world and how to make the gamble of evaluation pay off in improved programs. It includes observations about when to hold 'em, when to fold 'em, and how to know when the dealin's done.

THE POLITICAL NATURE OF DEFINITIONS

Evaluation's political inherency begins with definitions. What is evaluation? Of what does the practice of evaluation consist? Answers to these questions necessarily involve values, preferences, and definitions. There is no single accepted definition of evaluation. Different definitions of evaluation carry divergent implications for the perspectives on the political nature of evaluation. A review of a few of the variations in the content of definitions of evaluation reveals important differences in what various evaluators emphasize in their work.

(1) The classic approach of Ralph Tyler (1949) was to emphasize goals and objectives, so for him (and for the thousands of educators and researchers schooled in his approach), evaluation is the process of determining the extent to which the goals and objectives of a program are being attained. The process of clarifying goals and priorities is necessarily political in that it is necessary to make choices about what is desirable. However, two points should be noted about goals: (1) not all evaluations focus on goals, and (2) where goal attainment is the focus in evaluation, it is not necessary for all stakeholders to agree on goals inasmuch

as different outcomes can be measured for different stakeholders. There are also at least two prior and more important tasks than goals clarification: defining what evaluation is (or at least the intended nature and purpose of any specific evaluation); and deciding *who* will define evaluation's nature and purpose in any given situation.

I'll deal with these issues at greater length later, but first let's consider additional evaluation definition perspectives.

(2) Many social scientists emphasize scientific rigor in their evaluation models, and that emphasis is reflected in their definition of the field. For these social scientists, evaluation involves primarily the application of rigorous social science methods to the study of programs (e.g., Bernstein and Freeman, 1975; Rossi et al., 1979). These evaluators emphasize the importance of experimental designs and quantitative measures. Later in this chapter I'll discuss the political implications of this perspective with particular emphasis on the methodological biases this perspective brings to evaluation.

(3) Another common emphasis in evaluation definitions is on the comparative nature of the process: Evaluation is the process of *comparing* the relative costs and benefits of two or more programs. The principles and definitions that undergird evaluation models emphasizing the comparative nature of the process have emerged in part as a reaction to the narrowness of evaluation when defined as measuring attainment of a single program's goals (see Alkin and Ellett, 1984). The comparative perspective is most clearly political in the decision that must be made about what to compare to what. Many different comparisons—or none at all— are possible in an evaluation.

(4) Still another definitional variation comes from evaluators who highlight the valuation part of evaluation. From this perspective evaluation is the process of judging a program's value. This final judgment, this ultimate determination of relative merit or worth, is the sine qua non of evaluation (see Worthen and Sanders, 1973: 22-26, 120-122; Guba and Lincoln, 1981: 35-36). In his major plenary address to the 1985 joint meetings of the American Evaluation Association and the Canadian Evaluation

Society, Michael Scriven said that evaluators must truly *evaluate*—which to Scriven means *making judgments*. He concluded that specification of criteria for merit, i.e., necessary and sufficient criteria for success, is the most important problem facing the profession of evaluation.

(5) Some evaluation practitioners focus on the generation of data for decision making and problem solving. This perspective is different from making judgments or assigning relative values. The emphasis is on choices, decisions, and problem resolution. It is quite possible to decide that one thing is better than another (e.g., program X versus program Y) without making any concrete decision with regard to program X or program Y. When evaluation is defined as a problem-solving process (Gephart, 1981) or as a process that provides information for decision making (Thompson, 1975), some action process that goes beyond valuation is given primary emphasis in the definition. This approach involves the evaluator directly in the political processes of problem solving, decision making, and action taking.

(6) Finally, for the purposes of this discussion, there are those definitions that emphasize providing information to specific people. The broad definition I use as a basis for utilization-focused evaluation takes this approach.

> The practice of evaluation involves the systematic collection of information about the activities, characteristics, and outcomes of programs, personnel, and products for use by specific people to reduce uncertainties, improve effectiveness, and make decisions with regard to what those programs, personnel or products are doing and affecting. This definition of evaluation emphasizes (1) the systematic collection of information about (2) a broad range of topics (3) for use by specific people (4) for a variety of purposes [Patton, 1986].

This definition places emphasis on the information needs and interests of specific people, such needs including, but not limited to, information relevant to making decisions, judgments, comparisons, or goal attainment assessments.

Now then, we have six different emphases in various definitions of evaluation (goals, methods, comparisons, judgments, decisions, and information users). Nor do these cover all the possibilities. For example, in the study of how evaluations are used that formed the basis for *Utilization-Focused Evaluation* (Patton, 1986), we began with a collection of 170 "evaluations" on file in the Office of Health Evaluation. Fewer than half of those 170 federal health studies could be considered "evaluations" using any of the definitions just reviewed. This was because a large number of those studies were nonempirical think pieces (i.e., they included no systematic data collection or analysis) or they focused on general social indicators without reference to any specific program. Still, they were filed (defined!) as evaluations.

Let me now make several observations based on the preceding discussion. First, no single-sentence definition will suffice to fully capture the practice of evaluation. Second, different definitions serve different purposes, one especially important function being to serve as a foundation for a particular model of or perspective on evaluation. Third, there are fundamental disagreements within the field about the essence and boundaries of evaluation. These are political disagreements in the sense that different perspectives involve different values, and adherents compete for attention, allegiance, status, and resources. Fourth, people who propound a particular definition often have some ego investment in their special perspective, whether because they developed it, were trained according to it, or are part of a group in which that definition is esteemed; any critique of a definition, in such cases, can be taken as a personal attack, a good many people finding it difficult to separate criticism of their ideas from criticism of them personally. Fifth, people on the outside looking in (and many within the field) are often confused and uncertain about just what evaluation is. Sixth, there is no reason to expect an early end to either the disagreements or the confusion. As Samuel Butler explained the problem in "Higgledy—Piggledy,"

> Definitions are a kind of scratching and generally leave a sore place more sore than it was before.

UTILIZATION OF EVALUATIONS

There is widespread agreement that evaluations ought to be useful. However, since there is no universally excepted definition of evaluation, *there can be no universally accepted definition of utilization.* Any given definition of utilization will necessarily be dependent on and is derived from a prior definition of evaluation, whether that definition is implicit or explicit. As Eleanor Chelimsky has written: "The concept of usefulness . . . depends upon the perspective and values of the observer. This means that one person's usefulness may be another person's waste" (1983: 155).

Having a definition of use is important for evaluators because it directs our professional accountability. Our notions of use interlink with our definitions of evaluation to tell us what we are trying to accomplish. That, in turn, affects all of our design, methods, and measurement decisions. Therefore, the next few pages consider what the evaluation profession has learned about utilization. I shall then use this knowledge to develop premises for utilization-focused evaluation and offer a definition of use with far-reaching political implications. Finally, I shall discuss the practical implications for design and methods of this perspective that includes quite explicit attention to political considerations.

To organize this discussion about what we know I shall use the six honest serving men of Kipling:

I keep six honest serving men.
They taught me all I knew:
Their names are What and Why and When
And How and Where and Who.

WHAT IS USE?

Evaluations can have conceptual or action impacts. Conceptual impacts are those that affect thinking about a program. Such uses may lead to primary stakeholders (e.g., program staff, funders, administrators, and other decision makers) conceptualizing implementation or outcomes in new ways, understanding dynamics of the program more thoroughly, or shifts in program priorities. Action impacts are those that lead to observable changes in the actual operations of a program. These are most notable and dramatic when they involve changes in levels or types of funding, or changes in program delivery. Evaluations can also affect decisions. Evaluations may lead to decisions to continue or stop programs, or to do any of the large variety of things over which decision makers have control. A decision to do absolutely nothing new or different can be a major evaluation impact, but will not lead to any observable action or change as a result of the evaluation.

The research on utilization is typically biased toward action impacts. Earlier concerns in the evaluation literature about lack of utilization were based on narrow definitions of use limited largely to immediate action. It is clear, though, from discussions with people who actually use evaluations (Patton, 1986) that reinforcing or challenging ways of thinking are important impacts for decision makers attempting to reduce their uncertainties about programs.

The relative importance and utility of any specific evaluation can be judged only by the value attached to what happens by those who use the evaluation. There can be no absolute standard that values action over thinking, changes in a program over keeping things the same, or decisions to do something over decisions to wait. There simply can be no hierarchy of impacts, because the hierarchy is necessarily situational and depends on the values and the needs of the people for whom the evaluation is conducted.

WHAT IS USED?

Early research on use focused on the outcomes of evaluation, that is, the data, the recommendations, and the evaluation report. When the question was asked, "Was the evaluation useful?" the implicit assumption was that one was talking about the findings and recommendations of the evaluation.

As our understanding of the utilization process has increased, however, we have come to understand that evaluation processes can have significant impact quite apart from the findings of the evaluation. Indeed, evaluation processes can be used even if there are no findings, for example, if data collection falls apart and no report is ever written. Evaluation processes can be useful in helping program staff clarify what they are doing, establish priorities, focus resources and activities on specific outcomes, and identify areas of weakness even before data are collected. Evaluation processes are useful because they stimulate staff to think rigorously about their program in ways that might not happen without the forced stimulus of coming to grips with the demands of the evaluation.

WHO USES EVALUATION?

There are multiple and varied interests around any evaluation. Administrators, elected officials, funders, program staff, clients, community leaders, and the general public may all have an interest in an evaluation, but the degree and nature of their interests will vary. We have learned that these different constituencies use evaluations in different ways. Program staff are most likely to benefit from the evaluation process, that is, the processes of clarifying goals, looking at the linkages between implementation and outcomes, and thinking about ways to increase effectiveness. Funders and the community people are most likely to use published data and written findings. Administrators are often likely to use the evaluator as a management consultant.

The kind of use also varies. An evaluation is likely to be used to affect the thinking and conceptualization of people more distant from the day-to-day operations of the program, to affect actions taken by those actually involved in the day-to-day delivery of the program, and to affect the decisions taken by those with overall responsibility for the program, that is, funders and administrators.

We have also learned that the extent to which these various constituencies are well served will vary from evaluation to evaluation. *No single evaluation is likely to be able to serve all constituencies equally well.* Either implicitly or explicitly, any evaluation design inevitably includes biases toward the information and process needs of some constituencies more than others. The implications of this are considered at length later in this chapter.

WHEN IS EVALUATION USED?

The early literature on use of evaluation focused on *immediate* action impacts. Subsequent researchers found that evaluation use was more likely to be incremental than immediate. This means that, in many cases, evaluation processes make a difference over time and that evaluation findings are discussed and used over a period of time. This incremental nature of evaluation use flows in part from the incremental nature of most decision making. There are not a great many clear, specific, and immediate decisions taken in the implementation of most programs. Rather, decision making tends to be a process of moving in directions that are not always explicit and do not always come from decisive moments of action. There remains, I believe, a preference in the research literature on utilization in the direction of preferring immediate, concrete and short-term impacts to more diffuse and longer term impacts. This is partly in response to the problem of observing use, that is, that more immediate impacts are easier to get at and are more visible. However, incremental impacts over a longer period of time may be more important in many cases.

HOW IS EVALUATION USED?

There are many dimensions one might consider here. I want to focus on two, more by way of example than because they are definitive, although they have been particularly important in the evaluation utilization literature. Evaluation use can be planned or unplanned, and can be formal or informal. Planned use occurs when the intended use of the evaluation is identified at the beginning and then subsequent utilization is judged by planned or intended use. Unplanned use occurs when, in the typical case, the evaluation is designed without particular attention to questions of utilization and questions of use are left until the data are collected and analyzed.

In looking at utilization, limiting attention to the explicitly stated expectations for use can miss longer term, unintended, and unplanned uses, any of which may be quite important.

Another aspect of how evaluations are used that has become important is whether use is formal or informal. The early research on utilization focused on formal uses—that is, public, observable, and explicit uses of published findings. We have since learned that informal uses are often more important. This is the transfer of findings by word of mouth, in unplanned discussion groups, and in one-to-one interactions between the evaluator and program staff, administrators and/or funders. Such informal interactions often go well beyond official evaluation findings, and it is in the informal process of utilization that the evaluator himself or herself is likely to be used in a consulting role as much as or more than in the formal evaluation findings.

WHERE IS EVALUATION USED?

The problem of where evaluation is used has emerged most directly in efforts at satisfying the different needs of evaluation users at the local, state, and national levels. Framed in this way the question of where is closely related to the question of who. But the question of where the evaluation is used is a larger dimension in that evaluation designs and potential uses at the national level are quite different from those aimed at local utilization. In a perfect world, the kind typically demanded by political rhetoric, a single evaluation would be useful at all levels, from the local agency up through the national government. In reality, the information needs of these different units are dramatically disparate. National officials and program funders have their own evaluation needs and systems. The national funder imposes data collection requirements on local units that locals often perceive to be useless, while data collected entirely by local initiative seldom meet the needs of either federal governments or national funders. Local units tend to prefer highly idiosyncratic and situationally specific data. Larger units tend to prefer standardized data that make aggregation and comparisons easier. All of the dimensions of utilization vary according to where the evaluation is used. One of the greatest challenges for evaluations that are part of management information systems is responding to utilization needs at these different levels.

WHY IS EVALUATION USED?

The "why" of evaluation use has focused most often on the distinction between formative and summative evaluations. Indeed, the classic formative-summative distinction was intended to define different kinds of evaluation use, that is, evaluations aimed at program development and improvement versus evaluations aimed at major go/no-go decisions and/or major funding decisions. In practice, however, the "why" question is considerably more complex than this. The reasons evaluations are used, or not used, run the gamut of human motivations and schemes. There are highly political reasons why evaluations are used, or not used. There are personality dimensions to this problem. There are personal value reasons, and matters of personal integrity and motivation. There are reasons having to do with human factors, context factors, and characteristics of the evaluation. Indeed, the question of why evaluations are used leads directly to the research literature that reports on the factors that affect evaluation use, that explain utilization, and that describe varying conditions under which utilization takes different forms. *Indeed, most of the research on utilization has focused on identifying the factors that contribute to use rather than on variations in utilization itself,* this later point having been the focus of my discussion thus far.

James Burry (1984) has done a thorough review of the evaluation utilization literature aimed at a synthesis of factors that appear to have a bearing on the degree to which evaluation information may be used. He organizes the various factors in three major categories: human factors, context factors, and evaluation factors.

Human factors reflect evaluator and user characteristics with a strong influence on use. Included here are such factors as people's attitudes toward and interest in the program and its evaluation, their backgrounds and organizational positions, and their professional experience levels.

Context factors consist of the requirements and fiscal restraints facing the evaluation, and relationships between the program being evaluated and other segments of its broader organization and the surrounding community.

Evaluation factors refer to the actual conduct of the evaluation, the procedures used in the conduct of the evaluation, and the quality of the information it provides [Burry, 1984].

The primary weakness of this synthesis and the corresponding framework developed by Alkin et al. (1979) is that the factors are undifferentiated in terms of importance. The Burry synthesis represents a checklist of factors that can influence evaluation, and the literature that is synthesized suggests the conditions under which certain factors will emerge as important, but no overall hierarchy is suggested by the synthesis, i.e., a hierarchy that places more importance on certain factors as necessary and/or sufficient conditions for evaluation utilization. In the next section I want to take on this problem of differentiating the relative importance of various factors that explain utilization of evaluation by reviewing the premises of what has come to be called Utilization-Focused Evaluation (Patton, 1986).

UTILIZATION-FOCUSED EVALUATION PREMISES

The first premise is that concern for use should be the driving force in an evaluation. At every point where a decision about the evaluation is being made, whether the decision concerns the focus of study, design, methods, measurement, analysis, or reporting, the evaluator asks: "How would that affect the use of this evaluation?"

The second premise is that concern for use is ongoing and continuous from the very beginning of the evaluation. Utilization isn't something one becomes interested in at the end of an evaluation. By the end of the evaluation, the potential for utilization has been largely determined. From the moment decision makers and evaluators begin conceptualizing the evaluation, decisions are being made that will affect use in major ways.

The third premise is that evaluations should be user-oriented. This means that the evaluation is aimed at the interests and information needs of specific, identifiable people, not vague, passive audiences. Therefore, the first step in utilization-focused evaluation is identifying the primary intended users of the evaluation. This includes recognition that no single evaluation will meet the information needs of all potential stakeholders. Some will be better served than others. Whose interests are primarily served should be explicit. The evaluator and stakeholders must determine who the primary potential users are, and aim the evaluation at those users. This means that the highest priority in utilization-focused evaluation is *intended use for intended users*. Eleanor Chelimsky concurs with this priority when she emphasizes that the most important kind of accountability in evaluation is utilization that comes from "designed tracking and follow-up of a predetermined use to predetermined user" (1983: 160). Chelimsky calls this a "closed-looped feedback process" where "the policy maker wants information, asks for it, and is interested in and informed by the response." From this perspective, the most important political accountability question in researching the utilization of evaluation is whether the evaluation has its intended use. This solves the problem of defining utilization, addresses the question of who the evaluation is for, and builds in a time frame, since the predetermined use would necessarily have a time frame.

A fourth premise is that, once identified, the primary intended evaluation users should be personally and actively involved in making decisions about the evaluation. (The practicalities of how to manage this are discussed later in this chapter.) Working actively with people who have a stake in the outcomes of an evaluation (the "stakeholders") is aimed at increasing the potential for use by building a genuine commitment to and understanding of the evaluation over the course of the evaluation process. Such an approach recognizes the importance of the "personal factor" (Patton, 1986) in evaluation use. People who are *personally* interested and involved in an evaluation are more likely to use evaluation findings. The best way to be sure that an evaluation is targeted at the personal concerns of stakeholders is to involve them actively at every stage of the evaluation.

A fifth premise is that attention to utilization involves financial and staff time costs that are far from trivial. The benefits of these costs are manifested in greater use. These costs should be made explicit in evaluation proposals and budgets so that utilization effects are not neglected for lack of resources.

A sixth premise is that a variety of factors affect utilization. These factors include community variables, organizational characteristics, the nature of the evaluation, evaluator credibility, political considerations, and resource constraints (Alkin et al., 1979). In conducting a utilization-focused evaluation, the evaluator and primary intended users attempt to be sensitive to and aware of how these various factors affect the potential for utilization. An analysis of the factors that may affect the usefulness of an evaluation should be undertaken early in the evaluation process. These factors, and their actual effects on utilization, are then monitored throughout the utilization-focused evaluation process.

THE POLITICAL IMPLICATIONS OF
UTILIZATION-FOCUSED EVALUATION

Utilization-focused evaluation is explicitly political in its emphasis on fostering intended use by intended users. Identifying intended use by intended users and agreeing with them on intended use requires up-front choices—inherently political choices—about whose interests will focus the evaluation. This approach is built, in part, on what is sometimes called "the stakeholder assumption."

The "stakeholder assumption" is the idea that key people who have a stake in an evaluation should be actively and meaningfully involved in shaping that evaluation to focus the evaluation on meaningful and appropriate issues, thereby increasing the likelihood of utilization. In recent years, as evaluators have become increasingly concerned about utilization, the stakeholder assumption has received widespread attention. Doubts have been raised about the validity of the assumption. Nick Smith, for example, president of the Evaluation Network during 1980, wrote in his column in the Evaluation Network Newsletter that the assumption was being accepted without sufficient empirical evidence to support the supposed relationship between stakeholder involvement and utilization of findings.

> Although this (the stakeholder assumption) appears to be a widely held belief, no one has bothered to test it empirically. From a recent 16-state study of local district school accreditation evaluations, I have found that data from school board members and administrators with first-hand experience in such evaluations do not agree with this assumption. These individuals do not want to be personally more involved in such studies, nor do they believe that their involvement will make the evaluation results more useful to them. In fact, for these school board members and administrators, the correlation between their judgments of a past evaluation's utility to them was only 0.3, while there was a 0.7 correlation between their judgments of the evaluation's quality and its utility. Hardly strong support for the considerable effort now being expended at the local, state, and federal level to increase the involvement of various groups in evaluation [Smith, 1980: 39].

Smith's doubts about the validity of the stakeholder assumption provide an opportunity to clarify my own interpretations about what the stakeholder assumption means in practice. His critique includes some common misconceptions about the collaborative approach to utilization-focused evaluation that give rise to the issues outlined above.

First, there is the question of the nature of the relationship between stakeholder involvement and utilization. Smith states the relationship as a "necessary" condition. In the sentence preceding the excerpt quoted above, he said he was addressing "the currently popular assumption that increased involvement of clients and decision makers in evaluation activities will *necessarily* result in increased utilization of evaluation findings" (Smith, 1980: 39, emphasis added). From my point of view, the stake-holder assumption is somewhat overstated by Smith. I have never suggested, or heard others suggest, that increased stakeholder involvement in an evaluation will necessarily result in increased utilization. Nothing one can do, as near as I can tell, will guarantee utilization. But the *odds* for use are increased.

(Remember the gambler metaphor that opened this chapter. The odds are often heavily against use at the beginning. The utilization-focused process is aimed at tipping the odds in favor of use over the course of the evaluation. That's what is meant by learning to play well the stakeholders one is dealt.)

Second, there is a hint of a trade-off in Smith's skepticism implying that one must choose between stakeholder involvement and high quality data. Many evaluators assume that methodological rigor will inevitably be sacrificed if nonscientists collaborate in making methods decisions. This need not be the case. The ideal expressed in the standards for evaluation (Joint Committee on Standards, 1981) includes both utility *and* accuracy. Other research confirms Smith's findings that decision makers are concerned about "quality" of data, but quality includes both "truth tests" (accuracy) and "utility tests," the latter being a concern for relevance and applicability (Weiss and Bucuvalas, 1980).

Third, Smith's point is directed entirely at the quantity of stakeholder involvement in an evaluation. The variable "level of involvement" is somewhat ambiguous, but the implication is that it refers to amount of involvement in terms of time. In contrast, the emphasis in utilization-focused evaluation is on careful selection of the people with whom one works and the *quality* of the evaluation group process. *The quantity of interaction time is often inversely related to quality.* More on this later.

Fourth, while I expect Smith is correct in saying that there is a dearth of empirical evidence that "increased involvement" (if he means greater quantity) leads to greater utilization, there is substantial evidence that high-quality involvement of the right people (primary stakeholders and information users) contributes substantially to utilization (Patton, 1986). I noted earlier that James Burry of UCLA has done perhaps the most thorough review to date of research on utilization. At a 1985 conference on evaluation use sponsored by the UCLA Center for the Study of Evaluation, with support from the National Institute of Education, I asked Jim Burry if his review of the literature suggested any particular factors as particularly important in explaining use. He answered without hesitation:

> There's no question about it. The personal factor is far and away the most important. You're absolutely right in saying that the personal factor is the most explanatory variable in evaluation use. The research of the last five years confirms the primacy of the personal factor.

Another framework that supports the importance of the personal factor is the "Decision-Oriented Educational Research" approach of Cooley and Bickel (1985). While the label for this approach implies a focus on decisions rather than people, in fact the approach is built on a strong "client orientation." The client orientation means that the primary intended users of decision-oriented educational research are clearly identified and then involved in all stages of the work through ongoing dialogue between the researcher and the client. Cooley and Bickel present case evidence to document the importance of being client oriented.

Support for the importance of the personal factor also comes from the work of the Stanford Evaluation Consortium, one of the leading places of ferment and reform in evaluation during the late '70s and early '80s. Cronbach and associates in the Consortium summarized major reforms needed in evaluation thinking by publishing a provocative set of 95 theses, following the precedent of Martin Luther. Among their theses was this observation on the personal factor:

> Nothing makes a larger difference in the use of evaluations than the personal factor—the interest of officials in learning from the evaluation and the desire of the evaluator to get attention for what he knows [Cronbach et al., 1980: 6].

There is a growing evaluation and policy analysis literature—an empirical literature—that supports the proposition that utilization of evaluation is enhanced by *high-quality* stakeholder involvement in and commitment to the evaluation process (e.g., Fairweather et al., 1974; Weiss, 1977; Patton, 1978; Alkin et al., 1979; Braskamp and Brown, 1980; Stevens and Tornatsky, 1980; Lynn, 1980; Dickey, 1981).

A fifth observation about the stakeholder assumption is that evaluators should not expect much initial enthusiasm among stakeholders for the idea of participating actively in a research process. Past experiences are not likely to have been very positive. Most stakeholders are quite happy to leave evaluation to evaluators. They're also quite happy to ignore the resultant evaluation findings. Like a child who wants to avoid bad-tasting medicine (medicine, by definition, being bad tasting), stakeholders would typically prefer to avoid being subjected to distasteful doses of evaluation (evaluation, by definition, being distasteful), even if they believe it's good for them. The evaluation practitioner, like the medical practitioner, must often cajole and otherwise persuade stakeholders to do what ought to be done. Getting cooperation and participation has to be worked at. Initial resistance is no reason to fall back on traditional patterns of operating alone, at least not if the evaluator is really committed to utilization. In my experience, if stakeholders won't get involved at the beginning of an evaluation, they probably won't pay it much heed at the end.

If utilization is viewed as use of the evaluation process and not just as final findings, then stakeholders must be involved in the entire process for the process to have the most impact. Much of the impact of evaluations on stakeholders comes through personal engagement in the difficult processes of goals clarification, issues identification, operationalizing outcomes, matching research design to program design, determining sampling strategies, organizing data collection, interpreting results, and drawing conclusions. These processes take stakeholders through a gradual awakening to program complexities and realities, an awakening that contains understandings and insights that will find their way into program developments over time, only some of which will be manifested in concrete decisions. Utilization begins as soon as stakeholders become actively involved in evaluation because that involvement, properly facilitated, forces them to think about program priorities and realities. The stakeholder assumption, then, includes the expectation that stakeholders need to expend time and effort to figure out what is worth doing in an evaluation, they need help in focusing on worthwhile questions, and they need to experience the full evaluation process if that process, which is really a learning process, is to realize its potential, multilayered effects.

The focus on stakeholder interests and involvement in utilization-focused evaluation presents a political view of evaluation that is substantially different from Palumbo's view (Chapter 1) that evaluators can and should represent "the public interest" rather than specific interests. The stakeholder assumption makes it clear that there are inevitably multiple publics. Thus there is no single, overriding public interest for the evaluator to represent. Claims to the contrary open up the possibility—and danger, from my point of view—that evaluators will use the pretense of representing "the public interest" to represent their own vested interests and values, a ruse already routinely used by politicians of all political persuasions.

Identification and organization of primary intended users is not just an academic exercise performed for its own sake. The purpose of involving specific people who can use information is to enable them to establish direction for and commitment to the evaluation every step along the way. The personal factor is important from initiation of the study through the design and data collection stages as well as in the final report and dissemination parts of the process. If decision makers have shown little interest in the study in its earlier stages, our data suggest that they are not likely to suddenly show an interest in using the findings at the end of the study. They won't be sufficiently *prepared* for use.

Thus the centrality of the personal factor in contributing to evaluation use has implications for all aspects and stages of program evaluation, not just at the stage where findings are disseminated. The remainder of this chapter investigates those implications—implications for how an evaluation is conceptualized, how methods decisions are made, and how analysis is done.

PRACTICALITIES

In training evaluators in the strategy of utilization-focused evaluation, I am often pressed to be specific about how I actually organize and consult with a group of decision makers, information-users, and stakeholders. While my commitment to and belief in situational responsiveness makes me wary of laying out any single and absolute approach to organizing and facilitating groups, the realities of evaluation practice, especially time constraints and limited resources, have led me to develop some strategies for making the most of scarce consulting time. These experiences and ideas are shared in the hope that they help stimulate your thinking about your own consulting patterns, while providing some practical suggestions that you may be able to adapt to your own style. In sharing these ideas, I am not recommending imitation of the specifics. Rather, I'm providing a description of one consulting pattern and style that can be used for making comparisons, drawing contrasts, and stimulating development of your own consulting style. The process I shall describe refers specifically to what I've called the active-reactive-adaptive style of utilization-focused evaluation aimed at facilitating the work of an evaluation task force (Patton, 1986). It is a process that is inherently political in orientation in that it builds on and takes into account the vested interests of primary stakeholders and uses that knowledge to facilitate evaluation use.

PURPOSE OF A TASK FORCE

The reasons for organizing a task force in conducting an evaluation are discussed at length in *Practical Evaluation* (Patton, 1982: 55-98). In brief, an evaluation task force is organized to make major decisions about the focus, methods, and purpose of the evaluation. The task force is a vehicle for actively involving key stakeholders in the evaluation. This helps guarantee that the evaluation is relevant, appropriate, and useful. Moreover, the very processes involved in making decisions about an evaluation will typically increase stakeholders' commitments to use evaluation results while also increasing their knowledge about evaluation, their sophistication in conducting program evaluations, and their ability to interpret evaluation findings. Finally, the task force allows the evaluator to share responsibility for decision making and utilization by providing a forum for the political and practical perspectives that best come from those stakeholders who will ultimately be involved in using evaluation results.

Several things can be accomplished with a group or evaluation task force that are less likely to occur with individuals.

(a) An environment of openness can be established to reduce suspicions and fears about what is going on in the evaluation. The key stakeholders who participate in the process know how decisions are made and who was involved in making them. This can reduce political paranoia.

(b) Participants in the group process become sensitized to the multiple perspectives that exist around any program. They are exposed to divergent views, multiple possibilities, and competing values. Their view is broadened, and they are exposed to the varying agendas of people with different stakes in the evaluation. This increases the possibility of conducting an evaluation that is responsive to different needs, interests, and values.

(c) New ideas often emerge out of the dynamics of group interaction.

(d) A sense of shared responsibility for the evaluation can be engendered that is often greater than the responsibility that would be felt by isolated individuals. Commitments made in groups, in front of others, are typically more lasting and serious than promises made to an evaluator in private.

(e) An open forum composed of various stakeholders makes it difficult to suppress touchy questions or negative findings. Issues get raised and findings get publicized that otherwise might never see the light of day.

(f) The evaluator has the opportunity to observe firsthand the interactions among various stakeholders and to assess their interpersonal relationships. This information can be very helpful in developing utilization strategies.

(g) A certain momentum can often be established through group processes that helps reduce delays or roadblocks resulting from the attitudes or actions of one person.

(h) The evaluator(s) and stakeholders in a group process will often jell into a kind of support group. It's not the evaluator against the world. The other participants in the group can lend support, help, and understanding.

(i) The group will often continue to function after the evaluation is completed. Participants can develop a shared commitment to follow through on utilization of evaluation findings and recommendations. After all, in most cases the evaluator is present for only a limited period. Stakeholders stay with the program after the evaluation is over. A task force can become a repository for evaluation knowledge and carry forward an appreciation of evaluation processes. The members of the group can carry on what the evaluator helps to establish.

Of course, all of these outcomes of group dynamics assume an effective group process. The extent to which utilization is enhanced by a group process depends on (1) who participates in that process and (2) the questions dealt with by the group, that is, the focus and quality of the process.

Any group of people rapidly becomes greater than the sum of its parts. Bringing together a group of incompetents seems to increase geometrically the capacity for incompetent and misguided action. On the other hand, bringing together a group of competent, politically sensitive, and creative people makes it possible for them to stimulate each other and create something that is more useful than any of them individually might have created. Shared decision making may mean compromise; it can also mean powerful chain reactions leading to increased energy and commitment, especially commitment to use evaluation findings in which group members have developed some *stake* through their involvement in the evaluation decision making process.

COMPOSITION OF THE TASK FORCE

Several criteria are important in attempting to form an evaluation task force. Not all of these criteria can be met to the same degree in every case, but it is helpful to have in mind a basic framework for the composition of the task force group. (1) The members of the task force should represent the varied groups and constituencies that have an interest and stake in the evaluation findings and their utilization, including client interests. (2) Task force members should either be people who have authority and power to use evaluation findings in decision making, or to influence others who do have such power and authority. Again, this includes representatives of the program's clients who may be powerless as anonymous individuals but whose interests can be organized and taken into consideration for evaluation purposes. (3) The task force members should believe that the evaluation is worth doing. (4) The task force members should care how the results are used. (5) The task force members should be willing to make a firm commitment of time, including a commitment to attend all of the evaluation task force meetings. One of the things that causes the most problems in working with an evaluation task force is to have different people show up at different meetings, and to have such inconsistent attendance that the process never really moves forward, and has to be begun anew with each new meeting.

SIZE

The minimum number I would expect to have is three, in order to have some variation in viewpoints, and the most I would want to work with is ten. A group larger than ten begins to become quite cumbersome for decision making. For certain activities it may be appropriate and helpful to work with a much larger group. For example, I may do a goals-clarification exercise with the entire program staff, or have a large meeting to discuss findings. These activities, however, are sponsored by the task force participants in deciding when to hold larger group sessions and the purpose of such sessions.

The composition and size of a task force is limited for very pragmatic reasons. Not every stakeholder can or should participate, though an attempt should be made to represent all *major* stakeholder constituencies and points of view. The evaluator should be fair, but practical, in working with program administrators, funders, clients, program staff, and public officials to establish a task force (and imbue it with the necessary authority to make decisions). In this regard I find the advice of Guba and Lincoln (1981: 37) to be impractical when they assert that "it is unethical for the evaluator . . . to fail to interact with any known audience in the search for concerns and issues." They direct the evaluator to address "the broadest possible array of persons interested in or affected by the evaluand, including audiences that are unaware of the stakes they hold" While evaluators need to take care that the interests of program clients and the powerless are represented, there are practical limits to identification and organization of decision makers and information users. Fairness and a healthy regard for pluralism are guiding lights in this regard.

CHAIRING THE TASK FORCE

I prefer to have one of the task force participants act as chair of the group. The chair's responsibility is to convene meetings, to see that agendas for meetings are followed, and to keep discussions on the topic at hand. Having a stakeholder chair the task force helps symbolize the responsibility and authority of the group. The evaluator is a consultant to the group, and is paid to do the nitty-gritty staff work for the evaluation, but the task force should assume responsibility for the overall direction of the process. As facilitator, trainer, and collaborator the evaluator will command a good deal of floor time in task force sessions. However, an effective evaluator can accomplish everything needed by working with the chair, rather than being the chair.

ACTIVITIES

In facilitating the work of the task force, the evaluator must be able to help focus the activities of the group so that time is well used, necessary decisions get made, and participants do not become frustrated with a meandering and ambiguous process. To make the best use of task force time, it is helpful to minimize time spent on decisions about the group process and maximize the time spent on decisions about substantive evaluation issues. Thus I recommend that the evaluator *not* begin by asking the task force members how they want to make decisions, but rather that the evaluator provide the chair with an outline or agenda of the kinds of decisions that have to be made, and then move the group through the process of decision making, *focusing at all times on substantive issues.* A lot of time can be wasted while people try to figure out how they're going to operate. When the group is convened, the facilitator should have a clear idea of how the group will operate so that participants can rapidly get down to business and accomplish the necessary tasks. This also means that each task force meeting should have definite closure so that members know what has been accomplished and what has to happen next. An inexperienced chair may need considerable preparatory help from the evaluator to keep the task force task-oriented. What follows is a description of a bare bones process.

At a *minimum,* I expect to hold four two-hour meetings with the task force.

(1) *Focus/conceptualization session:* The purpose of the first meeting is to establish the focus of the evaluation. This means the group must consider alternative evaluation questions, issues, problems, and goals to decide the purpose and direction of evaluation. Some kind of group process is necessary to help

participants consider alternatives or to generate options (e.g., Patton, 1978, Chapter 5; Patton, 1981; Bertcher, 1979). In any case, the product of the first meeting is a focus identifying the basic direction of and purpose for the evaluation.

(2) *Methods and measurement options:* The second meeting is devoted to consideration of different ways of conducting the evaluation, given the focus determined in the first meeting. The evaluator presents varying kinds of measurement approaches and different designs that might be used. Time considerations and utilization possibilities are discussed with the clear intention of narrowing down the methods and measurement possibilities to those that are manageable, credible, and practical. Issues of validity, reliability, generalizability, and appropriateness are also discussed—in *lay* terms. What kinds of data are needed to answer the evaluation questions that emerged in the first meeting? What kind of design makes the most sense? What's an appropriate sampling approach? What comparisons should be made? The purpose of this second session is to provide clear direction for evaluation methods and measurement.

(3) *Design and instrument review:* Between the second and third meetings the evaluator will design the instruments to be used and write a concrete methods proposal specifying units of analysis, control or comparison groups to be studied, sampling approaches and sample size, and the overall data collection strategy. In reviewing the proposed design and instruments, the task force members should make sure that they understand what will be done and what *will not* be done, what findings can be generated and what findings *cannot* be generated, and what questions will be asked and what questions *will not* be asked. The third meeting will usually involve some changes in instrumentation—additions, deletions, revisions—and adjustments in the design. Basically, this meeting is aimed at providing final input into the research methods before data collection begins. The evaluator leaves the meeting with a clear mandate to begin data collection.

The third meeting is also often a good time to do a mock utilization session where task force members consider specifically how various kinds of findings might be used given simulated evaluation results. "If we get these answers to this question, what would that mean? What would we do with those results?" If that question cannot be answered *before* data collection begins, then there is a good chance (we're still gambling on probabilities) that question will not be answerable when data collection is over, an indication that more work needs to be done on the utilization focus of the evaluation.

(4) *Data interpretation session:* The fourth and final meeting in this minimum scenario of task force activities focuses on data analysis, data interpretation, and recommendations. Following data collection, but before the writing of the final report, the evaluator assembles task force members to review initial findings. The evaluator has arranged the data and organized it so that the task force members can deal with it, understand it, and interpret it. However, at this point the evaluator stops short of providing interpretations or recommendations. The purpose of this session is to allow task force members to get personally involved in the analysis and to consider the meaning of the findings. Out of this session will come further recommendations about the kinds of analyses that should be performed and insights about the meaning of the data. Recommendations will then follow from the findings. See *Practical Evaluation* (Patton, 1982) for details about how to arrange data for decision makers' analysis and how to move from findings to recommendations.

THE CONCERN FOR SCIENTIFIC INTEGRITY WHILE ESTABLISHING RAPPORT IN THE FACE OF THE POLITICAL REALITIES OF EVALUATION

One of the most common concerns I encounter in doing workshops on utilization-focused evaluation is worry that the evaluator may become coopted by stakeholders during the collaborative process. How can evaluators maintain their integrity if they become involved in close, collaborative relationships with stakeholders? How does the evaluator take politics into account without becoming a political tool of only one partisan interest? The nature of the relationship between evaluators and the people with whom they work is a complex and controversial one. On the one hand, there is a tradition in social science that researchers should maintain a respectful distance from the people they study to safeguard objectivity and minimize the introduction of personal and political bias. On the other hand, there is the human relations perspective, which emphasizes close interpersonal contact as a necessary condition for building mutual understanding. Evaluators thus find themselves on the proverbial horns of a dilemma: getting too close to decision makers may jeopardize scientific objectivity, but staying too distant from decision makers may jeopardize utilization of findings by failing to build rapport and mutual understanding. A program auditor at a U.S. General Accounting Office (GAO) workshop put the issue somewhat less delicately when he asked, "How can we get in bed with decision makers without losing our virginity?"

My immediate response was:

"The only way to completely safeguard your supposed virginity (of which I must admit I'm unconvinced is still possible to lose, or, if still in place, is worth saving) is not to play the dating game with stakeholders at all. That way you don't risk losing anything. You also don't risk winning. You have to ante something to play. Nothing ventured, nothing gained."

A more serious answer, I believe, lies in keeping decision makers and stakeholders focused on the empirical nature of the evaluation process. In everyday life people operate on the basis of relatively unconscious assumptions and selective perceptions. They are not used to testing the validity of their assumptions and perceptions. Quite the contrary, they typically admit into their consciousness only that information that reinforces existing values, attitudes, and behavior patterns. People are socialized to operate in accordance with a fairly limited set of cultural patterns, strong patterns of behavior and perception that resist not only change, but resist even examination.

The empirical basis of evaluation involves making assumptions and values implicit, testing the validity of assumptions, and carefully examining a program to find out what is actually occurring. *The integrity of an evaluation depends on its empirical orientation.* Likewise, the integrity of an evaluation group process depends on helping participants adopt an empirical perspective. A commitment must be engendered to really find out what is happening, at least as nearly as one can, given the limitations of research methods and scarce resources. Engendering this kind of commitment and helping task force participants adopt an empirical orientation involve the evaluator in the roles of teacher and trainer.

The evaluator begins building this empirical orientation at the very first task force meeting when the purpose of the evaluation is discussed and major evaluation questions or issues are clarified and identified. In *Utilization-Focused Evaluation* (Patton, 1986), I listed seven criteria for good evaluation questions, the first two of which emphasize directly the empirical nature of evaluation.

(1) It is possible to bring data to bear on the question, i.e., it is truly an *empirical* question.
(2) There is more than one possible answer to the question, i.e., the answer is not predetermined by the phrasing of the question.
(3) The primary users *want* information to help answer the question.
(4) The intended users feel they *need* information to help them answer the question.
(5) The identified and organized stakeholders want to answer the question for themselves, not just for someone else.
(6) They care about the answer to the question.
(7) The intended users can indicate how they would use the answer to the question, i.e., they can specify the relevance of an answer to the question for future action.

The integrity of the evaluation rests firmly on the first two criteria. The relevance of the evaluation depends on the remaining five criteria. Emphasizing the empirical nature of evaluation doesn't mean that values and politics are ignored. The making of judgments and decisions necessarily involves values. But value and political questions in and of themselves are not answerable empirically. It is critical, therefore, to separate the empirical questions from the values questions in focusing an evaluation.

When stakeholders first begin discussing the purpose of an evaluation, they often do so in nonempirical terms. "We want to *prove* the program's effectiveness." Proving effectiveness is a public relations job, not an evaluation task. This statement tells the evaluator about that person's attitude toward the program, and it indicates a need for diplomatically, sensitively, but determinedly, reorienting that stakeholder from a concern with public relations to a concern with learning about and documenting actual program activities and effects. The evaluator need not be frightened by such public relations statements. It's best to get such inclinations out in the open. Then the work begins of moving toward an empirical process.

> *Program Director*: "We want to prove the program's effectiveness."
> *Evaluator*: "What kind of information would do that?"
> *Program Director*: "Information about how much people like the program."
> *Evaluator*: "Does everyone like the program?"
> *Program Director*: "I think most everyone does."
> *Evaluator*: "Well, we could find out just how many do, and how many don't. So there's a reasonable evaluation question: 'What are participants' attitudes towards the program?' Later we'll need to get more specific about how to measure their attitudes, but first let's consider some other things we could find out. Assuming that some people don't like the program, what could be learned from them?"
> *Program Director*: "I suppose we could find out what they don't like and why."
> *Evaluator*: "Would that kind of information be helpful in looking at the program, to find out about its strengths and weaknesses so that perhaps you could improve it in some ways?" (This is a deliberately leading question, very hard to say "No" to).
> *Program Director*: "Well, we know some of the reasons, but we can always learn more."
> *Evaluator*: "What other information would be helpful in studying the program to find out about its strengths and weaknesses?" (Here the evaluator has carefully rephrased the original concern

from "proving the program's effectiveness" to "finding out about the program strengths and weaknesses."

* * * * *

In the dialogue above the evaluator chips away at the decision maker's biased public relations perspective by carefully allowing an empirical perspective to emerge. At some point the evaluator may want to, or need to, address the public relations concern with a bit of a speech (or sermonette).

> I know you're concerned about providing the program's effectiveness. This is a natural concern. A major and common purpose of evaluation is to gather information so that judgments can be made about the value of a program. To what extent is it effective? To what extent is it worthwhile?
>
> The problem is that if we only gather and present positive information about the program, it may lack credibility. You're sophisticated people. You know that if you read a report that only says good things about a program you figure something is being covered up. In my experience an evaluation has more credibility and usefulness if it's balanced. Everyone knows that no program is perfect, and I've never seen a program yet in which everyone was happy and everyone achieved all their goals. You may find that it's better to study and document both strengths and weaknesses, areas of effectiveness, and areas of ineffectiveness, and then show that you're serious about improving the program by presenting a strategy for dealing with weakness and areas of ineffectiveness. By doing that you establish your credibility as serious program developers who can deal openly and effectively with inevitable problems.

Sometimes the opposite bias is the problem. Someone is determined to kill a program, to present only negative findings, and to "prove" that the program is ineffective. In such cases the evaluator can emphasize what can be learned by finding out about the program's strengths. Few programs are complete disasters. An empirical approach means gathering data on *actual* program activities and effects, and then presenting those data in a fair and balanced way so that information-users and decision makers can make their own judgments about goodness or badness, effectiveness or ineffectiveness. Such judgments, however, are separate from the data. In my experience, evaluation task force members will readily move into this kind of empirical orientation as they come to understand its usefulness and fairness. It's the evaluators job to help then achieve understanding and adopt that perspective.

There is considerable nuance and skill involved in dealing with politically sensitive issues and making the shift to an empirical orientation. A common problem in an initial task force meeting is that evaluation questions and issues are stated in value-laden, nonempirical terms. For example, decision makers may want to study *improvements* brought about by a program. Are services improving? Are clients being helped? Are program participants doing better? Are staff becoming more effective?

Assessing improvement involves making a judgment about whether or not an observed impact is desirable or undesirable. It is important to separate the issues of improvement from the related but quite different issue of impact or change. Improvement involves a judgment about whether or not something is better, whereas impact involves the more limited question of whether or not the change is for better or worse. It is crucial throughout the evaluation process that empirical observations about program impact be kept separate from judgments about whether or not such impact constitutes improvement or effectiveness.

Questions of right or wrong, better or worse, are not simple empirical questions. To formulate evaluation questions solely in value terms can sabotage an evaluation from the beginning. The empirical question is not improvement but change, and the extent of change.

The evaluator can do two things when stakeholders suggest that the evaluation focus on such value-laden issues as improvement or effectiveness. First, the evaluator can work with stakeholders to determine what empirical information and data are needed to make judgments about improvement or effectiveness.

Second, the evaluator can help make a shift from asking absolute, dichotomous questions ("Is the program effective?") to asking relative, continuum-based, and open questions ("To what extent and in what ways is the program effective?"). Thus the initial issue of "proving the program's effectiveness" becomes a set of empirical evaluation questions:

To what extent and in what ways have clients changed?
What are the attitudes of clients about the program?
What are the relative strengths and weaknesses of the program?
What do staff and clients do in the program?

These are empirical questions. When these kinds of questions are asked in an evaluation the evaluators have established a solid foundation for a credible process that has integrity. Answers to these questions can be used by a variety of people to make judgments about the program. Of course, decisions will still have to be made about specific issues for intensive study, what data to gather, and how to report findings. Continuing judgments are necessary to maintain balance, credibility, and fairness. Undergirding all such decisions is the evaluator's commitment to keeping the focus on the *empirical* nature of the evaluation process.

FAIRNESS AS AN EVALUATION CRITERION IN PLACE OF OBJECTIVITY

In the previous section on maintaining one's integrity while establishing rapport, I have deliberately not emphasized (or even mentioned) the term "objectivity." The concern about integrity usually goes hand-in-hand with a fear of losing objectivity, or at least being accused of losing one's objectivity. A parallel concern is being sure that the evaluation gets at the *truth*. Elsewhere I have discussed at greater length the illusiveness of truth and objectivity (Patton, 1986; 1980: 267-283). Without going into a lengthy philosophical discussion, let me suggest that from a practical perspective, utilization-focused evaluation replaces the search for truth with a search for useful and balanced information, and replaces the mandate to be objective with a mandate to be fair and conscientious in taking account of multiple perspectives, multiple interests, and multiple realities. In this regard, Egon Guba suggests that evaluators could learn a great deal by adopting the stance of investigative journalists.

> Journalism in general and investigative journalism in particular are moving away from the criterion of objectivity to an emergent criterion usually labeled "fairness.". . . Objectivity assumes a single reality to which the story or evaluation must be isomorphic; it is in this sense a one-perspective criterion. It assumes that an agent can deal with an object (or another person) in a nonreactive and noninteractive way. It is an absolute criterion.
>
> Journalists are coming to feel that objectivity in that sense is unattainable. . . .
>
> Enter "fairness" as a substitute criterion. In contrast to objectivity, fairness has these features:
>
> It assumes multiple realities or truths—hence a test of fairness is whether or not both sides of the case are presented, and there may even be multiple sides. . . .
>
> It is adversarial rather than one-perspective in nature. Rather than trying to hew the line with the truth, as the objective reporter does, the fair reporter seeks to present each side of the case in the manner of an advocate—as, for example, attorneys do in making a case in court. The presumption is that the public, like a jury, is more likely to reach an equitable decision after having heard each side presented with as much vigor and commitment as possible.
>
> It is assumed that the subject's reaction to the reporter and interaction between them heavily determines what the reporter perceives. Hence one test of fairness is the length to which the reporter will go to test his own biases and rule them out.
>
> It is a relative criterion that is measured by *balance* rather than by isomorphism to enduring truth.
>
> Clearly, evaluators have a great deal to learn from this development [Guba, 1981: 76-7].

THE EVALUATOR AS DATA CHAMPION

In working to facilitate the utilization of evaluation findings, the evaluator can play the role of data champion. This is quite different from being a program advocate or program champion. The evaluator can, and I believe should, strongly advocate use of evaluation findings. This includes urging stakeholders and decision makers to deal with and take seriously the implications of the findings. Those implications may, and likely will, be perceived as for or against the program in some important ways. But the evaluator's job is to advocate using the evaluation to inform action, not to do the program's public relations lobbying. To do so is to undermine the integrity of the profession.

Ultimately, there are no simple rules one can follow to guarantee evaluator integrity. Evaluators can expect to be attacked by those who don't like or may be hurt by evaluation processes and findings. Integrity is a matter of working out one's own personal and professional standards, and then working to adhere to them, while being ready to examine and learn from likely failings along the way.

THE POLITICAL NATURE OF DATA
COLLECTION DECISIONS

Once primary intended users are identified and the focus of the evaluation is determined, methods decisions must be made. There are a variety of methodological options to consider. In utilization-focused evaluation, the evaluator has no intrinsic rights to unilaterally make critical design and data collection decisions. Quite the contrary, it is crucial that intended users participate in the making of measurement and methods decisions so that they understand the strengths and weaknesses of the data—and so that they believe in the data. Utilization potential can be severely diminished if stakeholders are excluded at the critical operationalization stage when making data choices.

The primary focus in making evaluation methods decisions should be on getting the best possible data to adequately answer primary stakeholders' evaluation questions given available resources and time. The emphasis is on *appropriateness and credibility*—measures, samples, and comparisons that are appropriate and credible to address key evaluation issues.

A consensus has gradually emerged in the professional practice of evaluation that evaluators need to know a variety of methodological approaches in order to be flexible and responsive in matching research methods to the nuances of particular evaluation questions and the idiosyncrasies of specific stakeholder needs. Evaluators are encouraged to use multiple methods to overcome the weaknesses of any one particular approach (Reichardt and Cook, 1979).

The problem is that this ideal of evaluators being situationally responsive, methodologically flexible, and sophisticated in using a variety of methods runs headlong into the realities of the evaluation world. Those realities include limited resources, political considerations of expediency, and the narrowness of disciplinary training available to most evaluators, training that imbues them with varying degrees of methodological prejudice.

The problem of methodological prejudice has been a major concern in evaluation. Much of that concern has centered on a debate about the relative merits of qualitative and quantitative methods. This debate had its origins in competing traditions within the social sciences, so as evaluation research emerged as a special application of social science methods, the debate carried over into evaluation.

The concerns that sparked the debate remain relevant because much social science training is still quite narrow. Most social scientists are most comfortable with those methods that are central to their primary discipline. They have been trained to study the world in a particular way. That particular way of viewing the world becomes so second nature that it takes on the characteristics of a world view, or a paradigm. The paradigms debate has been a prominent and persistent topic in the evaluation literature (Rist, 1977; Cronbach, 1975, 1980; Reichardt and Cook 1979; Heilman, 1980; Guba and Lincoln, 1981) and a regular feature at meetings of professional evaluators.

A paradigm is a world view, a general perspective, a way of breaking down the complexity of the real world. As such, paradigms are deeply embedded in the socialization of adherents and practitioners: paradigms tell them what is important, legitimate, and reasonable. Paradigms are also normative, telling the practitioner what to do without the necessity of long existential or epistemological consideration. But it is this aspect of paradigms that constitutes both their strength and their weakness—their strength in that it makes action possible, their weakness in that the very reason for action is hidden in the unquestioned assumptions of the paradigm.

> Scientists work from models acquired through education and through subsequent exposure to the literature often without quite knowing or needing to know what characteristics have given these models the status of community paradigms. . . . That scientists do not usually ask or debate what make a particular problem or solution legitimate tempts us to suppose that, at least intuitively, they know the answer. But it may only indicate that neither the question nor the answer is felt to be relevant to their research. Paradigms may be prior to, more binding, and more complete than any set of rules for research that could be unequivocally abstracted from them [Kuhn, 1970: 46].

Evaluation research was initially dominated by the natural science paradigm of hypothetico-deductive methodology. This dominant paradigm emphasized quantitative measurement, experimental design, and multivariate, parametric statistical analysis as the epitome of "good" science. This basic model for conducting evaluation research came from the tradition of experimentation in agriculture, which gave us many of the basic statistical and experimental techniques most widely advocated in evaluation tests.

By way of contrast, the alternative to the dominant quantitative-experimental paradigm was derived from the tradition of anthropological field studies. Using the techniques of in-depth, open-ended interviewing and participant observation, the alternative paradigm relies on qualitative data, naturalistic inquiry, and detailed description derived from close contact with the targets of study.

In utilization-focused evaluation, neither of these paradigms is intrinsically better than the other. They represent alternatives from which the utilization-focused evaluator can choose; both contain options for primary stakeholders and information users. *Issues of methodology are issues of strategy, not of morals* (cf. Homans, 1949). Yet it is not easy to approach the selection of evaluation methods in this adaptive fashion. The paradigmatic biases in each approach are quite fundamental. Great passions have been aroused by advocates on each side. Kuhn (1970: 109-110) has pointed out that this is the nature of paradigm debates:

> To the extent that two scientific schools disagree about what is a problem and what is a solution, they will inevitably talk through each other when debating the relative merits of their respective paradigms. In the partially circular arguments that regularly result, each paradigm will be shown to satisfy more or less the criteria that it dictates for itself and to fall short of a few of those dictated by its opponent. . . . Since no paradigm ever solves all problems it defines and since no two paradigms leave all the same problems unsolved, paradigm questions always involve the question: Which problems is it more significant to have solved?

There is not space to fully review the methods debate in evaluation. The point for our purposes here is that different methods are *not* perceived as equally valuable, rigorous and meaningful. Methods decisions, then, have political implications because the types of data collected will have different degrees of credibility among different groups. This differential credibility is a factor to be taken into consideration in making methods decisions.

EVALUATION OPTIONS
AND POLITICAL INTERESTS

The trappings of scientific measurement can often disguise the political choices that have been made in an evaluation. Deciding what to measure, and how to measure it, is not a purely technical issue. There are always options. Deciding among options is in part directed by evaluator and stakeholder interests, values, and concerns for status, credibility, and funding. Moreover, the political and cultural values held may be so deeply embedded that they hardly appear at all as matters of values and politics.

An excellent example is the United States National Assessment of Educational Progress (NAEP). The intensely political nature of this evaluation has been well documented by Olson (1976). Much of the politics involved measurement decisions around the question: What should all children in the United States know?

> It is possible to see how much meaningful educational progress can be measured by looking at what, as the National Assessment was constructed, was deemed offensive: for example, questions touching family, finances, references to specific minority groups, literary passages with sexual references, and questions dealing with birth control or religion. Exercises dealing with human rights were deemed offensive unless more exercises were added "dealing with . . . responsibilities in a free society." Deleted also were references to sex, unwed mothers, divorce, whiskey, the FBI, the president, communism, and specific organizations such as the Ku Klux Klan and labor unions; references to violence or cruelty; exercises with *inappropriate* words or phrases, such as "sportive ladies leave their doors ajar;" exercises that might be interpreted as putting national heroes or the police and other authorities in an unfavorable light; and exercises about the Civil War that suggest the North was better than the South. Senator Joe McCarthy, that demagogue and hate maker of the 1950s, is to be presented, according to the National Assessment, in the light that is neither too critical nor too favorable [Olson, 1976: 9-10].

Olson goes on to review in some depth the literature portion of the NAEP. Goal one of the NAEP specified that children should "understand the basic metaphors and themes through which man expresses values and tensions in Western culture."
Olson comments:

First of all, goal one—understand the basic metaphors and themes through which man expresses values and tensions in Western culture—leaves out those one million Americans who come from Japanese and Chinese cultures; it leaves out nearly one million Native Americans, as well as that part of literary heritage of Chicanos which depends upon Native American rather than Hispano sources; it also leaves out those African or Afro-Caribbean works which express the independent civilizations and identities of black people. The works which are mentioned for recognition are: *Little Red Riding Hood, Moby Dick, Little Bo Peep, The Turtle and the Hare, Sherlock Holmes, Alice in Wonderland, Winnie the Pooh, Charlotte's Web, Don Quixote, Casey at the Bat, The Village Blacksmith, The Charge of the Light Brigade* and *Tom Sawyer.* The important literary characters are Noah, Samson, Adam, Venus, David, Gallahad, the Trojan Horse, Job, Daniel Boone, the Ugly Duckling, Rumpelstiltskin, Paul Bunyan, Cupid, and Thor.

No one would knock the list of works that are proposed for recognition (save perhaps those bromide of bromide pieces, *The Village Blacksmith* and *The Charge of the Light Brigade*), but one wonders why only the sacred scriptures of Northern Europe and ancient Greece and Rome are brought in for recognition. Why not the Navajo Twins, or Quetzalcoatl and his epic, or Ananzi, or the sacred heroes whose thoughts are recorded in the *Bhagavad-Gita.* The answer is that Africa, South America, and native peoples in North America do not matter, according to the National Assessment. The ancient peoples who created *The Night Chant* lose out to *The Village Blacksmith* [Olson, 1976: 13-14].

Whether one agrees or disagrees with Olson's perspective, his criticisms of the NAEP make it clear that the methods decisions made were controlled by representatives of a dominant political culture that led to measurement decisions that reinforce and place the greatest value on the political and cultural priorities of that dominant group— "dominantly middle class and predominantly white" (Olson, 1976: 6). Those stakeholders not involved appear from Olson's analysis to neither understand, believe in, or find credible the National Assessment of Educational Progress. But those dominantly middle class and predominantly white stakeholders who were involved in the NAEP appear to have *believed* that their questions and measures were universally fair, appropriate, objective, and unbiased. The deeply political nature of the NAEP was disguised by the trappings of scientific methods and "objective" standardized testing. I would assert that *no* national test can possibly be fair to all the possible stakeholders of the American educational system. Therefore, it is incumbent on those involved to, at a minimum, be explicit about *who* and what they represent.

CONCLUDING ASSERTIONS AND JUDGMENTS ABOUT EVALUATOR'S POLITICAL INHERENCY

This chapter has focused on issues of evaluation design and use to illustrate evaluation's political inherency. That political inherency is derived from and based on the fundamental premises outlined below.

Assertion: Different stakeholders have different evaluation information needs, different interests, and different perspectives on the program.

Assertion: No evaluation can answer all stakeholders' questions or represent all interests equally well.

Assertion: There is no single, overriding public interest to represent in evaluation because there are multiple publics and multiple interests around any program.

Conclusion: Any given evaluation *will* represent some interests and serve the information needs of some people more than others.

Definition: Serving some interests more than others is a political act in that those interests served may become more powerful and influential through the use of evaluation information.

Judgment: Since any evaluation will inherently and inevitably serve some stakeholder interests more than others, evaluators ought to explicitly acknowledge who the primary stakeholders are whose interests shape the evaluation. These primary stakeholders should then be the primary intended users of the evaluation.

Definition: The first and most important meaning of utilization is intended use by intended users.

Judgment: Utilization should be the driving force in evaluation.

Assertion: Intended use by intended users (utilization) is most likely to occur if these primary intended users are actively involved in shaping the evaluation—including participation in making decisions about the evaluation's purpose, design, methods and analysis.

Definition: The integrity of evaluation, given its political inherency, resides in the focus on bringing high quality and credible data to bear on genuinely empirical questions. Serving the information needs of primary stakeholders does not mean manipulating the results to come out a certain way; rather it means focusing the evaluation on the questions of primary interest to intended users, and then doing a fair and balanced job of answering those questions rigorously and credibly.

Conclusion: The issue for evaluators is not whether evaluations are political, since they cannot be otherwise. The issue is how explicitly the evaluator deals with, facilitates and negotiates political considerations in the context of concerns for use, practicalities, rigor, integrity, accuracy, fairness and credibility.

Maxim: Life consists not in holding good cards, but in playing those we do hold well. Evaluation consists not in being dealt good stakeholders, but in playing well those we are dealt.

CAVEAT EMPTOR.
CAVEAT EVALUATOR.
FINIS

REFERENCES

Alkin, Marvin C., Richard Daillak, and Peter White (1979) Using Evaluations: Does Evaluation Make a Difference? Newbury Park, CA: Sage.

Alkin, Marvin C. and Fred Ellett (1984) "Evaluation Models," in International Encyclopedia of Education. New York: Pergamon.

Bernstein, Ilene and Howard Freeman (1975) Academic and Entrepreneurial Research. New York: Russell Sage.

Bertcher, Harvey J. (1979) Group Participation: Techniques for Leaders and Members: A Sage Human Services Guide, vol. 10. Newbury Park, CA: Sage.

Braskamp, Larry and R. D. Brown [Eds.] (1980) Utilization of Evaluative Information. San Francisco: Jossey-Bass.

Burry, James (1984) "Synthesis of the Evaluation Use Literature." Evaluation Productivity Project, Center for the Study of Evaluation, UCLA.

Chelimsky, Eleanor (1983) "Improving the Cost Effectiveness of Evaluation," pp. 149-170 in Alkin and Solmon (eds.) The Costs of Evaluation. Newbury Park, CA: Sage.

Cooley, William W. and William E. Bickel (1985) Decision-Oriented Educational Research. Boston: Kluwer-Nijhoff.

Cronbach, Lee J. and Associates (1980) Toward Reform of Program Evaluation. San Francisco: Jossey-Bass.

Cronbach, Lee J. (1975) "Beyond the Two Disciplines of Scientific Psychology." American Psychologist 30: 116-117.

Dickey, Barbara (1981) Utilization of Evaluations of Small-Scale Educational Projects. Educational Evaluation and Policy Analysis 2, 6: 65-77.

Fairweather, G.W., D. Sanders, and L. Tornatsky (1974) Creating Change in Mental Health Organizations. New York: Pergamon.

Gephart, William J. (1981) "Watercolor Painting," pp. 247-272 in Nick L. Smith (ed.) Metaphors for Evaluation. Newbury Park, CA: Sage.

Guba, Egon G. (1981) "Investigative Reporting," pp. 67-86 in Nick L. Smith (ed.) Metaphors for Evaluation. Newbury Park, CA: Sage.

Guba, Egon G. and Yvonna S. Lincoln (1981) Effective Evaluation: Improving the Usefulness of Evaluation Results Through Responsive and Naturalistic Approaches. San Francisco: Jossey-Bass.

Heilman, John G. (1980) "Paradigmatic Choices in Evaluation Methodology." Evaluation Rev. 4, 5: 693-712.

Joint Committee on Standards for Educational Evaluation (1981) Standards for Evaluations of Education Programs, Projects, and Materials. New York: Mc-Graw-Hill.

Kuhn, Thomas (1970) The Structure of Scientific Revolutions. Chicago: University of Chicago Press.

Lynn, Laurence E. (1980) Designing Public Policies: A Casework on the Role of Policy Analysis. Santa Monica, CA: Goodyear.

Olson, Paul (1976) A View of Power: Four Essays on the National Assessment of Educational Progress. North Dakota Study Group on Evaluation, University of North Dakota. (December)

Patton, Michael Q. (1980) Qualitative Evaluation Methods. Newbury Park, CA: Sage.

Patton, Michael Q. (1981) Creative Evaluation. Newbury Park, CA: Sage.

Patton, Michael Q. (1982) Practical Evaluation. Newbury Park, CA: Sage.

Patton, Michael Q. (1986) Utilization-Focused Evaluation (2nd ed.) Newbury Park, CA: Sage.

Reichardt, Charles S., and Thomas D. Cook (1979) "Beyond Qualitative Versus Quantitative Methods." In T. D. Cook & C. S. Reichardt (eds.), Qualitive and Quantitative Methods. Newbury Park, CA: Sage.

Rist, Ray C. (1977) "On the Relations Among Educational Research Paradigms: From Disdain to Detente." Anthropology and Education 8: 42-49.

Rossi, Peter H., Howard E. Freeman, and Sonia R. Wright (1979) Evaluation: A Systematic Approach. Newbury Park, CA: Sage.

Smith, Nick L. (1980) "Studying Evaluation Assumptions." Evaluation Network Newsletter (Winter): 39-40.

Stevens, William F., and Louis G. Tornatsky (1980) "The Dissemination of Evaluation: An Experiment." Evaluation Rev. 4, 3: 339-354.

Thompson, Mark (1975) Evaluation for Decision in Social Programmers. Lexington, MA: D. C. Heath.

Tyler, Ralph W. (1949) Basic Principles of Curriculum and Instruction. Chicago: University of Chicago Press.

Weiss, Carol H. [Ed.] (1977) Using Social Research in Public Policy Making. Lexington, MA: Lexington Books/D. C. Heath.

Weiss, Carol H., and Michael Bucuvalas (1980) "Truth Test and Utility Test: Decision Makers' Frames of Reference for Social Science Research." American Sociological Review (April): 302-313.

Worthen, Blaine R., and J. R. Sanders (1973) Educational Evaluation: Theory and Practice. Worthington, OH: Charles A. Jones.

5

WHAT SHOULD EVALUATION MEAN
TO IMPLEMENTATION?

ANGELA BROWNE
AARON WILDAVSKY
University of California at Berkeley

Evaluation research is a robust area of activity devoted to collecting, analyzing, and interpreting information on the need for, implementation of, and impact of intervention efforts to better the lot of humankind by improving social conditions and community life [Peter Rossi and Howard Freeman, quoted in Palumbo and Nachmias (1983): 67-79].

Most everyone who writes on the subject of evaluation is tempted to invent their own labels and to offer a personal conceptualization of this activity. This intellectual ferment may be attributed to the fact that evaluation is a rapidly growing branch of social research. This growth began in the midsixties, fed by the vast infusion of federal funds for evaluation social programs of the Great Society. Disappointment with the results of these programs has led evaluators to extend their reach to cover the various theoretical perspectives and the sources of error in practice they soon discover.

But in order for evaluation to be effective in its expanding domain—to be of use during implementation—it must be aimed at generating data that can be used to improve the implementation process. Evaluation must also allow future implementation processes (and their designers, organizations, operators, and critics) to learn from errors. Because implementation is always occurring, evaluators, having extended their reach to this arena, can contribute to a continuing refinement in comprehension of why programs and policies do or do not work. Implementers can help them do so by understanding the differences between the various forms that evaluation takes.

In asking "What should evaluation mean to implementation," this chapter looks both at the separation of implementation and evaluation and at the connections that do exist between them. Having infringed on the tasks of implementers, evaluators also take over their problems—which involves reconciling knowledge with power.

EVALUATION AS IMPLEMENTATION

According to Dennis J. Palumbo and David Nachmias:

> The field of evaluation is undergoing an identity crisis. From its initial surge in the 1960s when evaluation research clearly was dominated by a single methodology and evaluation researchers believed that its potential was unlimited, it has undergone a metamorphosis. Rather than a single orientation, a number of alternative approaches to evaluation have sprung up and a nagging doubt about its future has crept into a number of recent publications [1983: 1].

Ernest House writes that "the current evaluation scene is marked by vitality and disorder. The scale, ubiquity, and diversity of evaluation activities make comprehension difficult, even for those operating within the field" (quoted in Palumbo and Nachmias, 1983: 1). Yet,

> it has not always been this way. During the 1960s and early 1970s the ideal type of evaluation research that was conducted then . . .

was aimed at determining whether goals were being achieved; it was not much concerned with the relationship between the evaluator and program manager; and it optimistically believed that evaluations would automatically be used to improve the socio-political processes. Today there is considerable doubt about all of these things [Palumbo and Nachmias, 1983].

It is the plunge into the cold bath of implementation that has given evaluation the chills.

The main trend in evaluation research, Howard E. Freeman and Marian A. Solomon say, is its emphasis on relevance. This trend manifests itself by an interest in utilization of evaluation. Programs should be designed "to build a shared understanding and, if possible, to achieve consensus on evaluation requirements and strategies to maximize the applicability of results and increase the likelihood of program improvement" (1981). This trend toward utilization (real implementation) is the same one that Daniel Mazmanian and Paul Sabatier posit as their preferred direction for implementation studies (Pressman and Wildavsky, Ch. 10; Mazmanian and Sabatier, 1983). Yet the closer evaluators come to program managers, the greater the temptation of evaluators to fudge the results (Wildavsky, 1972). Indeed, the disappointment with lack of utilization has led some analysts to argue in favor of a political model in which evaluators take a partisan stance, marshaling evidence in favor of the policies they are asked to evaluate. Since evaluation inevitably turns up negative aspects of programs, Palumbo and Nachmias believe its results will be rejected. "Thus," they conclude, "it is not possible for the evaluator to be independent or engage in scientific 'objectivity.'" Needless to say, such severe criticism from within the evaluation community is bound to be contested.

The failure to implement evaluation, that is, to utilize its results, has led to challenges to prevailing assumptions. This line of thought and action is made brutally clear by Palumbo and Nachmias:

Most evaluations that are done today assume that decision makers analyze the situation first, then act; the assumption is that decision makers, *before they act*, identify goals, specify alternative ways of getting there, assess the alternatives against a standard such as costs and benefits, and then select the best alternative (the rational model). But if organizations in fact do the opposite—if they act first and then analyze what they did—then evaluations based on the rational paradigm will be out of resonance. . . . Rationalistic evaluations are likely to miss the mark because organizations (decision makers, individuals in organizations) are not looking for the one best way or most efficient alternative for solving a problem. They are instead searching for support for action already taken, and for support that serves the interest of various components of the policy shaping community (Walker, 1981). Evaluations, therefore, should *not* seek "objective truth," but attempt to discover what societal needs have been met by the action that has been taken. They should *not* attempt to see if policy goals have been achieved because . . . they cannot do this; instead, they should determine which stakeholders' interests are served by organizational action [1983: 9-11].

The substitution of partisan analysis for enlightenment as the primary function of evaluation is bound to be controversial.

Contact with implementation has spread the utilization virus. Are evaluators to become poor politicians, then, abandoning the concern for error that made them methodologically rigorous and politically neutral[1], or can they make use of their newly found organizational sophistication to improve their work without sacrificing its quality?

AN IMPLEMENTER'S GUIDE TO
THE CHARACTERISTICS OF EVALUATION

Concern over the dollar volume of expenditures on evaluation and related services has been intensified by suspicion that evaluation research has a low level of utility. Three common criticisms of evaluation are:

(1) *Weak methodology.*—Validity and credibility are endangered by problems of proper procedure.

(2) *Irrelevance.*—Research findings either lack timeliness or would not, in any event, make a difference to decision making.
(3) *Underutilization.*—The resulting information is not disseminated or, if received, is not used (Freeman and Solomon, 1981: 16; Knott and Wildavsky, 1980; Weiss and Bucuvalas, 1980).

Though evaluation is undoubtedly, as Carol Weiss terms it, a "growth enterprise," it is growing not only in size but in scope, threatening to become coterminous with policy analysis itself (1972: 34). This conceptual imperialism, we believe, is grounded in the desire to produce perfect policy. As soon as a major category of policy defects is uncovered, recommendations are made to improve the evaluation process. Soon enough the purview of the evaluator becomes so broad (does the expert's desire for power and professionalization lurk here?) that it is difficult to say what evaluation is not.[2]

Let us begin by trying to say what evaluation *is*. Peter Rossi and Richard Berk provide a broad description, which includes evaluation as policy analysis during implementation:

Evaluation research may be conducted to answer questions that arise during the formulation of policy, in the design of programs, in the improvement of programs, and in testing the efficiency and effectiveness of programs that are in place or being considered. Specific policy questions may be concerned with how widespread a social problem may be, whether any program can be enacted that will ameliorate a problem, whether programs are effective, whether a program is producing enough benefits to justify its cost, and so on [1981: 287].

As evaluative activity increases, it strives to develop a clear identity separate from that of merely a stage in policy formulation. This distinct identity may be enhanced by considering evaluators' answers to five basic questions about their craft, with an emphasis on the last two questions:

(1) When?
(2) Where?

(3) For whom?
(4) What?
(5) Why?

WHEN?

Evaluation can occur at any time. It may be "retrospective," a characterization that many definitions of evaluation prefer,[3] inquiring into how well a program has done in the past, or "prospective," considering how a program is likely to do in the future. If it continues during a program, it is "formative." If it is both formative and retrospective, then it is "ongoing." When it occurs before and after a treatment is administered, it is "integrative" (Dunn, 1981: 51-6).

The evaluative questions asked will vary according to time phase. The emphasis on outcome measures, selection of investigative methods, and even the purpose of an evaluation will be affected by its timing.

Retrospective and prospective evaluation.—Retrospective evaluation, depending as it does on history, cannot be accomplished without efforts to implement the program in question. So we can say that without implementation there can be no retrospective evaluation. Only prospective evaluation can conceivably occur without a prior record of implementation. We doubt whether it is helpful to designate as evaluation the analysis of a program without a past, that is, without consequences to evaluate.

Continuous evaluation.—Evaluation can occur once or continuously, by a single study or by many. A "continuous evaluation" is performed "proactively to help improve a program as well as retroactively to judge its worth" (Stufflebeam and Webster, 1981). At its best, evaluation is "a social procedure that is the cumulative result of many efforts rather than just one" (Wildavsky, 1979: 7). The effects of purposive evaluative behavior can be additive, resulting in continuing advances in the perceptual capacities of actors in the policy process. Perhaps this was an underlying intention of the recently proposed "Master Plan for Services to California's Children and Youth," which noted that program objectives "often are not clearly stated, measurable, or agreed upon, which makes it difficult to accurately evaluate their degree of accomplishment," and that "these programs do not operate in isolation of other children services and social and economic events." This predicament generates "a need to develop mechanisms to accurately and continuously measure and evaluate the quality of children services. Evaluation is necessary to determining the redirection of funds and for decision making regarding future program development (Office of Statewide Health Planning, 1980: 14). Thus evaluation becomes a generic activity aiming at enlightenment.

Continuous evaluation is an attempt to generate perpetual feedback. "Responsive evaluation" is one through which evaluators learn about their clients' perceived needs for information (Stake, 1975). Since client behavior is part of the process of implementation, information about the perceptions in terms of which they act is essential.

WHERE?

As evaluators descend from the general, formal, and national locus to the specific, less formal, and local setting, they intervene in the system of information generation at increasingly lower levels, which affects the nature of their evaluations. Structure and formality increase at higher levels of bureaucracy and organization. Rules are written, studies are planned, meetings are held. At local levels, evaluation may be managed by "peak associations," such as leagues of cities, or not done at all, except informally.

There are organizations especially devoted to evaluation. These range from units within government, such as the General Accounting Office, to not-for-profits like the Council on Municipal Performance, to private-for-profits, like the big management consultants or the famous "beltway bandits" that ring the nation's capital. Independence, objectivity, and capability vary across and within all these categories. The perspectives from which they do their work vary with their clientele, as we can see by looking at exactly for whom the evaluation is being performed.

FOR WHOM?

Evaluators are naturally obligated to their sources of funding; they must address their employer's or sponsor's evaluative concerns. However pressing and clearly defined these concerns, evaluators may perceive the existence of other interested parties. There are numerous stakeholders in the delivery of a publicly funded social service. Among them may be the recipients of the service, the socio-political groups within the community in which the service is delivered, the congressmen who voted to fund this service, the political party with which the related policy is identified. Additional stakeholders who are responsible for the implementation of this service delivery program include overseeing agencies of government, administrators, managers at the local level, and first-line service workers. If the service is contracted, the provider may have an added interest in the findings of an evaluation about its activities.

Multiple perspective evaluation.—The recognition of multiple stakeholders may have a liberating effect on the otherwise constrained evaluative focus. Perceptions of program goals and underlying values may expand. "The focus, use and power of evaluation will vary, then," Michael Patton concludes, "depending on who is identified as the relevant decision maker(s) and information user(s)" (1978: 145). The sponsoring client's need for information is frequently distorted by the push and pull of the multiple stakeholders' interests in the outcome. And whether there are multiple and conflicting stakeholders or a single unified stakeholder in the evaluative process, there always remains the possible discrepancy between the values of the employer and those of the evaluator.

WHAT?

When evaluative energy is expended without a primary motivation to analyze, the scope of the study is narrowed by omitting policy implications from among the research questions. The research questions address the efficiency of selected processes,

(Freeman, 1977: 25; Matry et al., 1981: 4) but generally they do not focus on the relationship between these processes of implementation and their implications for future policy change.[4]

Pseudo-evaluation.—Certain forms of evaluation purport to study both process and outcome but do not actually do so. William N. Dunn labels studies that employ evaluative techniques but do not evaluate outcomes as "pseudo-evaluations" (1981: 343). In their delineation of thirteen forms of evaluation in education, Daniel L. Stufflebeam and William J. Webster describe two forms of pseudo-evaluation, both "politically oriented." A "politically controlled study" is initiated by a client who must defend or maintain his "sphere of influence." A second form of pseudo-evaluation, consisting of a "public relations inspired study," is based on a "propagandist's information needs" for data that construes a positive image of a policy or program (1981: 71). Other pseudo-evaluations are merely innocuous assessments that do not ask questions relevant to policy.

Quasi-evaluation.—In between process and outcome lies what is called "quasi-evaluation." This "question-oriented" evaluation begins with a query, such as, "How many people does this program serve?" or "How can we be certain it is serving them?" Techniques are employed to answer these questions. Questions designed to generate information about outcomes (i.e., how did these outcomes occur, and what is the distribution of valued outcomes among the population?) are not given priority. The quasi-evaluative "focus . . . is too narrow or is only tangential to the questions of worth." (Stufflebeam and Webster, 1981: 73). Variables that might affect implementation are ignored.

Accountability studies and standardized testing programs are common quasi-evaluations. Standardized tests have been widely used since the 1930s to evaluate the quality of education. Performance of individual students is monitored and summed; the teacher's time is accounted for. Now the desire for accountability has spread beyond education. Clients, advocates, taxpayers, groups, and opponents of many social programs have created a demand for competing measures of accountability such as process equity and process effectiveness in service delivery

(Hoisington, 1977: 207). The implementers of social programs are held accountable for their actions, as if their actions guaranteed the desired outcomes. The program is not questioned; its operators must fulfill its specifications, even when these specifications are irrelevant, vague, even counterproductive.[5]

"Objectives-based" quasievaluations intend to discover whether or not specific goals are being achieved. Without questioning the desirability of the objectives themselves, the use of experimental designs allows investigators a limited focus on suspected causal relationships.

Goal-fixed evaluation.—As Huey-Tsych Chen and Peter H. Rossi designate it (1981), "Goal-fixed evaluation is a quasi-evaluation that focuses on expected outcomes. Evaluation is conducted on the basis of "policy-program objectives that have been formally announced" (Dunn, 1981: 345). A good example was the Office of Economic Opportunity's use of project evaluation at the local level of federally funded programs: "Very often," R. O. Washington concludes, "this form of evaluation simply compares project results with performance objectives on baseline conditions" (Washington: 2).

Restriction to formal objectives narrows the focus of evaluation. Accreditation-certification studies, for example, specify guidelines for professionals, lay persons, or self-reporting institutions to determine whether an institution is "fit to serve [the] designated functions." Guidelines such as these restrict the outlook of evaluators in any field of study (Stufflebeam and Webster, 1981: 76). Consider the evaluator of a suicide prevention hotline. The prespecified goal of the project may be to prevent anonymous callers from committing suicide. If so, an output measure, such as the number of calls per month, reveals very little about implementation—about potential suicide victims' use of the hotline, the needs of callers, or the hotline's success in meeting these needs.

Fixed-objective evaluations are confined to description—what has or has not happened. Pseudo- or quasi-evaluations either ignore or obscure causality: "What," not "why," is their question. Each of these forms of evaluation serves a purpose, but each is inherently limited in its capacities to produce knowledge relevant to policy implementation: the evaluator may suspect something is wrong but, without knowing why, cannot, on that basis, devise better policies. By contrast, comprehensive evaluations strive to clarify causality by connecting inputs and processes to outcomes.

Comprehensive evaluation.—"Comprehensive evaluation" is the ideal form, Howard Freeman argues, combining analysis of process and of program impacts as they relate to previously specified goals (1977: 26-27). The synergism of process and impact data in comprehensive evaluation has the potential for an increased understanding of what is happening and why. There are many fields, however, in which it is difficult to identify significant process variables and their relationships to outcomes because the multitude of factors influencing implementation have yet to be delineated. One of these fields is family services. The interactions between a counselor and a client family during a given number of sessions can be represented in terms of total hours, number of times voices were raised, or other quantitative depictions of activity. Yet even when the prespecified goal seems clear enough—removal of the family's need for family service—the process of achieving this outcome may be obscure. Some of the crucial causal variables may actually exist outside the treatment program (for example, income level, public health, maturation of family members) (Schuerman, 1975). Comprehensive evaluation is only as comprehensive as the understanding of the process.

Inferential evaluation.—Barclay Hudson tells us that "inferential evaluation" goes beyond facts to attempt a clarification of cause and affect relationship," asking "was Y caused by X?" (1975). Value is not emphasized, but causality is. A program given credit for positive outcomes (families improve their quality of life due to counseling, for example) or receiving criticism for failure (e.g., a crime has not been prevented due to poor policing) may be the benefactor or the victim of poor causal reasoning.

The problem of identifying causality is prominent in the evaluation of group home-treatment programs. To date, Michael Jang and Herbert Hatanaka report, there is only "fragmentary evidence" that "demonstrates the efficacy of programs for particular adolescent problems." Lacking a sound information base, "most group home studies deal with the issue of effectiveness in a roundabout way by first examining salient attributes of these programs and only later inferring their effectiveness in helping the adolescent residents" (Jang and Hatanaka, 1980: 58-59). In an effort to avoid such fallacious inferences, research is designed to "help make explicit the overlay of concepts and judgment that is needed to extract causal inference from inert facts" (Hudson, 1975: 81). This identification and separation of causal factors is desirable, if, in fact, it can be accomplished. In inferential evaluation, alternative causes and objectives can be considered. Insight into causality is freed from the confines of a single model. But prefixed goals continue to limit the study of outcomes in that the questions remain fixed. "Did X cause Y?" is a good question; even better would be "If not Y, then what did X cause?" or, "If not X, then what caused Y?" The discovery and evaluation of these connections have political overtones.

The objectives of public policy are likely to be multiple, conflicting, and vague (Wildavsky, 1979: 10-11, 21-25). The price of agreement among stakeholders is likely to be vagueness, allowing them to fight their battles another day. Policy and program objectives are multiple so as to create a sufficiently broad coalition of support. Contradiction comes in because objectives held by different interest groups (for example, lowest cost per person placed versus finding jobs for the hard-core unemployed; quality versus cost of medical care) may well be opposed. It follows that evaluators may be hard put to discover single, specific, compatible objectives to use as criteria for judging policy. As programs to carry out policy evolve, moreover, the objectives of the stakeholders may change. New information about the workability of programs is gained during their implementation. Unforeseen consequences occur that may accomplish objectives that, while generally considered desirable (say, preschool education helps mobilize parents for community action), were on no one's explicit agenda. Yet the new objectives, new workability issues, and new unanticipated consequences are unlikely to be examined if the evaluation criteria are restricted to formally predetermined goals.

Goal-free evaluation.—The escape from this myopic goal-oriented research design into "goal-free" evaluation is proposed by Michael Scriven, who claims that "consideration and evaluation of goals" is "unnecessary" and that it may "contaminate" the findings. An evaluator should seek out "actual" rather than "alleged effects." The evaluator, in knowing as little as possible about goals and "program rhetoric," will be free of a condition in which the researcher sees exactly that which is being sought (Scriven, 1972).

Whether or not goals are realized, there may be outcomes of a program or policy that do not relate to the original goals. This is a natural result of the "complex web of exchanges" required to formulate and implement a policy "that changes the rules of the game, but not necessarily the interests of the consumers" (Jacobs, 1980: 250). Students of health and medical policy are particularly aware of perverse consequences. Each of the public and private "players" involved in the distribution and consumption of health care have different goals. Public funders may have partisan motives. Private-sector providers are generally profit-oriented. The consumer of a medical service is presumably health-oriented. But the distribution of "health" is not necessarily the actual objective of the funders and suppliers. And the acquisition of "health" by service recipients is not always the outcome of a health-care program. Among the actual effects of the Medicare program, for example, is the growth in health-care expenditures. Whether this results in improved health among the recipients of the service is difficult to say. Suppliers may be responsible for inducing unessential demand, while overlooking cases of actual need. Or medical care may, in large measure, be irrelevant to most health problems (Wildavsky, 1977). A goal-fixed approach to the evaluation of health programs and policies may overlook competing goals, undesigned consequences, and conflicts in the underlying definitions of health. A goal-free evaluation may escape these confines.

Goal-free evaluation has its share of shortcomings. This creative approach to program evaluation necessarily involves the covert imposition of the evaluator's perspectives and preferences as distinguished from the overt kind involved in acceptance of fixed goals. And it is not geared to unearthing alternative theoretical explanations for outcomes. An evaluator must have some means of selecting from among the infinite range of potential perceptions and effects those which are to be studied. Goal-free evaluation does not specify criteria for such a decision. Evaluators are in a peculiar predicament: "There is no theoretical limit to how they must define the problem to which they apply their skills. The limits are political" (Nakamura, 1983).

When expected benefits do not occur, programs are considered to be less than effective. In these instances, which are common, it appears that programs cannot bear evaluative scrutiny. Yet closer inspection may reveal weaknesses in the evaluation itself.

Both programs and evaluations of them may be ineffective, Chen and Rossi write, but the actual

> problem lies in the articulation of research design and program design. Evaluation researchers have not adequately mapped social programs onto the research designs that are used. . . . There is nothing wrong with the formal structure of conventional research paradigms, nor are there necessarily serious defects in the programs. Rather the problem lies in the extent to which programs have been properly interpreted by evaluation researchers [Chen and Rossi, 1981: 39].

Implementation may have been successful but ability to evaluate program effectiveness may be lacking. Here we have the evaluator's dilemma: is it the implementation or the evaluation that has failed?

Multigoal evaluation.—A variety of potential outcomes are identified in multigoal evaluation. Recognition of possibilities is greatly expanded, but in a more structured way than in a goal-free evaluative free-for-all. The evaluator looks at program goals and beyond them to treatment effects. In so doing, the "conventional official-goal-fixed approach" (i.e., passive evaluative behavior) is abandoned. Instead, evaluators actively develop theoretical models to lead to discovery of a wider range of potential impacts.

Chen and Rossi describe the role of social science evaluation as one that reviews "all of the outcomes deemed possible by social science theory" from "the pool out of which outcomes are to be selected for evaluation testing" (1981: 46). This theory-driven method would contribute to the body of social science research. But it may have little effect on the implementation of policy unless it can provide program operators with more substantial information on modes of improvement.

True evaluation.—A "true evaluation," Stufflebeam and Webster say, "sets out to identify and assess, for society or some segment of society, the merits of competing policies" (1981: 71). "True" is not opposed to "false" evaluation but is merely a designation for a more comprehensive approach to the subject. It differs from inferential evaluation (which reviews multiple sources of causality) and from multiple-goal evaluation (which considers a variety of impacts) in that a wider range of values are involved. In their eyes, a "policy study" is an example of true evaluation. Costs and benefits of alternatives are evaluated to determine "which of two or more competing policies will maximize the achievement of valued outcomes at a reasonable cost" (1981: 76-77).

Difficulties with certain studies arise when stakeholders propose competing policies while they value similar outcomes or when conflicting stakeholders propose similar policies while valuing contrasting outcomes. Politicians often seek agreement on a general policy, postponing what the parties to the bargain think they are going to get out of it or how.[6] Either way, the difficulty encountered in inferential evaluation remains: causality cannot be guaranteed. Competing stakeholders not only propose alternative policies and value contrasting results, but their underlying assumptions of causality may be radically different without any certain method of deciding between them.

Decision-theoretic evaluation.—Dunn's "decision-theoretic evaluation" also addresses outcomes, but these are "explicitly valued by multiple stakeholders" (Dunn, 1981: 348). By combining sponsor-initiated studies with client and consumer-oriented studies, a more global picture of the values at stake may be produced. Stakeholders may have intended or even hidden goals. Decision-theoretic evaluators strive to unearth these goals and weigh them against and along with the publicly stated ones.

A version of this form of evaluation may be especially useful in the evaluation of programs aimed at "prevention" of a known evil. A social investment in prevention is often viewed as an expenditure for an evil that does not yet exist. The economic value of a prevention program (such as immunization drives, antismoking and proseatbelt campaigns, water fluoridation, and prenatal screening for birth defects) consists of the avoidance of future costs. Yet imagining these costs may involve considerable conjecture on the part of all of the competing stakeholders (Scheffler and Paringer, 1980). These preventative programs appear prima facie to be desirable, but interspersed among them may be not a few nostrums, and deciding which ones ought to be implemented may take more knowledge than anyone can command.

Metaevaluation.—An "evaluation of evaluation" is advocated to ensure its continued refinement (Cook and Gruder, 1979). These "metaevaluations" may be conducted either during or after the primary evaluation. They may examine the research design, evaluative techniques, and the conclusions. A review of the literature can be included. Evaluations of similar programs may be compared. Reevaluation and even replication of the original study can verify or question its results.

An independent, simultaneous, heterogeneous evaluation of evaluation is the ultimate metaevaluation. It is conducted by persons who are not connected with the primary evaluators. It is concurrent and thus able to avoid maturation and various other time-related threats to its own validity.[7] And this metaevaluation applies different evaluative techniques, in order to better test the primary findings (Cook and Gruder, 1979: 480-84).

Validity, credibility, and relevance are increased with such a metaevaluation. But, is it feasible? Will the expense be prohibitive? Not necessarily. The simultaneous secondary evaluation need not be large and costly. Several small metaevaluations, coupled with a small primary evaluation, may each be a fraction of the size of

one larger primary evaluation. Thomas D. Cook and Charles
Gruder argue that

> in some circumstances several independent evaluations might
> require a total number of respondents and sites that is not larger
> than a single evaluation would require. But even when it is
> advisable to have one large evaluation, it may still be useful . . . to
> yoke this to a smaller evaluation that is more explicitly focused
> [1979: 507].

Restricting the number of respondents, focusing on target
groups, limiting the research questions, and sharing responsibility
for the product of an evaluation are all part of the simultaneous
evaluative activity. In a sense, otherwise overabundant and
superfluous evaluative behavior is streamlined by such metaevalua-
tive behavior. A potentially beneficial aspect of metaevaluation is
the pressure coevaluators may exert on themselves to examine
carefully the construct validity of their models. A potentially
destructive aspect may be the encouragement of feelings that,
since the evaluations differ, anything goes; in the end, superfluous
evaluation may be encouraged or at least permitted. Every Eden,
even the enlightenment of evaluation, has its serpent.

WHY?

Swimming in a sea of complexity, evaluators begin to wonder if
it is all worthwhile: why should they struggle so hard to produce
information about programs and policy if no one is going to use
it? Recall two of the common criticisms of evaluation: irrelevance
and underutilization. By involving themselves into the maelstrom
of policy making, evaluators hope to make their profession
meaningful. If the evaluative information is actually absorbed by
a policy implementing organization, it should affect policy
outcomes.

It follows that information users (often these are implementers)
should work with evaluators to analyze and interpret the data.
The dissemination of information is a cooperative effort. Hence
evaluators have to involve decision makers and information users

who work at all levels of implementation in all stages of the evaluation.

Yet even the continuous and responsive production of feedback does not guarantee that the information will be recognized and absorbed. When the information is absorbed, it may not be utilized. Implementation is, after all, the acid test of evaluation.

Utilization-focused evaluation.—If the wrong questions are asked by evaluators, Michael Patton contends, they are wrong because they are not going to generate information that will be utilized. In his utilization-focused evaluation, evaluation designs should have a "built-in utilization component appropriate to the unique circumstances they encounter" (1978: 20). This form of evaluation requires the identification of decision makers and information users. Relevant questions are listed and focused. User need and not just program relevance is emphasized. According to Patton, the fundamental question should always be: "What difference would it make to have this information? How would the information be used and how would it be helpful?" (1978: 286). In this model of evaluation for implementation—the active imposition of a framework by the evaluator on clients in order to elicit their reactions—the evaluator is "active-reactive-adaptive" (1978: 289). Clients will react by contributing their own goals, perceptions, and questions. This dialogue is supposed to lead to the adaptation of the research design, via clarification of the issues. Whose objectives should be implemented, those of the adapter or the adapted, is presumably up for grabs.

Utilization-focused evaluation involves the people who intend to implement the evaluation research. These participants are asked to define the questions to be asked by evaluators (1978: 20).

Interactive evaluation.—"Interactive evaluation" brings implementers right into the very act of evaluation. Evaluation, Jolie Bain Pillsbury and Kathy Newton Nance explain, should become "the shared responsibility of evaluators and direct delivery staff." "Direct delivery," of course, is another term for "implementation." Together, evaluators and staff define questions and construct a process of analysis. A "continuous feedback loop becomes an integral part of service delivery" (1976). Presumably, mutual agreement and commitment to evaluation is generated when this happy circumstance occurs so that staff no longer view outside evaluators as threatening. Pillsbury and Nance extend interactive evaluation from the programmatic levels to the decision-making levels of organization and policy. Thus the organization becomes self-evaluating.

Though responsive evaluators attempt to adapt their behavior to the demands of each new task, this may not be enough to guarantee the utility of an evaluation. Utilization-focused research is only as effective as a program or policy is evaluable. Continuous evaluation of something that has not been constructed to be evaluable is wasted work.

Evaluability assessment.—During the latter half of the 1970s, the United States and Canadian governments became concerned about the inevaluability of programs. "Evaluability assessment" (also known as "exploratory evaluation" and "accountability assessment") was developed in response. According to Joseph Wholey, it is "being used to stimulate agreement on realistic, measurable program objectives, appropriate program per-formance indicators, and intended uses of program performance information" (1981). Program objectives are analyzed for their consistency with program design, for the likelihood that they can be realized, and for their measurability. Proposed information utilization procedures are scrutinized. An evaluability assessment can provide advance warning when a proposed treatment process will be impossible to evaluate.

In evaluability assessment, evaluation has come a long way from an activity to determine whether a policy is working, to an integral part of policy design so one can tell whether it works. Error detection is no longer incidental; it becomes integral to evaluation.

Learning evaluation.—Is it possible that a hybrid of all of the evaluations—a continuous, responsive, utilization-focused, inter-active evaluation, accompanied by evaluability and metaevalua-tions—would contribute to "gradual, cumulative improvement" in processes, programs, and policies? (Hargrove, 1975: 55). Would it overcome the common criticism of irrelevance and underutilization in evaluation?

How would such an evaluation become relevant to policy? Must the evaluation findings be fed back to the locus of initial policy decisions? Or are evaluations conducted during policy and program implementation relevant to policy as soon as they affect implementation itself?

In that the attempted fulfillment of policy objectives is a test of the workability of a program, any policy implementation is already based on a tacit policy evaluation. How far beyond the informal connections between implementation and evaluation, the question is, should formal studies go? Should they, for instance, go to the very objectives that are supposed to be evaluated? An explicit evaluation that promotes the amending of objectives is self-forming. This morphogenetic or self-organizing evaluation might ask, "What are the emerging issues?" rather than, "Is this program reaching predetermined policy goals?"

Either the old objectives may be inappropriate to new circumstances, or they may be vague or contradictory. Thus a new program may be forced to develop its objectives during implementation rather than prior to it. In the emerging field of mental health care for the victims of violent crime, for instance, Susan Salasian proposes an ongoing evaluation of services on a case-by-case basis. As a victim's course of psychological recovery is unpredictable, the successful program must be continuously responsive around a flow of information regarding the client's mental health (1980: 25).

Existing programs are forever confronted with new programmatic issues. At this level of operation, evaluation is a necessary component of program development and implementation. A morphogenetic evaluation could be part of a "continual in-house trial policy," such as that maintained by the California Youth Authority. The CYA contends that it has learned from its trial programs (e.g., community parole centers and within-institution counseling), which are conducted at only one or two facilities at a time. CYA claims to have a better record than "other organizations with different approaches to correctional change." Although many of its findings are negative, the information generated allows CYA to refrain from further investment in "fruitless" programs, and to seek out and develop the best methods of lowering recidivism rates.[8] Going along with the fad for naming new types, we can call the CYA approach Hippocratic evaluation—doing no harm when you cannot do good.

SEPARATING IMPLEMENTATION FROM EVALUATION

In the world of action, implementation and evaluation are often carried on by the same people—public officials. They act and observe, observe and act, combining program execution with intelligence about consequences, so as to reinforce or alter behavior. Doing well or doing badly, hardly conscious of the analytic distinctions involved, participants in the policy process act simultaneously as evaluators of the programs they implement and implementers of the programs they evaluate.

It has to be so. Even where there is a formal attempt to separate policy from administration, whether this is between the legislative and executive branches or between policy analysis units and program administration, the vast bulk of activity is carried on in the field. Outside forces are overwhelmed in numbers and expertise by men and women inside the organization. Given the size and scope of contemporary government, most intelligence about events and their consequences has to come from close to the ground.

It is well to understand that formal evaluators, being once (if they work in agencies) or twice (if they are part of overhead units, like the Office of Management and Budget or the General Accounting Office) or three times (if they are outside government) removed from the scene of action, cannot substitute for or replace public officials themselves.[9] This would be undemocratic; it would also be cognitively unfeasible. If mankind sees "through a glass darkly," what shall we say of those who see almost entirely through other people's prisms?

Because implementation and evaluation take place together in organizations, the character of these organizations matters more than one can say for quality of the endeavor. Yet the world continues to be one that evaluators never made. No skill can replace the organizational context or make up merely out of the mind for the antievaluative proclivities of some kinds of organizations. Failure is inherent in an enterprise that runs counter to deep-seated tendencies in the organizations through which the work has to be done. No one gets it all, as President Kennedy said, and no evaluator should expect to be successful most of the time.

In the world of theory, distinctions may be made that are, of necessity, blurred in practice. There, if we have the wit, we can control concepts instead of being dominated by them. In that world of abstractions, evaluation may be distinguished from implementation. The question is whether it is intellectually satisfying and practically useful to do so.

By blurring the distinction, evaluation becoming preoccupied with utilization and implementation taking up monitoring, the two subfields merge into a single-seamed concern with policy analysis. Designing policies to be evaluable and implementable, discovering new alternatives, bringing in new values and constituencies, recommending choices among possible programs, establishing coalitions to support preferred programs, and more, much more, from political feasibility to organizational incentives, become part of the task of evaluators-cum-implementers. A sense of power and responsibility is gained. A sense of differentiation, appropriateness, and hence professionalization is lost.

Evaluators are able to tell us a lot about what happened—which objectives, whose objectives, were achieved—and a little about why—the causal connections. Cumulating evaluations should add to the store of information relevant to policy. The broader the viewpoints from which evaluation is done, the more valuable the information generated. Were they particularly fortunate or perspicacious, evaluators might just barely know a little about which instruments of policy are likely to be efficacious in securing desired results, without necessarily recommending particular policies.

Selling evaluation goes with the job. Making it more attractive to different constituencies or organization units is part of being persuasive. So is writing well. Why shouldn't evaluators go "whole hog" by superintending the actual implementation of programs themselves?

Evaluators have tried to become implementers. This is both good and bad—good because evaluation becomes more relevant, bad because it becomes less knowledgeable. Being useful is one thing; acting as if one were responsible for implementation is another. Monitoring the consequences of programs, which up until now has been the central core of evaluation, requires a certain openness to go where the evidence leads. The evaluator must always be prepared to discover that the consequences (or objectives) hitherto considered are not the only ones. That breadth of vision is sacrificed when evaluation becomes indistinguishable from implementation. Where an absence of interest in utilization is stultifying, an exclusive concern with immediate use results in subordination of intelligence to action. In the end, if this path is taken, only self-serving evaluations will be made. Why care, then, whether evaluations whose conclusions are prejudged are utilized or not? If we care, it is only to see that there is as little of this sort of "evaluation" as possible. Demarcating the domain of implementation helps maintain the distinctiveness and integrity of evaluation.

Implementation might be conceived, following Jan-Erik Lane, as joining the traditional public administration concern with the executive to the newer interest in evaluation (Lane, 1983). The evaluator collects and analyzes data to provide information about program results. The implementer consumes this information, using it to check on past decisions and to guide future actions. Implementation is, as we said, about learning from evaluation. It is in their production and consumption of information (that is, learning) that implementers and evaluators engage in complementary relationships.

These two generic aspects of policy analysis share an interest in the clarification of objectives. There must be prior objectives against which to measure subsequent achievement. But objectives need not, indeed should not, "be forever." Both implementation and evaluation are concerned with the relationship between resources and objectives, though in different directions. Evaluation is concerned with the causes of outcomes and implementation with utilizing causal knowledge to alter outcomes. If, as we claim, however, implementation takes place within an evolutionary framework, it becomes difficult to assume the prior existence of objectives against which to assess accomplishment. Objectives cannot be held constant while they are changing. Neither can the policy preferences of different people. It is intelligent to alter objectives to fit resources,[64] to adjust programs to face facts, as well as to fit resources to objectives.

In his perceptive paper, Lane asks, "Is implementation analysis the same as evaluation analysis? The concept of implementation as evolution amounts to a strong denial of any identity between the two, because if objectives and outcomes continuously interact, how could the outcomes be evaluated in terms of a fixed set of objectives?" Evaluators need not stand still when they need to keep moving. They are wise, then, not to fix prematurely on immediate utilization amidst the flux of life, wise also to infuse their own evaluations with multiple possibilities, some of which may be more important in the future than they are now. The conceptual distinction between evaluation and implementation is important to maintain, however much the two overlap in practice, because they protect against the absorption of analysis into action to the detriment of both.

NOTES

1. And can they do this without impeding implementation? Negative evaluations that are incorrect can cause good programs to be terminated, or they can create unfavorable public opinion. Slow evaluations can impede implementation of decisions based on awaited findings (Cook, 1983).

2. William Meyers refers to the "entrepreneurial willingness" to accept evaluation contracts "bearing little relationship to . . . previous competence" of social research firms (Meyers, 1981: 43-44).

3. In 1976, the Symposium on the Use of Evaluation by Federal Agencies reached a consensus on the definition of evaluation that included the stipulation that evaluation be retrospective (Chelimsky, 1977: 5).

4. For analysis of the differences between outputs, outcomes, and inputs, see Levy et al (1973).

5. The concept of "accountability" in clinical social work practice (as well as in other fields) is related to several unresolved issues, one of which is whether accountability has

increased at all. Some say that a "pseudoaccountability" has developed in response to public and administrative pressures. They allege that quantities of insignificant data are collected in time-consuming and costly ways, with little bearing on the substance of clinical social work (Haselkorn, 1978).

6. A seminal study of the dynamics of agreement is E. Pendelton Herring, The Politics of Democracy (New York: Rinehart, 1940).

7. "Maturation" is a process in which the subjects under study change due to the passage of time, such as "growing older, growing hungrier, growing more tired." (Campbell and Stanley, 1966: 5).

8. Glaser (1976: 158-159). Many issues covered in the literature on ethics in social experimentation are pertinent to the evaluation of social experiments and programs. "Large scale experimentation is so new that the moral and ethical dilemmas it raises have not yet been addressed systematically." (Rivlin and Timpane, 1975: 2, 115-118).

9. Of course, public officials' "every proposal to evaluate has political impact." This singles out a program for evaluation, signaling its vulnerability (Cronbach, 1980: 163-164).

10. See the extensive discussion in Wildavsky, 1979.

REFERENCES

Campbell, Donald T. and Julian C. Stanley (1966) "Factors Jeopardizing Internal and External Validity," in Experimental and Quasi-Experimental Designs for Research. Chicago: Rand McNally.

Chelimsky, Eleanor (1977) An Analysis of the Proceedings of a Symposium on the Use of Evaluation by Federal Agencies, vol. 2, November 17-19, 1976. MacLean, VA: Metrek.

Chen, Huey-Tsych and Peter Rossi (1981) "Multi-Goal, Theory-Driven Approach to Evaluation: A Model Linking Basic and Applied Social Science." Evaluation Studies Review Annual 6: 40-41.

Cook, Thomas (1983) "Book Reviews." Knowledge 4 (March): 463-465.

Cook, Thomas D. and Charles Gruder (1979) "Metaevaluation Research." Evaluation Studies Review Annual 4: 469-513.

Cronbach, Lee J. (1980) Toward Reform of Program Evaluation. San Francisco: Jossey-Bass.

Dunn, William N. (1981) Public Policy Analysis: An Introduction. Englewood Cliffs, NJ: Prentice Hall.

Freeman, Howard F. (1977) "Boundaries of the Evaluation Research Field." Evaluation Studies Review Annual 1.

Freeman, Howard E. and Marian A. Solomon (1981) "Evaluation and the Uncertain '80s." Evaluation Studies Review Annual 6: 1-23.

Glaser, Daniel (1976) Routinizing Evaluation: Getting Feedback on the Effectiveness of Crime and Delinquency Programs, National Institute for Mental Health, Department of Health, Education, and Welfare, publication no. ADM 76-369 Washington, DC: Government Printing Office.

Hargrove, Erwin C. (1975), The Missing Link: The Study of the Implementation of Social Policy. Washington, DC: Urban Institute.

Haselkorn, Florence (1978) "Accountability in Clinical Practice." Social Casework 59 (June): 330-36.

Hoisington, Sumner J. (1977) "Accountability in Social Welfare," in Encyclopedia of Social Work. National Association of Social Workers.

Hudson, Barclay (1975) "Domains of Evaluation." Social Policy 6 (September/October): 79-81.

Jacobs, Philip (1980) The Economics of Health and Medical Care (Baltimore: Univ. Park Press.

Jang, Michael and Herbert Hatanaka (1980) "Group Homes for Adolescents: A History, Ideology, and Organizational Analysis." Office of Human Development Services, Grant No. 18-P-0017-9-01 San Francisco: Institute for Scientific Analysis.

Knott, Jack and Aaron Wildavsky (1980) "If Dissemination Is the Solution, What Is the Problem?" Knowledge (June): 537-78.

Lane, Jan-Erik (1983) "The Concept of Implementation." Statsventenskaplig Tidskrift 86: 17-40.

Levy, Frank, Arnold Meltsner, and Aaron Wildavsky (1973) Urban Outcomes. Berkeley and Los Angeles: Univ. of California Press.

Matry, Harry P., Richard E. Winnie, and David M. Fisk (1981) Practical Program Evaluation for State and Local Governments. Washington, DC: Urban Institute.

Mazmanian, Daniel and Paul A. Sabatier (1983) Implementation and Public Policy. Palo Alto, CA: Scott, Foresman.

Meyers, William R. (1981) The Evaluation Enterprise. San Francisco: Jossey-Bass.

Nakamura, Robert (1983) Personal communication (May 16).

Office of Statewide Health Planning, State of California (1980) Proposed Master Plan for Children and Youth: Executive Summary (Public Hearing Draft). Author.

Palumbo, Dennis J. and David Nachmias (1983) "The Pre-Conditions for Successful Evaluation: Is There an Ideal Type?" Policy Sciences 16: 67-79.

Patton, Michael Quinn (1978) Utilization-Focused Evaluation. Newbury Park, CA: Sage.

Pillsbury, Jolie Bain and Kathy Newton Nance (1976) "An Evaluation Framework for Public Welfare Agencies." Public Welfare 36 (Winter): 47-51.

Pressman, Jeffrey and Aaron Wildavsky (1984) Implementation (3rd ed.) Berkeley: Univ. of California Press.

Rivlin, Alice M. and P. Michael Timpane [eds.] (1975) Ethical and Legal Issues of Social Experimentation. Washington, DC: Brookings Institution.

Rossi, Peter H. and Richard A. Berk (1981) "An Overview of Evaluation Strategies and Procedures." Human Organizations 40: 287.

Salasian, Susan (1980) "Evaluation as a Tool for Restoring the Mental Health of Victims." Evaluation and Change, Special Issue.

Scheffler, Richard M. and Lynn Paringer (1980) "A Review of the Economic Evidence on Prevention." Medical Care 18 (May): 473-84.

Schuerman, John R. (1975) "Do Family Services Help?" Social Services Rev. 49 (September): 367.

Scriven, Michael (1972) "Prose and Cons About Goal-Free Evaluation." Evaluation Comment: The Journal of Education Evaluation 3 (December): 1-7.

Stake, Robert A. (1975) Evaluating the Arts in Education: A Responsive Approach. Columbus, OH: Charles E. Merrill.

Stufflebeam, Daniel L. and William J. Webster (1981) "An Analysis of Alternative Approaches to Evaluation." Evaluation Studies Rev. Annual 6: 70-85.

Washington, R. O. (n.d.) Program Evaluation in the Human Services. Milwaukee: University of Wisconsin.

Weiss, Carol (1972) Evaluation Research. Englewood Cliffs, NJ: Prentice-Hall.

Weiss, Carol H. and Michael J. Bucuvalas (1980) "Truth Tests and Utility Tests: Decision-Makers' Frames of Reference for Social Science Research." Amer. Soc. Rev. 45 (April) :302-313.

Wholey, Joseph S. (1981) "Using Evaluation to Improve Program Performance." Evaluation Studies Review Annual 6: 59-60.

Wildavsky, Aaron (1972) "The Self-Evaluating Organization." Public Administration Rev. 32 (September/October): 509-520.

Wildavsky, Aaron (1977) "Doing Better and Feeling Worse: The Political Pathology of Health Science." Daedalus 106 (Winter) :105-123.

Wildavsky, Aaron (1979) Speaking Truth to Power: The Art and Craft of Policy Analysis. Boston: Little, Brown.

6

POLICY TERMINATION
AS A POLITICAL PHENOMENON

PETER DeLEON
Columbia University

It's not that I'm afraid to die. I just don't want to be there when it happens [Allen, 1971].

Within the past few years, the study of policy termination[1] has experienced two subtle but important shifts in emphasis. The preponderance of earlier work on policy termination had two prevalent characteristics. First, it focused on the termination of the sponsoring organization (Brewer, 1978; Kaufman, 1976) as a means of ending outworn or inadequate policies or programs. Consequently, institutional "fixes" were at the heart of policy recommendations regarding the revitalization of defined social objectives (Hirschman, 1970; Biller, 1976). Second, most of the motivation for policy termination stressed reducing organiza-

Author's Note: *I am indebted to a number of students in the Masters of Public Administration program at Columbia University for both asking insightful questions regarding termination processes in general and providing excellent case histories of specific instances.*

tional inefficiencies or, better yet, promoting greater governmental economies (e.g., Shubik, 1978; Levine et al., 1982).

These emphases are not difficult to understand and rationalize. In the first instance, organizations are highly visible, often symbolic targets that, if terminated, could conceivably end a number of seemingly inadequate programs and policies. Better to do away with the entire Office of Economic Opportunity, some would claim, than the piecemeal dismembering of the War on Poverty by gradual, glacial programmatic attrition. In the second case, the emphasis on economies and efficiencies fits comfortably into the analyst's nominal preference for objective, rational analysis. If a program were demonstrably inefficient in its delivery of services, or if the desired service could be provided at a lower cost, then these facts could serve as prima facie evidence arguing for the elimination of that program.

However desirable or convenient such perspectives might have been, they have been revealed as deficient in both concept and practice. In conceptual terms, Kaufman's (1976) seminal study posed the question *Are Government Organizations Immortal?* and found that they basically were. Only 15% had been organizationally disbanded. Little new evidence is in hand to refute his observations. Since Kaufman, in spite of the avowed objective of two administrations to cut back to the size of the government bureaucracy, only two important federal agencies have been eliminated, the Community Services Administration in 1981 (Shribman, 1981; Ink, 1982) and the Civil Aeronautics Board in 1984 (Cooper, 1984; Molotsky, 1985). A third office, the Renegotiation Board, which had the responsibility for discovering and recovering excessive profits in defense procurement contracts, was quietly phased out in March 1979 (Singer, 1979). And two major funding agencies, the Law Enforcement Assistance Administration (LEAA) and the National Institute for Education (NIE), closed their doors in April 1982 (*New York Times,* 1982a) and October 1985 (Savage, 1985), respectively.

Managerial procedures designed to help eliminate programs have been largely unsuccessful. "Sunset" clauses, while widely hailed and enacted, have been ineffective in curtailing organizations except when applied against minor bureaucracies such as accrediting boards (Carlson, 1982; Cooper, 1984: 1822). PPBS and ZZB have never fulfilled the retrenchment promises of their proponents (Wildavsky, 1979a; Brewer and deLeon, 1983: 441-443). As a point of empirical fact, in the face of limited budgets and growing deficits, the "death" of government organizations has continued along the torpid trend traced by Kaufman.

A columnist once posed the institutional query, "What Will Outlive Even Eternity?" and concluded that government organizations would (Bethell, 1979). While immortality clearly implies a much longer lifespan than one should normally care to countenance, it does seem that government institutions are, by and large, exempt from the usual ravages of age—although not necessarily senility—if institutional death is the criterion by which they are to be judged. Thus if one is going to address with any prescriptive intent the issue of termination as part of the policy process, it appears that the organizational level of analysis is inappropriate.

In practical terms, these initial perspectives were again found wanting. Shubik (1978) examines how the notion of "efficiencies" in government is intuitively attractive but, in many cases, operationally inapplicable. The serpentine lattice of conflicting groups and their incongruent objectives presents multiple problems in defining what the desired service is, what the respective (and occasionally conflicting) organizational goals are, or even who the proposed recipients are. Downs and Larkey (1981) detail how expected efficiencies seldom occur as the result of agency reductions. Who wins and who loses is an elusive calculus. For instance, what parties have been well served (or hurt) by the deregulation of the airlines, especially in light of the charge that the airlines (particularly American Airlines) have cut back on their aircraft maintenance to ensure their profit margins, even if safety suffers (Dahl, 1985). Are job training programs meant to aid the business communities, the chronically underemployed, or those on social welfare? In short, efficiency is an attractive but usually elusive standard.

Compounding this basic confusion is the difficulty in arriving at reliable, consensual measures of efficiency. The Census Bureau has admitted that it has trouble arriving at a definition, let alone a measure of poverty (Herbers, 1982b), thus making the evaluation of antipoverty programs a problematic exercise. The Assistant Secretary of Labor for Employment and Training testified that "when we came here . . . they couldn't even measure what was right and what was wrong . . . because nobody was really looking at performance. . . . There is no standard measure out there that everybody will accept as a basis for success or failure of the program." (quoted in Lanoutte, 1982: 241) Similar shortcomings can be found in national defense, as critics ask whether the billions of defense dollars are being "well spent" (Gordon, 1983a and 1983b; Ognibene, 1981; Keller, 1985; Gerth, 1985; S.V. Roberts, 1985), or whether federally administered education programs should be replaced by local initiatives (e.g., compensatory education; see Stanfield, 1982). In short, the evaluation measures necessary for thoughtful and effective termination actions have not been present (deLeon, 1983).

Nominally, economic savings would provide sufficient rationale for organizational reductions, especially in the post Proposition 13 era, with two-trillion-dollar national debts, Gramm-Rudman-Hollings acts, and budget-balancing constitutional amendments. But careful analysis has revealed that economics rarely drive decisions to eliminate agencies. The CAB, as it prepared itself to be phased out of its organizational existence as a result of the 1978 Airline Deregulation Act, reduced its staff from 830 to 351 but its budget was reduced by only 25% (Cooper, 1984). When the Reagan administration proposed eliminating the Department of Energy (DOE), it originally estimated the potential savings at $1.3 billion for the first year; this figure was later reduced to $1 billion over three years and, finally to $250 million. A subsequent GAO study reported that even the last figure was "not adequately documented and does not reflect a full assessment of potential reorganizational expenses" (quoted by Sun, 1982). Thus when DOE Undersecretary Fiskc was testifying on why his Department should be dismantled, he stated that "This isn't being done for savings. . . . There will be some savings, I am sure, but it is not being done because there is a cost savings of this much or that much" (Anonymous, 1982b). And the now-defunct Renegotiation Board was estimated to have saved the government $1.3 billion in excessive profits since its creation after the Korean War (Light, 1979).

There are, therefore, scant grounds to argue that economics is the driving force in the decision to mandate significant reductions in public sector institutions. This point might be much more arguable in the case of private sector organizations where there is a much more tractable financial "bottom line" that most decision makers can accept. Still, even in this arena, economics is not always dominant, and the evidence is mixed (see Behn, 1978a).

Finally, the "lessons" of the last few years are less than clear cut, and even somewhat contradictory. Dwight Ink, the last head of the Community Services Administration (CSA), was quoted at the time (Shribman, 1981) as being somewhat nostalgic over the final bolting of the CSA doors. Later, he reflected on how splendidly his bureaucracy had implemented its own demise (Ink, 1982). His main regret was not for the over 1,000 employees who lost their jobs, but that CSA had only two months in which to execute its organizational hara-kari. On the other hand, the CAB had six years between the passage of the 1978 Airlines Deregulation Act, which mandated its end, and its institutional taps on December 31, 1984. There was ample time for expected staff attrition, and many of its remaining personnel were absorbed into the Department of Transportation; only 38 people were actually released. C. Don McKinnon, CAB's last administrator, lamented that the CAB's death throes would have been better managed had the agency had only six months rather than six years (Molotsky, 1985).[2] The Renegotiation Board was apparently terminated because it was doing its job, that is, recovering excessive profits from defense contractors for the government. Repeated efforts by the Carter administration and Congressional supporters to reauthorize and refund the Board were absolutely rejected by its Congressional opponents—largely representing stages with large defense industries—until the Board and its functions were completely eliminated (Light, 1979). Military reformers claim that the Renegotiation Board was in fact phased out because it was doing its job too well (Singer, 1979). In the CSA and CAB examples, their respective administrators implied that their particular circumstances and actions would not translate easily into guidelines for other future agency closings. Lastly, the NIE and LEAA were exclusively funding agencies. Even though these organizations were dismembered, their funding functions were transferred whole cloth to other agencies—in the case of NIE, literally down the hall.

In summary, it would appear that research in policy termination has not made great advances since Bardach (1976) and his collaborators first began to explore the subject in 1976. Indeed, the cynic could argue that too many case studies and misspecified criteria have served only to retard whatever understandings might have been made. These observations are perhaps puzzling, for it is clear that the motivations and demands for policy termination have not abated since the late 1970s. If anything, they have grown as a result of diminished governmental resources as reflected by decreasing budgets and public concerns. CSA administrator Ink said that he found no useful precedents to guide his agency's closing (Cooper, 1984). Legislators call for "rational decremental budgets" (Tarschys, 1981) in an era of financial constraints. The Reagan administration has been consistently insistent in its demands that entire agencies—such as AMTRAK, the Small Business Administration, and the Economic Development Administration (EDA)—be completely eliminated (*New York Times,* 1985; Rauch, 1985a). Nor is this a strictly federal phenomenon; states are faced with financial retrenchments (e.g., Kirlin, 1982) as are municipalities (Levine et al., 1982). Even the noted welfare states of Europe are being forced to similar procrustean exercises (Chapman, 1980-81; Brand, 1982; Nordheimer, 1983; *Wall Street Journal,* 1983; Tarschys, 1983; Lewis, 1984).

This confluence suggests the subtle shifts in termination research alluded to at the beginning of this chapter, namely, transitions away from the nominal "cost/benefit" types of analyses and institution attentions to the more realistic but less manageable criteria of ideology in terminating programs. This emphasis has led to a more political accounting of who benefits and who loses in any termination exercise (deLeon, 1982) and therefore a more realistic assessment as to the feasibility of planned termination. That is, what types of policy evaluations have the potential for motivating and shaping the termination activities?

This second set of perspectives on termination was initially broached by Bardach (1976) when he described terminators as "economizers" and "reformers."[3] As noted above, most termination researchers, perhaps seduced by numerous examples from private business and its economic cachet, followed the "economizers" line of thought. Recent studies of the end of the no-tuition policy at the City University of New York (Glazer, 1984), and the reduction in federal grants for municipal services (Nathan and Doolittle, 1985) still fundamentally adhere to this model. However, practical evidence has revealed economics and efficiencies to be principally a post hoc rationale rather than the motivating impetus. Economics alone surely cannot explain why the Clinch River breeder reactor development program survived for as long as it did (Lefevre, 1985); indeed, economics would have argued for its cancellation long ago (Lanoutte, 1983). Nor can economics defend the Reagan administration's decision to resurrect the B-1 strategic bomber program that the Carter administration had chosen to kill (cf. Wade, 1977, with Ingersoll, 1981). Termination research must increasingly explore ideology and its resulting political positions as the root cause for termination decisions (Cameron, 1978; deLeon, 1983). In other words, it is the reformers rather than the economizers who would appear to be calling the termination auction. If one is to understand the lifespan of program and policies, one must examine the ideologies and values that underpin those policies as well as the objectives of actors who are involved.

Similarly, it would seem that evaluators' attentions should be refocused on terminating more discrete programs and policies rather than entire agencies or institutions. This reflects the low number of termination experiences over the past decade. As Biller (1976) hypothesized and Kaufman (1976) supports, institutions are, in fact, deliberately created for longevity. It is little wonder that they endure. Therefore, evaluators would be better advised to find more vulnerable targets if they are to be relevant in policy-termination decisions. As deLeon (1978) noted, these would be on the programmatic level.

While the elimination of an entire organization might sweep away a complete raft of programs in one fell swoop, its multiple clientele could assemble defenses that would blunt the termination's thrust and leave all the programs intact. For instance,

AMTRAK critics would be better served to reduce subsidies to parts of the railway system rather than abolish the organization itself. The Department of Energy has been able to bulwark itself against President Reagan's campaign promise and subsequent proposals to do away with it by assembling an unholy coalition of divergent energy advocates (Miller, 1981); but, in the meantime, it has lost its solar, conservation, and coal programs, as well as some of its user subsidy programs (Corrigan, 1982). The Small Business Administration could more likely be reduced by the elimination of certain types of loan programs rather than by a wholesale attack on the agency itself (Rauch, 1985a). The Legal Services Commission's (LSC) programs and clientele are being steadily atrophied and surrendered while Congress and the President feud over the LSC's mission and ultimate fate (Boyd, 1983; Paltrow, 1982; Drew, 1982). A reduction of over 1,900 persons (approximately 25%) of the Department of Education's staff has debilitated its women's educational equity, migrant education, adult education, and civil rights training programs (Pear, 1983a). As a spokesperson for the National Education Association characterized the Reagan administration's termination efforts, it "has given up trying to wipe out the Department of Education, but they are apparently trying to starve it" (Pear, 1983a: 7).

As a result of these altered attentions, policy researchers are necessarily paying closer heed to what deLeon has called "partial termination" (1978; also Brewer and deLeon, 1983: 386). Again, this reflects the robust nature of organizations and specific policies, which can muster and maintain sizable constituent defenses when threatened. As Mark Twain observed in a similar situation, reports of their deaths have been greatly exaggerated. For instance, the Bureau of Alcohol, Tobacco, and Firearms marshaled the National Rifle Association and the liquor industry to fend off the Reagan reorganization plans for the Bureau's functions to be parcelled out to other divisions of the Treasury Department (Wines, 1982). More recently, one need only look at the discrepancy between the organizational and policy cuts presented in the Reagan administration's FY85 budget submissions and the subsequent congressional authorizations to appreciate this fact of institutional life. As the *New York Times* headlined, "Proposals for Spending Cuts Echo Many Rejected Before" (Rosenbaum, 1985). Therefore, one must look to the gradual, marginal reductions of programs (rather than organizations) that are failing to meet their prescribed objectives if evaluators are to propose effective termination strategies. The decrements are measured in particular programs, occasionally aggregated into policy packages (Brewer and deLeon, 1983: 386).

In short, policy termination must be viewed as an exercise in *political* rather than *analytical* decision making, that is, as an exercise in values with most "adjustments" being made on the margin. It is the mirror image of Wildavsky's (1979) representation of budgetary politics, because it deals with decrements rather than increments (Tarschys, 1981). This article explores these two facets of policy termination to illustrate how ideology—either revealed or hidden—is the motivating and defining force behind termination activities and how, for political reasons, these termination actions must perforce be directed towards the level of individual programs.

This emphasis on political rather than analytic desiderata presents a particular challenge for the evaluation community in terms of termination activities. Even though many of its more cognizant members (e.g., Suchman, 1967; Caro, 1976) have long recognized the primacy of the political contexts in which they must operate, many evaluators still feel more secure in their methodological sanctuaries. Political ideologies remain removed from the evaluators' fields of comfortable expertise. Yet, of course, politics is the arena in which they must exercise their skills if their evaluation efforts are to prove relevant and effective (Palumbo, 1986; Weiss, 1986) for termination purposes. This essay specifically addresses this charge.

IDEOLOGY AND POLICY TERMINATION

Cameron (1978) hypothesized that political values and ideology play the key role in termination decisions. He illustrated his case with examples from the mental health system in California as it operated in the 1970s. Since his study, the Reagan administration has overwhelmingly substantiated Cameron by proposing a welter of agency and policy terminations openly based on two related ideological tenets: the decentralization of government services from the federal to the local level and the relative efficiency of the private—as opposed to the public—sector in the distribution of goods and services.

The Reagan administration has thoroughly endorsed the decentralization of government services in a number of specific areas. A 1982 draft report by the Department of Housing and Urban Development claimed that:

> Too often the Federal Government has been called upon to intervene, to insulate individuals, businesses and communities from the consequences of changes brought about by evolving technology, shifting market conditions and altered social attitudes. Intervention can do more harm than good by slowing the processes of individual and collective adjustment to changes [quoted in Herbers, 1982a: 20].

The final report was hardly less assertive, stating that "in the past, the federal government has too often mandated an unassailable social objective and left it to others to pay the bill. . . . State and local governments have amply demonstrated that, property unfettered, they will make better decisions than the federal government acting for them" (quoted in May, 1982). President Reagan neatly summarized the philosophy driving these decisions: "We are committed to restoring the *intended* balance between the levels of government" (quoted in R. Wade, 1982; emphasis added).

Economic development falls into the same category of value-driven termination criterion. The Reagan administration has consistently proposed the elimination of the Appalachian Regional Commission and the Tennessee Valley Authority (excepting only its power generating roles). No agency has come under more sustained attack than the Economic Development Administration. Carlos Campbell, the Assistant Commerce Secretary for Economic Development, bluntly stated the Reagan administration's position:[4]

Increasing federal spending for programs under the Economic Development Administration is really counterproductive.... You either believe in free enterprise or you are a socialist.... Either you believe the state is supreme over people and that's the source of jobs or you reject that theory [quoted by Stanfield, 1983: 1739].

Candidate Reagan campaigned for the abolition of the Department of Education. His Secretary of Education defined the "prime reason for eliminating the Department of Education: Federal regulatory power" (Hunter, 1982). A 1981 White House "fact" sheet on the rationale for abolishing the Department spoke only in philosophic terms:

Creation of the Department of Education symbolized the progressive intrusion of the federal government into an educational system that had traditionally drawn its strength from diversity, adaptability and local control. The organizational arrangements for federal support for education to be proposed will emphasize assistance and discourage federal intervention [quoted in Stanfield, 1981: 1907].

An administration spokesperson reiterated the ambivalent but forceful theme a few weeks later: "The principal thing, whatever agencies control education programs, is to make sure that the [federal] education system dictates to the schools as little as possible. Education decision making must be rooted in the states" (Stanfield, 1981: 1907). Stanfield observed that "Whether it's a foundation or an education assistance agency is less important than the diffusion of power and the reduction in general size" (1981: 1909). Or, as in the case of compensatory education funds, Secretary of Education Bell testified that "The rationale for the budget cuts was not based upon any alleged failure of Title I. I know . . . that our Title I programs are successful" (Stanfield, 1982: 201). Yet the administration asked the Congress to slash a billion dollars from compensatory education programs because:

it's simply [something] the federal government shouldn't be doing. Education is the province of the states and localities . . . and no matter how effective a federal program may be, it still intrudes on the state and local domains [Stanfield, 1982: 201].

Similar rationales have been proposed for the elimination of local job training programs, arguing that these are the legitimate and primary concern of local governments and private enterprises, since they are the principal beneficiaries (Lanoutte, 1982). Any federal support for continued job training would be via the block-grant mechanism. This creates a fierce competition for scarce funds and could thus eliminate the program entirely.

A second philosophic theme motivating the Reagan administration's termination activities is adherence to the free market model. Certainly the belief in the wisdom of the unregulated market supported the long-standing economist's drive toward the deregulation of the airline (Behrman, 1980) and interstate commerce (Mosher, 1979) industries. But Reagan's staunch opposition toward government support for what he considers to be private sector enterprises represents a dominant theme in his governmental symphony: As Fuerbringer (1985) summarizes the score, the administration budget plan offers it an opportunity to achieve an enduring goal—to shrink the government. Harmonics seemingly outweigh harmony in the Reagan orchestration.

This return of government activities to the private sector— often referred to ungracefully as "privatization" (Hanke, 1985)— surfaced in a wide number and range of administration proposals, with former CMB Director David Stockman being cast as the administration conductor. Arguing for the termination of AM-TRAK, he testified to Congress that "There are few programs . . . that rank lower than AMTRAK in terms of the good they do, the purpose they serve and the national need they respond to" (quoted in Stuart, 1985b). Highly controversial farm aid programs were not screened from this value filter. Agriculture Secretary Block defended proposed cutbacks in his Department's farm aid programs with the avuncular advice:

I'm painfully aware of the difficulties many farmers are having today. But I'm equally certain American agriculture has a great future if it's willing to compete for exports at world market prices. We can't do that if we continue with a farm policy built on false prices, false hopes and high dependence on the government [quoted in King, 1985].

Stockman's now famous testimony was even sharper and more tendentious:

> For the life of me I can't figure out why taxpayers have the responsibility to go in and refinance bad debt willingly incurred by consenting adults who went out and bought farmland when prices were going up and thought they could get rich.

In no area, however, are the ideological stimuli for program termination provided by a faith in the efficacy of the private sector more pronounced than in the case of the Department of Energy. President Reagan, in a 1980 campaign speech, asserted that "President Carter called for the 'moral equivalent of war' and created the Department of Energy, which is the bureaucratic equivalent of surrender" (Solomon, 1982a: 1). The department's mandated sunset review document was even more elaborate and explicit:

> Many of the department's programs are no longer valid within the context of the federal role in the energy sector of the economy. . . . In view of the demonstrated success of energy markets in those cases where they have been allowed to function freely, and given the limited role and responsibilities of the federal government in this sector of the economy, it is no longer necessary or appropriate to maintain a Cabinet-level Department of Energy. The department was established to address a set of problems that were peculiar to their time and that were largely the result of a philosophy that stressed executive government intervention in the energy market in the first place [quoted in Solomon, 1982b: 1].

Two important observations can be made from these trends. First, it is an ideological stance rather than rigorous analysis or evaluation that drives the current termination activities. Repeatedly one finds scant regard for analytic underpinning when designating targeted agencies or programs. "At issue," cautions deLeon (1983: 640), "is not so much the legitimacy of these reductions but the apparent lack of standards by which they are assessed or, when standards are established, how they are derived." Cameron (1978: 306) pointedly summarizes the situation:

> Legitimizing the proposal involves a systematic effort to delegitimize the policy it is designed to supplant. This frequently takes the simplistic form of "the right and the good" versus the "wrong and immoral. . . ." But the simplistic approach that gives ideology its coalescing force results in ill-considered policy choices: data that are inconsistent with the ideology are ignored or explained away; rigid adherence to credo becomes more important than inquiry into the potential risks attending the prospect of contingencies.

Based on a value-dictated set of criteria, one can readily ignore questions such as the effectiveness of private job training programs (Serpick, 1982; Lanoutte, 1982), the privitization of local services (Herbers, 1983), the ability of states and municipalities to assume programs previously funded by federal sources (Herbers, 1985; Stanfield, 1982; Nathan and Doolittle, 1984) and even the basic equity of budget reductions (Pear, 1983b). Gross budget cuts are brusquely proposed without the benefit of analysis, thus leaving the implementation of the reductions to others, with little thought as to their immediate effect (Rauch, 1985b) or their social distribution. For instance, the entire issue of privitization is extremely contentious (e.g., cf. Hanke, 1985, with Berger, 1984, and Bendick and Levinson, 1984) but amenable to empirical research; yet the level of discourse has rarely gone beyond the purely polemic.

The second point is that the dependence on ideological rationale cuts both ways. Just as it can lead proponents to recommend policy terminations without supporting documentation, it makes defending the programs much easier. Supporters are not forced to argue the economics or effectiveness of their favorite threatened policies. AMTRAK is clearly a subsidy program, but few are debating the size or the distribution of the subsidy. When CBM Director Stockman declared that AMTRAK was "the litmus test" for Congressional resolve to reduce the national debt, its defenders simply retorted that "AMTRAK is indispensable for the welfare of the country" (Stuart, 1985a). Again, analysis seemed secondary, almost irrelevant when Wicker (1985) described "young David's tantrum." Congressional proponents of the EDA dismiss the administration's reduction requests with a wave of the ideological hand: "They just have philosophical problems with the EDA," and "We think the agency's broad rural economic development mission is a good and appropriate one for the federal government to have." (quoted in Stanfield, 1983: 1739) The Legal Services Corporation does not have to defend itself against charges of misappropriated funds (e.g., GAO, 1985a, 1985b; also Shenon, 1985) if it can find sufficient support for its fundamental existence.[5]

Thus one can easily and often find the opposing camps at philosophic and political loggerheads over the issue of policy termination with little ground for resolution, let alone hope for compromise. Given the turf and rules, the ideological basis for termination would as a matter of natural course, apparently, render few victories.

PROGRAMMATIC TERMINATIONS

We have argued that ideology has been the principal impetus underlying most policy termination efforts but that such broad criteria fail to cut a wide swath, that their victims are more shibboleth than substance, more posture than policy. The Reagan administration has found it extremely difficult to eliminate agencies as a way to reduce the size of government. Despite repeated assaults on social welfare (Blustein, 1985) and education (Maeroff, 1985) policies, most of the administration's rare termination achievements have been recorded on the level of individual programs, and even those have been on a piecemeal, seemingly uncoordinated basis. CMB Director Stockman recognized that specific agency budgets, each argued on its particular

merits, represent the "best, last, and only opportunity we will
have in this decade or maybe for decades to come, to determine
whether or not we can fundamentally restructure and bring under
control this far-flung bloated, sprawling, $1 trillion national
budget" (Fuerbringer, 1985).

DeLeon (1978) and Behn (1978b) hypothesized that programs
are more vulnerable to termination activities than policies or
organizations as a function of their political exposures and
relatively limited constituencies. For these reasons, it is not
surprising that termination activities have focused on the programmatic level, regardless of their motivation (e.g., ideological or
economic). Examples abound. Rather than attack the entire
cadre of Veterans Administration entitlements, "Reagan would
deny free Veterans Administration medical care to veterans with
nonservice-related medical problems unless their incomes were
below a certain level" (Rauch, 1985b: 302). Certain AMTRAK
passenger subsidies are more likely to be successfully deleted than
if the entire agency were disbanded. The administration chose not
to deny the entire Higher Education Act funding; instead, it
concentrated its efforts on the $1.6 billion student college loan
program and middle income families (Friendly, 1985).

This strategy has not always been successful. While there
certainly have been some major reductions in EDA- and CETA-
type programs, viewed as a whole, "Mr. Reagan's legacy on
domestic spending shapes up as or of a retrenchment than the
revolution it is often called" (Blustein, 1985). The affected middle
class families marshalled their academic and Congressional allies
to defeat soundly reductions in federal student loan programs.
Farming lobbies have postponed and probably defeated the
administration's proposals to restrict farm credits and loans.
Reagan's antipathy toward Federal education programs have
surely hurt specific programs (Pear, 1983a; Maeroff, 1985) but
the overall thrust of the federal role in educations seems largely
untouched, at least in terms of function:

> Mr. Reagan began his Presidency by trying to cut $654 million
> from the education budget in the remaining months of the 1981

fiscal year. Instead, Congress increased appropriations to the Education Department from $14.1 billion to $14.8 billion. The initial interplay between Mr. Reagan and Congress set a pattern. The President has regularly sought to pare Federal funds for education and each time the lawmakers have increased funds over what they were the previous year [Maeroff, 1985].

In cases in which agencies have been abolished, their programs in terms of function have usually been continued elsewhere. The LEAA and NIE were grant-giving agencies for law enforcement and education research. Although both have surrendered their organizational identities, their programmatic functions have been assumed by other agencies. Apparently oblivious to congressional reservations regarding the worth of education research (Savage, 1985), the closing of the NIE merely transferred education research support to other agencies within the Department of Education. Similarly, restrictions in HEW funding resulted in OEO sponsorship of education programs in performance contracting.

This is not to suggest that program termination is a futile exercise, a contemporary version of tilting with windmills. Rather, it is to reaffirm what termination researchers have long held, that termination is never an easy activity, even under conditions that would appear most conducive. The limited acceptance of the Grace Commission's budget-cutting and agency-reduction recommendation provides numerous examples. The Reagan administration has held all the termination-facilitating cards: It is ideologically disposed to a severe reduction in the size of the federal government, a large and growing budget deficit heaps further fuel on the budget-cutting fires, and an immensely popular President has enjoyed two overwhelming electoral victories. Yet even with these sweeping mandates, the Reagan administration has been unable to reduce noticeably the size of the budget or the number of organizations. "The deficit 'starved' few programs to death, even in cases—such as the Small Business Administration and the Economic Development Administration—where many liberals questioned the programs' worth"

(Blustein, 1985: 1). If programs are more vulnerable than policies or organizations to termination, it should be recognized that this is a relative statement, that in political point of fact, there are few easy termination targets.

Still, it is reasonable to claim that programs have been ended more readily than policies or institutions and that this might therefore be the appropriate level for such activities. There are, however, two caveats that must be considered. First, many times individual programs are singled out because of their relative vulnerability, which is to say, their lack of articulate and powerful supporters. Thus middle-class education entitlement programs are left unscathed while housing programs that mainly benefit the very poor or the elderly bear a disproportionate brunt of the budgeteer's axe. Pear (1983b) estimates that over 40% of the FY84 budget cuts in social welfare programs would affect households earning under $10,000. Leaving aside the question of equity, selecting programs for elimination primarily because they are attractive "windows of opportunity" rarely presents a coherent pattern for program termination. Stitching together a crazy quilt of unrelated programs for elimination would hardly be the most persuasive argument before Congress and the American public that there is a coherent intellectual pattern underlying the proposed deletions.

The second reservation attached to the programmatic focus is that in many cases it represents little more than a temporary holding action. "Paring programs rather than pulling them out by the roots . . . leaves open the possibility that the programs will grow back when the political climate changes, as some did following the historic budget cuts of 1981"(Blustein, 1985: 1). The demise and resurrection of the B-1 bomber is only one example. The pattern of minor programmatic reductions followed by slow but steady restorations has been repeatedly seen in Washington over the past few years. The lesson is clear. Programmatic terminations should at best only be viewed as short term remedies to such fundamental questions as the reduction in the size and scope of public sector organizations. This is not to claim that such reductions are trivial, but it is to suggest that they should not be viewed as a set of ends unto themselves, that whatever victories are obtained are more likely to be Pyrrhic than permanent. "Perhaps, then, the thematic metaphor should be that termination is more Dracular than Draconian. That is, programs and policies rarely die, regardless of their contemporary irrelevance or inefficiency. . . . Changing conditions and percepts will almost certainly create opportunities for long-dead programs to be reborn." (Brewer and deLeon, 1983: 448)

"IT'S NOT OVER 'TIL IT'S OVER"

This essay has argued that the "usual" grounds for termination—e.g., the economies and efficiencies that are the evaluators' professional stock in trade—have been much less the guiding rationale than fundamental questions of values and ideologies. Furthermore, termination efforts are better directed for political reasons at specific programs rather than institutions or general policies, even if the latter are more reflective of ideological concerns. If these observations are valid, they raise some important tensions that must be considered by evaluation researchers and practitioners.[6]

Returning to Bardach's (1976) distinction between reformers and economizers, we have argued that the former would appear to be more influential in producing the termination drama. But, as we have seen, it is not clear that the reformer is more effective, that the reformer's zeal brought to the political stage can be easily turned aside with a counter-zealot's parry. One is forced to argue interpretations instead of evidence, with edification being the primary victim.[7] This is especially true when the data are prone to conflicting interpretation, such as the area of "welfare dependency" (cf. Murray, 1985, with Levitan, 1985). Robinson (1982) and Thompson (1984) have documented how even technology-based debates are fundamentally couched in values and therefore often refuse to be heard by either party. These values can be covertly inculcated in mathematical models that would otherwise appear to add precision to the controversy (Greenberger et al., 1983; Wynne, 1984). The broad brush wielded by the reformer cannot always be effectively moved from the pallet to the canvas.

At the same time, we have seen that an approach on the programmatic level yields spotty results, that it rarely portrays or produces a clearly articulated philosophy, which is the hallmark of the reformer. For instance, why should the CAB be more vulnerable in the move toward deregulation than the Interstate Commerce Commission (cf. Cooper, 1984, with Mosher, 1979)? The general inability of the Congress to cancel military development and acquisition programs reflects the confusion and deliberate obfuscation surrounding the roles of specific weapons and missions. Why should one technically inadequate antiaircraft program (DIVAD, or the Sergeant York system) be canceled while a similarly flawed surface-to-air missile system (the Patriot) is permitted further development? Furthermore, many of the programmatic terminations would appear to be transitory, as effective as throwing tacks in the way of the *Wehrmacht*. One might wish to canonize Sisyphus as the patron saint of the professional policy terminator.

This is, in many ways, an unfairly morose depiction. It might be a gloomy, but hardly groundless description of the actualities of policy termination. Yet, it is not an admission of defeat or even despair. There are many examples of deliberate and successful examples of policy termination and organization terminations (e.g., see Brewer and deLeon, 1983: Ch. 14). Even though they are not numerous, they do indicate that such successes are possible. More important, however, is the observation that such excisions are often necessary if the body politic is to remain vital, that is, to respond as it must to the exigencies and opportunities of the political moment. To deny the possibility of institutional death would be to guarantee policy and institutional scleroses. In the stark assessment of Carl Jung, "Only that which can destroy itself is truly alive" (quoted by Wildavsky, 1979b: 62).

Sports sage Yogi Berra once reminded a skeptic that, athletically speaking, "It ain't over 'til it's over" (Blount, 1984: 86).[8] Much the same can be said for institutional terminations, especially as they are experienced in the political arena. Even in instances where an organization's existence would appear to have undesirable implications, it has been deliberately allowed to continue past its logical retirement. For instance, as a concession to financial solvency and lending institutions, New York city was forced by New York state during the city's fiscal crisis to accept the creation of an Emergency Financial Control Board (EFCB).[9] "The Legislature gave the board key powers to review and reject the city budget, estimates of city revenue and expenditures, and municipal labor contracts" (Gottlieb, 1985b: 14). In other words, the EFCB was mandated tremendous powers intimately affecting the governing of New York city, powers that would not be surrendered until the various city governmental loans and debt guarantees were retired. By 1985, at least a full year ahead of schedule, New York city was able to retire these debts, but chose not to pay them off completely, thus maintaining the existence of the EFCB. New York city government thereby consciously decided to retain an organization that restricted its governing powers even though the establishing crisis conditions of municipal bankruptcy had long since faded. In the assessment of the EFCB's Executive Director, Comer S. Coppie, "New York's is perhaps the most comprehensive and substantial recovery in the history of American cities and perhaps for any jurisdiction at the state or local level" (quoted in Gottlieb, 1985a: 20). Coppie continued to say that he was prepared for the relinquishment, or "sunsetting," of these powers. Yet New York city government demurred (Sam Roberts, 1985).

If progress is to be made in the study and practice of termination, two elements must be made clear. First, political expediency rather than evaluative elegance is the cutting edge. This observation forces termination researchers and practitioners to look beyond the straightforward issues of economies and efficiencies. They need to understand and articulate the underlying values that motivate the termination rationale and exercise. One might justifiably ask if such explications of political values represent a legitimate domain for the policy analyst (see Amy, 1984). The positivist tradition would argue to the contrary, but this review has amply documented how the mere command of the analytic evidence is not sufficient to decide or perhaps even leverage the termination debate. At best, an analytic advantage exposes only the value structures that are driving the termination selection process. If one wishes to operate effectively in the termination arena, one needs to address the inherent ideological motivations.

Second, it would appear that an organization's and policy's natural political defenses are too formidable for anything less than the most determined termination activities. It would therefore seem that termination efforts are best directed at individual programs, even if this level of attention might not be completely congruent with the ideological termination template. Lest one need to be reminded, politics is the art and practice of compromise. For the zealot to deny this reality is to surrender most of the reformer's opportunities.

In conclusion, this paper has explicitly argued that termination, even under the best of circumstances, is the most problematic of political activities. A policy initiative, however tedious and fractious (Polsby, 1984), is relatively simple in comparison; new policies are not openly goring entitled, established, and well-horned oxen. If policy termination is to be achieved with any guidelines and wisdom short of brute force or deception, we must have a realistic assessment of its concept and practice.

NOTES

1. For the immediate purposes, "policy termination" is used here in its broadest sense to represent actual agency terminations, basic policy redirections, program eliminations, partial terminations, and fiscal retrenchments.

2. One wonders if either administrator was familiar with Dr. Samuel Johnson's gallows aphorism: "Depend upon it Sir, when a man knows he is to be hanged in a fortnight, it concentrates his mind wonderfully." (Boswell's *Life of Johnson*, September 19, 1777).

3. Bardach (1976: 126) also referred to "Oppositionists, who dislike the policy at issue simply because, in their view, it is a bad policy." This essay will not discuss this termination sect because it would appear that most current termination activities are adequately captured by the economizing and reforming motivations; furthermore, the majority of the oppositionists' objections can be subsumed by the other two categories.

4. Campbell is nothing less than candid, especially in his position as the EDA administrator: "The EDA has been a pork barrel. I question the motive of members of Congress who vote for it." (Quoted by Stanfield, 1983: 1739).

5. Ideological battle lines over the LSC are already drawn and becoming increasingly entrenched; compare Drew (1982) with the *Wall Street Journal* editorial, "Not So Legal Services" (1985); also Shenon, 1985.

6. The concern here will be with the more strategic aspects of policy termination. Customized tactics need to be designed for each activity; good examples are provided by Biller (1976), Behn (1978b), and Caraley (1982).

7. This situation is not unusual (Bernstein, 1983) but is particularly debilitating in the context of the policy process.

8. In a more cultured vein, although a different sport, Dick Motta of the then Washington Bullets pro basketball team, told a corps of doubting reporters that "The opera isn't over until the Fat Lady sings."

9. The EFCB is composed of the governor, mayor, state and city comptrollers, a special city deputy comptroller, the board's executive director, and three private citizens jointly appointed by the mayor and governor. The team "Emergency" was later dropped from the Board's title.

REFERENCES

Allen, Woody (1971) Getting Even. New York: Random House.

Amy, Douglas J. (1984) "Why Policy Analysis and Ethics Are Incompatible." J. of Policy Analysis and Management 3, 4 (Summer): 573-591.

Bardach, Eugene C. (1976) "Policy Termination as a Political Process." Policy Sciences 7, 2 (June): 123-132.

Behn, Robert D. (1978a) "How Differences Between Private and Public Organizations Affect Their Abilities to Terminate Their Activities." Presented at the American Society for Public Administration, Phoenix, AZ: April 10.

Behn, Robert D. (1978b) "How to Terminate a Public Policy: A Dozen Hints for the Would-Be Terminator." Policy Analysis 4, 3 (Summer 1978): 393-413.

Behrman, Bradley (1980) "C.A.B." Ch. 3. in Wilson, James Q. (ed.) The Politics of Regulation. New York: Basic Books.

Bendick, Marc, and Phyllis M. Levinson (1984) "Private-Sector Initiatives or Public-Private Partnerships?" in Lester M. Salamon and Michael W. Lund (eds.) The Reagan Presidency and the Governing of America. Washington, DC: The Urban Institute.

Berger, Renee A. (1984) "Private-Sector Initiatives in the Reagan Era: New Actors Rework an Old Theme," in Lester M. Salamon and Michael S. Lund (eds.) The Reagan Presidency and the Governing of America. Washington, DC: The Urban Institute.

Bernstein, Richard J. (1983) Beyond Objectivism and Relativism: Science, Hermeneutics, and Praxis. Philadelphia: Univ. of Pennsylvania Press.

Bethell, Tom (1979) "What Will Outlive Even Eternity?" New York Times, December 26: A-27.

Biller, Robert P. (1976) "On Tolerating Policy and Organizational Terminations: Some Design Considerations." Policy Sciences 7, 2 (June): 53-76.

Blount, Roy (1984) "Yogi." Sports Illustrated 60 (April 2): 84-88.

Blustein, Paul (1985) "Recent Budget Battles Leave the Basic Tenets of Welfare State Intact." Wall Street Journal (October 21): 1, 16.

Boyd, Jo Ann (1983) "Despite Setbacks, Reagan's Assault on Legal Services Corp. Bears Fruit." National J. 15, 11 (March 13): 562-564.

Brand, David (1982) "Europe's Slump Swells Social Security's Costs, and Ax Begins to Fall." Wall Street Journal (November 1): 1, 14.

Brewer, Garry D. (1978)"Termination: Hard Choices, Harder Questions." Public Administration Rev. 38, 3 (May/June): 338-344.

Brewer, Garry D., and Peter DeLeon (1983) The Foundations of Policy Analysis. Ridgewood, IL: Dorsey.

Cameron, James M. (1978) "Ideology and Policy Termination: Restructuring California's Mental Health System," pp. 301-328 in Judith V. May and Aaron B. Wildavsky (eds.) The Policy Cycle. Newbury Park, CA: Sage.

Caraley, Demetrios (1982) Doing More With Less. New York: Graduate Program in Public Policy and Administration, Columbia University.

Carlson, Eugene (1982) "Success of Sunset Laws Varies as Fights Turn to Big Targets." Wall Street Journal (May 4): 29.

Caro, Francis G. [ed.] (1976) Readings in Evaluation Research. Russell Sage.

Chapman, Richard A. (1980-81) "Reducing the Public Sector: The Thatcher Government's Approach." Policy Studies J. 9, 8 (Special Issue #4): 1152-1163.

Cooper, Ann (1984) "The CAB Is Shutting Down, but Will It Set an Example for Other Agencies?" National J. 16, 39 (September 29): 1820-1823.

Corrigan, Richard (1982) "The Administration May Try Again to Kill Energy Aid for the Poor." National J. 14, 4 (January 23): 150-152.

Dahl, Jonathan (1985) "Airline Safety Snafus At American Airlines Inspire A Wider Probe." Wall Street Journal (November 6): 1, 38.

DeLeon, Peter (1978) "Public Policy Termination: An End and a Beginning." Policy Analysis 4, 3 (Summer): 369-392.

DeLeon, Peter (1982) "New Perspectives on Program Termination." J. of Policy Analysis and Management 2, 1 (Fall): 108-111.

DeLeon, Peter (1983) "Policy Evaluation and Program Termination." Policy Studies Rev. 2, 4 (May) 631-647.

Downs, George W., and Patrick D. Larkey (1981) "Fiscal Reform and Governmental Efficiency: Hanging Tough." Policy Sciences 13, 4 (September): 381-397.

Drew, Elizabeth (1982) "A Reporter at Large: Legal Services." The New Yorker 63, 2 (March 1): 97-113.

Energy Daily (1982b) "Delay in DOE Demise." (February 12): 10, 29: 2.

Friendly, Jonathan (1985) "Budget Ax Fails to Make Dent in Aid Programs for Students." New York Times (September 24): C-1, C-10.

Fuerbringer, Jonathan (1985) "Beyond Federal Deficits." New York Times (April 30): A-27.

General Accounting Office (1985a) The Establishment of Alternative Corporations by Selected Legal Services Corporation Grant Recipients. GAO Report BAO/HRD-85-51 (August 22). Washington, DC: Government Printing Office.

General Accounting Office (1985b) Legal Service Corporation Grants to Establish Three

New National Support Centers. GAO. Report No. GAO/HRD-85-54 (March 29). Washington, DC: Government Printing Office.

Gerth, Jeff (1985) "Pentagon Buying: Need for Businesslike Business." New York Times (May 15): A-1, B-10.

Glazer, Judith S. (1984) "Terminating Entrenched Policies in Educational Institutions: A Case History of Free Tuition." The Review of Higher Education 7, 2 (Winter): 159-173.

Gordon, Michael R. (1983a) "Pentagon Cost Overruns, a Venerable Tradition, Survive Reagan's 'Reforms,' " National J. 15, 2 (January 8): 56-60.

Gordon, Michael R. (1983b) "Pentagon May Face 'Readiness Crunch' If Weapons Buying Continues Apace." National J. 15, 4 (January 22): 157-161.

Gottlieb, Martin (1985a) "A Decade After the Cutbacks, New York Is a Different City." New York Times (June 30): 1, 20.

Gottlieb, Martin (1985b) "Private Moments Helped Solve Fiscal Crisis." New York Times (July 2): 1, 14.

Greenberger, Martin, et al. (1983) Caught Unawares: The Energy Decade in Retrospect. Cambridge, MA: Ballinger.

Hanke, Steve H. (1985) "Privatization: Theory, Evidence, and Implementation." pp. 101-113 in C. Lowell Harriss (ed.) Control of Federal Spending. New York: Academy of Political Science.

Herbers, John (1982a) "Administration Seeks to Cut Aid to Cities, Charging It Is Harmful." New York Times (June 20): 1, 20.

Herbers, John (1982b) "Measuring Poverty." New York Times (April 15): 13.

Herbers, John (1983) "Cities Turn to Private Groups to Administer Local Services." New York Times (April 23): 1, 9.

Herbers, John (1985) "States' Study Disputes Administration on Surplus." New York Times (February 9): A-8.

Hirschman, Albert O. (1970) Exit, Voice, and Loyalty. Cambridge, MA: Harvard Univ. Press.

Hunter, Marjorie (1982) "How to Dismantle Your Own Agency." New York Times, (February 2): 8.

Ingersoll, Bruce (1981) "Bl Back from Dead Stronger than Ever." Chicago Sun-Times (September 30): 21.

Ink, Dwight (1982) "CSA Closedown—A Myth Challenged." The Bureaucrat 11, 2 (Summer): 39-43.

Kaufman, Herbert (1976) Are Government Organizations Immortal? Washington, DC: Brookings Institution.

Keller, Bill (1985) "As Arms Buildup Eases, U.S. Tries to Take Stock." New York Times (May 14): A-1, A-20.

King, Seth S. (1985) "Block Defends Proposals to Cut Aid to Farmers." New York Times (February 7): A-18.

Kirlin, John J. (1982) The Political Economy of Fiscal Limits. Lexington, MA: Lexington Books.

Lanoutte, William (1983) "Dream Machine." Atlantic Monthly 251, 1 (April): 35-52, 85-86.

Lanoutte, William J. (1982) "Life After Death—CETA's Demise Won't Mean the End of Manpower Training." National J. 14, 6 (February): 241-244.

Lefevre, Stephen R. (1985) "Trials of Termination: President Carter and the Breeder

Reactor Program." Presidential Studies Q. 15, 2 (Spring): 330-342.

Levine, Charles H. et al. (1982) The Politics of Retrenchment. Newbury Park, CA: Sage.

Levitan, Sar A. (1985) "How the Welfare System Promotes Economic Security." Pol. Sci. Q. 100, 3 (Fall): 447-460.

Lewis, Flora (1984) "Sweden's Quiet Way." New York Times (January 24): 25.

Light, Larry (1979) "Renegotiating Board Dies; Victim of Industry Lobbying." Congressional Q. 37, 18 (May 5): 858.

Maeroff, Gene I. (1985) "After 20 Years, Education Programs Are a Solid Legacy of Great Society." New York Times (September 30): B-7.

May, Lee (1982) "U.S. Softens Urban Policy After Criticism." Los Angeles Times (July 10): 6.

Miller, Judith (1981) "Energy Dept.'s Backers Cross Ideological Lines." New York Times (December 29): 12.

Molotsky, Irvin (1985) "C.A.B. Dies After 46 Years; Airlines Declared 'On Own,' " New York Times (January 1): A-1, A-7.

Mosher, Lawrence (1979) "Trucking Deregulation—An Idea Whose Time Has Almost Gone?" National J. 11, 20 (April 19): 817-820.

Murray, Charles (1985) "Have the Poor Been Losing Ground?" Pol. Sci. Q. 100, 3 (Fall): 427-446.

Nathan, Richard P. and Fred C. Doolittle (1985) "Federal Grants: Giving and Taking Away." Pol. Sci. Q. 100, 1 (Spring): 53-74.

New York Times (1982) "Crime Panels Reviewed As U.S. Unit Nears End." April 12: A-11.

New York Times (1985) "The Reagan Budget: Capping or Killing Programs." February 5: A-18, A-19.

Nordheimer, Jon (1983) "Belt-Tightening in Europe Squeezes Welfare State." New York Times (December 8): 2.

Ognibene, Peter J. (1981) "In Military Procurement, More Bucks Don't Always Produce a Bigger Bang." National J. 13, 50 (December 12): 2192-2197.

Paltrow, Scot J. (1982) "Cutbacks Force Legal Aid to Reject Cases, Often Leaving Poor Helpless." Wall Street Journal (January 28): 25, 26.

Pear, Robert (1983a) "Department of Education Staff is Cut." New York Times, (August 2): A-1, A-7.

Pear, Robert (1983b) "40% of U.S. Benefit Cuts Said to Affect Households Earning Under $10,000." New York Times (August 26): 7.

Polsby, Nelson (1984) Political Innovation in America. New Haven, CT: Yale Univ. Press.

Rauch, Jonathan (1985a) "Small Business Agency Alive and Well Despite White House Attempt to Kill It." National J. 17, 36 (August 10): 1245-1248.

Rauch, Jonathan (1985b) "Reagan Budget Pursues His Political Goals, Lets Congress Fret About Bottom Line." National J. 17, 6 (February 9): 296-308.

Roberts, Sam (1985) " '75 Bankruptcy Scare Alters City Plans Into 21st Century." New York Times (July 8): 1, 13.

Roberts, Steven V. (1985) "Behind Military Budget Rises: Political Aims of Lawmakers." New York Times (May 17): A-1, D-22.

Robinson, John Bridger (1982) "Apples and Horned Toads: On the Framework-Determined Nature of the Energy Debate." Policy Sciences 15, 1 (November): 23-45.

Rosenbaum, David E. (1985) "Proposals for Spending Cuts Echo Many Rejected Before." New York Times (February 5): A-16.

Savage, David C. (1985) "Anatomy of U.S. Agency That Failed." Los Angeles Times (October 1) I: 1, 16.

Serpick, Joanne (1982) "Training the Unskilled—Will A Joint Public-Business Effort Do the Job?" National J. 14, 51-52 (December 18): 2168-2169.

Shenon, Philip (1985) "Federal Audits of Legal Aid at Issue." New York Times, (November 18): A-19.

Shribman, David (1981) "Death Comes to a Federal Agency." New York Times (September 19): 7.

Shubik, Martin (1978) "On Concepts of Efficiency." Policy Sciences 9, 2 (April): 121-126.

Singer, James W. (1979) "How the Renegotiation Board Went Out of Business." National J. 11, 16 (April 21): 642-645.

Solomon, Burt (1982) "DOE: 'Give Me Death.' " Energy Daily 10, 98 (May 25): 1, 4.

Solomon, Burt (1982b) "DOE Memoirs to Congress." Energy Daily 10, 28 (February 11): 1, 4.

Stanfield, Rochelle L. (1981) "Breaking Up The Education Department—School Aid May Be the Main Target." National J. 13, 43 (October 24): 1907-1910.

Stanfield, Rochelle L. (1982) " 'If It Ain't Broke, Don't Fix It,' Say Defenders of Compensatory Aid." National J. 14, 5 (January 30): 201-204.

Stanfield, Rochelle L. (1983) "EDA on Death Row—Congress Is Poised To Grant Another One-Year Reprieve." National J. 15, 34-35 (August 20): 1738-1739.

Stuart, Reginald. (1985a) "Rallying Round the AMTRAK: Deficits and All." New York Times (May 10): B-6.

Stuart, Reginald. (1985b) "Stockman Presses Senators to End AMTRAK Subsidy." New York Times (April 30): A-27.

Suchman, Edward A. (1967) Evaluative Research. Russell Sage.

Sun, Marjorie (1982) "Mathematical Magic." Science 217, 4561 (August 20): 713.

Tarschys, Daniel (1981) "Rational Decremental Budgeting: Elements of an Expenditure Policy for the 1980s." Policy Sciences 14, 1 (December): 49-58.

Tarschys, Daniel (1983) "The Scissors Crisis in Public Finance." Policy Sciences 15, 3 (April): 205-224.

Thompson, Michael (1984) "Among the Energy Tribes: A Cultural Framework for the Analysis and Design of Energy Policy." Policy Sciences 17, 3 (November): 321-339.

Wade, Nicholas (1977) "Death of the B-1: The Events Behind the Carter Decision." Science 197, 4303 (August 5): 536-539.

Wade, Richard C. (1982) "The Suburban Roots of the New Federalism." New York Times Magazine (August 1): 20, 21, 39, 46-47.

Wall Street Journal (1983) "Denmark Plans to Cut Outlays in 1984 Budget." August 18: 28.

Wall Street Journal (1985) "Not So Legal Services." (Editorial, October 4): 20.

Wicker, Tom (1985) "Young David's Tantrum." New York Times (May 3): A-31.

Wildavsky, Aaron (1979a) The Politics of the Budgetary Process. Boston: Little, Brown.

Wildavsky, Aaron (1979b) Speaking Truth to Power. Boston: Little, Brown.

Wines, Michael (1982) "Silencing Some Guns." National J. 14, 13 (March 27): 559.

Wynne, Brian (1984) "The Institutional Context of Science, Models and Policy: The IIASA Energy Model." Policy Sciences 17, 3 (November): 277-320.

PART III

POLITICS AND RESEARCH METHODS

7

THE COUNTENANCES OF FOURTH-GENERATION EVALUATION: DESCRIPTION, JUDGMENT, AND NEGOTIATION

E G O N G. G U B A

Indiana University

Y V O N N A S. L I N C O L N

University of Kansas

The history of evaluation has been characterized by dramatic change. The melange of evaluation models, principles, and advice that has emerged over more than a half century can be ordered and classified in many different ways (see for example Stake, 1973; House, 178; Stufflebeam and Webster, 1980; Guba and

Authors' Note: *We are indebted to our classes in program evaluation at Indiana University and the University of Kansas whose students helped us to evolve the principles developed in this paper in a systematic fashion. Their constant challenges to our thinking were instrumental in developing and refining our ideas. We also acknowledge a debt to Judy Meloy, graduate student at Indiana University, who assisted in sorting out the many ideas thrown into the hopper by our classroom students, and who read and commented on the draft.*

Lincoln, 1981). What appears in this chapter is yet another construction, arbitrary to be sure, but one that may nevertheless cast some light on how the field of evaluation came to be what it is today, and more important, how it is becoming what it is likely to be tomorrow.

It is our thesis that evaluation has moved through three generations of development and is currently entering the fourth generation. We shall describe these four generations, delineate the fundamental principles that underlie the fourth, show how both the concept of evaluation and the role of the evaluator are accordingly shifting, indicate some constraints on the continuing development of the "new" evaluation, and end with a brief discussion of the metaevaluation criteria that may be appropriate to it.

THE FOUR GENERATIONS
OF EVALUATION

The first generation of evaluation began to form in the early part of this century, but received a particular stimulus with the sudden availability of intelligence, aptitude, and achievement tests following World War I. This generation of evaluation may be characterized as *technical*, and the evaluator's role as that of *technician*. During this period evaluation meant little more than measurement—determining the status of individual pupils or groups of pupils with respect to norms that had been established for certain standardized tests. Pupils were seen as the "raw material" to be "processed" in the "school plant," presided over, appropriately enough, by the school "superintendent." The industrial metaphor is no accident, since this period of American history is well described as the era of scientific management, as Eisner (1979) and others have shown. Evaluation was seen as a means of determining whether pupils measured up to the "specifications" that the school had set—largely college preparatory specifications. That this technical sense of evaluation persists today cannot be doubted, as evidenced, for example, by the frequent practice of requiring pupils to pass such tests as part of their high school graduation or college admission procedures, by the use of such test scores in many states to rank schools and even individual teachers for effectiveness, and by the continued publication of texts that use the phrase "measurement and evaluation" in their titles (see, for example, Gronlund, 1985).

By the late 1920s the secondary schools of America were experiencing an influx of types of students that had earlier rarely gone beyond elementary levels; these students exhibited needs and aspirations that could not be met adequately by the prevailing college-preparatory curricula. Many of these students saw the secondary school as an opportunity to acquire the skills needed to rise above the social and economic status of their parents, but the schools were ill equipped to provide such teaching. Moreover, efforts to devise curricula that were more appropriate were defeated before they could receive a fair trial, because the secondary schools were inextricably locked into the Carnegie unit system. The chief obstacles in the path of altering this requirement were, not surprisingly, colleges and universities, which feared that if the Carnegie unit was abolished as the basis for accumulating secondary school credits they would be forced to accept high school graduates who were ill prepared to cope with their standard curricula.

The Eight Year Study, launched in 1933, was intended to determine the validity of that position. Thirty public and private secondary schools were given license to develop more responsive curricular with the understanding that their graduates would be admitted to cooperating colleges without necessarily having met normal Carnegie requirements. The purpose of the Eight Year Study was to demonstrate that students who were trained by using these unorthodox curricula would nevertheless be able to succeed in college. The period of eight years was selected to permit at least one cohort of such students to complete four full years each of secondary school and college work.

An immediate problem confronting the designers of the study was to devise a means for assessing whether the developing new curricula were working as intended—it would not be a fair test if students failed in college because the secondary curricula were inadequate. By a serendipitous occurrence, Ralph W. Tyler, a member of the Bureau of Educational Research at Ohio State University, the campus at which the Eight Year Study was headquartered, had for several years been working with selected Ohio State faculty to develop tests that would measure whether the students had learned what the professors had wanted them to learn. These desired learning outcomes were labeled *objectives*. Tyler was engaged to carry out the same kind of work with Eight Year Study schools, but with one important variation from conventional evaluation (measurement): The purpose of the studies would be to refine the developing curricula and make sure they were working. Program evaluation was born.

As the participant secondary schools began devising their new curricula, Tyler collected information about the extent of achievement of their defined objectives by the pupils in their programs. This information, taken with an analysis of the patterns of strengths and weaknesses that emerged, was then utilized to guide refinements and revisions—a process we today would be inclined to call *formative* evaluation, except that the results were not available until *after* rather than *during* a trial. This process was reiterated until the curriculum was found to produce an appropriate level of achievement.

Thus was born second-generation evaluation, an approach that was characterized by *description* of patterns and strengths and weakness with respect to certain stated objectives. The role of the evaluator came to be that of *describer*, although the earlier technical aspects of the role were also retained. Measurement was no longer treated as the equivalent of evaluation but was redefined as one of several tools that might be used in its service. When the five-volume results of the Eight Year Study were published in 1942, the third volume, which reported on the evaluation activities of the project (Smith and Tyler, 1942), drew widespread attention. Like Lord Byron, Tyler awoke one morning to find himself famous, the acknowledged leader of a new group of curriculum evaluators. Later he was to be recognized as the "Father of Evaluation" (Joint Committee, 1981).

But the objectives-oriented descriptive approach had some

serious flaws, although they were not very noticeable until the post-Sputnik period, when it proved inadequate to the task of evaluating the course-content improvement programs of the National Science Foundation (BSCS Biology, Project CHEM, PSSC Physics, and SMSG Mathematics) and of the then Office of Education (Project English and Project Social Studies); these programs were was the Federal government's response to the (purported) deficiencies of American education that had allowed the Russians to gain a march in space exploration. Because it was essentially descriptive in nature, second-generation Tylerian evaluation neglected, at least explicitly, an equally important matter, referred to by Robert E. Stake in his now-classic 1967 paper as the *other* countenance or face of evaluation: *judgment*. Stake noted:

> The countenance of evaluation beheld by the educator is not the same one beheld by the specialist in evaluation. The specialist sees himself as a "describer," one who describes aptitudes and environ- ment and accomplishments. The teacher and the school administra- tor, on the other hand, expect an evaluator to grade something or someone as to merit. Moreover, they expect that he will judge things against external standards, on criteria perhaps little related to the local school's resources.
>
> Neither sees evaluation broadly enough. *Both* description and judgment are essential—in fact, they are the two basic acts of evaluation [p. 109 as reprinted in Worthen and Sanders, 1973].

The call to include judgment in the act of evaluation marked the emergence of third-generation evaluation, a generation in which evaluation was characterized by efforts to reach *judgments*, and in which the evaluator assumed the role of *judge* while retaining the earlier technical and descriptive functions as well. This call, widely echoed in the profession, notably by Michael Scriven (1967), exposed several problems that had not been dealt with adequately in the earlier generations. First, it required that objectives *themselves* be taken as problematic; goals, no less than performance, were to be subject to evaluation. As a wag pointed out, something not worth doing at all is certainly not worth doing well. Further, judgment requires, as Stake pointed out, *standards* against which the judgment can be made. But the inclusion in a scientific and therefore putatively value-free enterprise like evaluation of standards, which must by definition of the genre be value-laden, was repugnant to most evaluators. Finally, if there is to be judgment, there must be a judge. Evaluators did not feel competent to act in that capacity, felt it presumptuous to do so, and feared the political vulnerability to which it exposed them. Nevertheless they were urged to accept that obligation, largely on the ground that among all possible judge-candidates, the evaluators were without doubt the most objective (Scriven, 1967).

In the final analysis the call to judgment could not be ignored, and evaluators soon rose to the challenge. A bevy of new evaluation models sprang up in 1967 and thereafter: neo-Tylerian models, including Stake's own Countenance Model (1967) and the Discrepancy Evaluation Model (Provus, 1971); decision-oriented models such as CIPP (Stufflebeam et al., 1971); effects-oriented models such as the Goal-Free Model (Scriven, 1973); neomeasurement models in the guise of societal experimentation (Campbell, 1969; Rossi and Williams, 1972; Boruch, 1974; Rivlin and Timpane, 1975); and models that were directly judgmental such as the Connoisseurship Model (Eisner, 1979). All of these post-1967 models agreed on one point, however: that judgment was an integral part of evaluation. All urged, more or less explicitly, that the *evaluator* be the judge. There were differences in the extent to which evaluators were represented as appropriate judges, ranging from the tentativeness of decision-oriented models, whose proponents hesitated to advocate an aggressive judgmental role because doing so seemingly coopted the very decision makers whom the evaluations were ostensibly to serve, to the assertiveness of the judgmental models, in which the evaluator was chosen precisely because of his or her connoisseurship qualities, assuring that the judgment could be trusted. Nevertheless it seems fair to say that during the decade and more following 1967, judgment became the hallmark of third-generation evaluation.

The fourth generation is presently emerging, as a new class of models takes its place on the evaluation scene. Commonly called response, these models take as their point of focus not objectives, decisions, effects, or similar organizers but the *claims, concerns, and issues* put forth by members of a *variety* of *stakeholding audiences*, that is, audiences who are in some sense involved with the evaluation. Such audiences include *agents* (e.g., developers, funders, implementers), *beneficiaries* (e.g., target groups, potential adopters), and (e.g., excluded target groups, potential beneficiaries of opportunities forgone by the decision to implement the particular evaluand) (Guba and Lincoln, 1981). The principles undergirding these responsive models may be noted to a greater or lesser degree in responsive evaluation (Stake, 1975), naturalistic evaluation (Guba and Lincoln, 1981), illuminative evaluation (Parlett and Hamilton, 1972), utilization focused evaluation (Patton, 1978) and adversarial evaluation (Wolf, 1979).

Fourth-generation models share one highly consequential belief: that of value-pluralism. Judgments must be made in terms of standards that derive from particular value postures. The judgments affect various stakeholding audiences, all of whom are at some degree of risk in the evaluation. But there is no assurance that the various audiences the value position that undergirds any particular set of standards; indeed, the evidence of the past 15 years is that American culture (and probably every other advanced culture) is characterized by value-pluralism. Thus it is more than merely possible that different stakeholder values might lead to *conflicting* judgments even *in the face of the same* "factual" evidence.[1] But if one group, say, finds an evaluand effective and appropriate, while another, on the same evidence, finds it ineffective and inappropriate, what is to be done at the point of action? Clearly the evaluator cannot arrogate to himself or herself the making of a judgment that would so obviously infringe the rights of certain of the stakeholders. Worse, such an act of evaluator judgment would *dishonor* the values of the infringed groups, and *exploit the power* of the evaluation to override their self-perceived interests. The evaluator therefore cannot ethically undertake to render judgments; what he or she must do instead is to act as mediator in a negotiation process. The theme of *negotiation* is the hallmark of fourth-generation evaluation, and the role of *negotiator and change agent* of the fourth-generation evaluator. We believe that these concepts will shape evaluation practice for the foreseeable future. It is the purpose of this chapter to explicate the form of that shaping.

FUNDAMENTAL PRINCIPLES GUIDING FOURTH-GENERATION EVALUATORS

We begin the task of explicating fourth-generation evaluation by outlining certain principles that guide evaluators practicing in this mode. These principles are generated from a consideration of five more or less axiomatic concepts that we shall take up in turn: value pluralism, stakeholder constructions, fairness, merit and worth, and negotiation. In two later sections we shall show how these principles coalesce to redefine evaluation and the role of the evaluator.

1. *The concept of value-pluralism.* Fourth-generation evaluation is the first that explicitly recognizes and deals with the possibility of value pluralism. The earlier generations tended to assume value consensus, even if only implicitly. It makes no sense, for example, to evaluate by objectives unless one implicitly assumes that the objectives are agreed to by all; indeed, it is difficult to imagine how objectives could be formulated in the first place without such agreement. In practice, disagreements are often papered over through the statement of grandiose and/or ambiguous objectives, so as not to generate resistance of lose constituencies. But in the end such a maneuver is self-defeating, because the evaluator *must* render the objectives into a specific form to be able to assess objectives/performance discrepancies. The evaluator "takes the heat" for the failure of the legislating parties to come to prior agreement. In similar fashion one cannot imagine a decision-oriented evaluation without assuming agreement on the criteria by which decision options are to be assessed. Nor can one do a goal-free evaluation without assuming consensus on some needs assessment against which the effects can be tested, particularly so since needs themselves are value-based (Guba and Lincoln, 1982a). The connoisseurship model assumes agreement

with the values to be brought to bear by the connoisseur.

Fourth-generation evaluators open the door to a consideration of value differences. But in doing so they introduce two complications, one methodological and one substantive. Methodologically, they relinquish some control over the evaluation as a process. They must include different value positions in consideration of what is to be studied, how, with what reports, and the like. They are consequently no longer able to provide a priori assurance to clients and stakeholders that the evaluation will be useful, because they are not in a position to determine whether consensus, even if only at the level of practical accommodation, will be possible. Substantively, they must now include *political elements* among those that will be taken account of in the evaluation. The evaluation becomes a political act as well as an investigatory process. Different political positions will have to be recognized and accommodated. Hence, fourth-generation evaluators operate according to the following principles:

> *Principle 1:* Conflict, rather than consensus, must be the expected condition in any evaluation taking account of value differences.
>
> *Principle 2:* The technical/descriptive/judgmental processes that have completely characterized evaluation practice in the past cannot alone deal with partisan discord; some means must be invoked to reach an accommodation among different value postures.
>
> *Principle 3:* The parties holding different value postures must themselves be involved if there is to be any hope of accommodation.

2. *The concept of stakeholder constructions.* Fourth-generation evaluation is rooted in a relativist ontology. The position of positivist science is that there exists an objective reality that goes on about its business independently of the interest that human beings may exhibit in it.[2] Compelling evidence is building up in the "hard" and life sciences such as physics and biology to suggest that this view is no longer tenable (Lincoln and Guba, 1985). Instead, the concept of a single objective reality onto which

inquiry can converge by continuous and systematic effort is being replaced by the concept that reality is *multiple* and *constructed* in form, so that inquiry continuously diverges (the more you know, the more of the unknown you contact). These constructions are made by persons, and it is in the minds of persons that one finds them, not "out there."

Fourth-generation evaluation also takes issue with positivism's epistemological position: that what there is to be known can be known objectively by an inquirer who is able to stand "outside" of it. Evaluations focus the attention of participants and stimulate them to synthesize, crystallize, and coalesce their ideas in order to form, create, and expand their realities. The evaluator thus becomes a major agent in the construction of the realities that define the evaluand, make claims for it, and raise concerns and issues about it. In a very real sense evaluations *create* reality rather than objectively discover it. But they do so in relation to the contexts in which the evaluands are found (including the expectations for the evaluand in relation to that context) and to the particular value patterns that are held by the various constructing stakeholders. Contexts and values thus play a vital role in reality definition. It is value differences that account for the different constructions made by different stakeholders in some given context (although the latter will also be constructed differently by the various parties), but the fact of differing constructions is usually hidden from the stakeholders themselves, who are prone to be aware only of that one admitted by their own values. Fourth-generation evaluation thus also operates according to these next principles:

> *Principle 4:* The evaluator is at times a who must learn what the consequences of stakeholders are, while recognizing that the very act of learning them helps to create those constructions.

> *Principle 5:* The evaluator is at times a *teacher* who communicates the constructions of other stakeholders to each stakeholding audience, and in the process, clarifies the value positions that account for them.

3. *The concept of fairness.* The fourth-generation evaluator, recognizing that different stakeholders may base their judgments on very different value patterns, is concerned that no one of them be given unfair preference in the evaluation. There is, finally, no metacriterion that can be used to distinguish more worthy from less worthy values (although for some purposes it may be possible to order values hierarchically); equity demands that the constructions, claims, concerns, and issues that stem from each value pattern be solicited and honored. The evaluator must project an *emic* (Pike, 1954), that is, an insider's view for *each* audience, and be prepared to accept it at face value unless and until that audience determines to change it.[3]

It may be taken as axiomatic that evaluation equitably carried out will inevitably upset the prevailing balance of power. Evaluation produces information, and information *is* power. To deny information to some groups is to disenfranchise them. Those holding power may argue for selective dispersal of information on such apparently sound grounds as efficiency, minimization of conflict, personal accountability, or even a "higher social good," but, as Cronbach (1980: 4) points out in the 19th of his 95 theses bearing on evaluation:

> An open society becomes a closed society when only the officials know what is going on. Insofar as information is a source of power, evaluations carried out to inform a policymaker have a disenfranchising effect.

Thus the fourth-generation evaluator adds the following principles to his or her repertoire:

Principle 6: The evaluator is ethically bound to solicit the constructions, claims, concerns, and issues of all identifiable stakeholders, and to clarify the values that undergird them.

Principle 7: Equity demands that the evaluator honor all constructions, claims, concerns, and issues by collecting information that is responsive to them (for example, validates or invalidates them) without regard to their source audience, and to disseminate that information so that it is equally accessible to all.

Principle 8: The evaluator must collect information in ways that expose "facts" useful both to protagonists as well as antagonists of an evaluand.

Principle 9: The evaluator must release findings continuously and openly so as to provide ample opportunity for the assessment of their credibility from all constructed points of view, and for their rebuttal should that be the desire of some audience(s).

4. *The concepts of merit and worth.* Both merit and worth are aspects of value, which it is the purpose of evaluation to assess, but they are very different from one another (Guba and Lincoln, 1981). Merit depends on *intrinsic* characteristics of the evaluand, those characteristics that the evaluand would retain regardless of the circumstances under which it is used. Thus we may speak of the temper of the steel or the flexibility of the handle of an axe; the scholarliness and writings of a professor; or the internal consistency, modernity, continuity, sequence, and integration of a curriculum. Worth, on the other hand, is an *extrinsic* assessment, which depends heavily on the context of use. Thus the worth of an axe may depend on the nature of the tree to be cut down or on the expertise of the cutter who uses it; the worth of a professor to an employing institution may depend on his or her ability to teach high-demand courses, set a good role model, or attract outside funding; and the worth of a curriculum may depend on its utility for teaching particular target groups in particular socio-economic and cultural contexts when used by teachers with particular training and experience. Merit may be assessed through an examination of the evaluand in relative isolation, while worth can only be assessed in terms of its ability to meet needs-in-context. Values have a "double dip" here: They are the basis for defining the needs whose fulfillment may be the purpose of the evaluand (although sometimes needs are met as a serendipitous side effect of an evaluand intended for some other purpose), as well as for setting the standards useful for determining how well the needs are "in fact" met. The possibilities for value conflict are thus noticeably exacerbated.

In light of these considerations the fourth-generation evaluator adds these three principles to the repertoire of guidelines:

Principle 10: While merit can be assessed in isolation, worth can be assessed only in relation to particular needs-in-context. Change the context and you change both needs and worth.

Principle 11: The evaluator cannot carry out an assessment either of needs or worth except with field-based methods that take full account of the local context.

Principle 12: Transferability of assessments of needs and/or of worth from one context to another depends on the *empirical* similarity of sending and receiving contexts.

5. *The concept of negotiated process and outcomes.* Once the concept of value pluralism is admitted and the criterion of fairness is invoked, it becomes plain that fair judgments can be reached only through negotiation, if at all. The basis for negotiation is collaboration—the inclusion of stakeholders in the evaluation process itself. Most past evaluations have been exogenous, that is, with control vested entirely in the hands of the professional evaluator. A few evaluations are *endogenous*, that is, with control vested in the hands of the audience(s), particularly if an evaluation is carried out by a single audience for its own purposes, such as a group of teachers who evaluate the discipline practices in their own building for the sake of improving their available time-on-task. But what is called for in light of the fourth-generation position is *full collaboration*, in the sense that evaluator(s) and stakeholder(s) or their representatives are *continuously* involved.[4]

The concept of collaboration has both a strong sense and a weak sense. In the weak sense, stakeholders are given an opportunity to react to findings and to the evaluator's constructions thereof. Such "member checks" (Lincoln and Guba, 1985) have both validational and ethical utility. It is of little use to impute a construction to an audience if that audience cannot identify its own position therein. Moreover, to persist in that erroneous construction is to exploit and to enervate the audience that it putatively represents.

In the strong sense, which the fourth-generation evaluator advocates, stakeholding audiences are given the opportunity to provide inputs *at every stage* of the evaluation: the charge, the goal, the design, the data collection and analysis instruments and methods, the interpretation, and so on. Clearly, soliciting and incorporating what are likely to be very divergent views will require an intensive *political* effort from the evaluator. Further, the strong sense of collaboration requires that the inputs that are proferred be *honored* as much as possible, limited only by competing inputs provided by other legitimate stakeholders (Torbert, 1981; Rowan, 1981). Again the political acumen of the evaluator is likely to be severely taxed. The evaluator will soon lose credibility if inputs, once sought, are apparently ignored; yet the inclusion of these divergent views into anything resembling a viable course of action requires extreme political dexterity, persuasiveness, compromise, and, let it be noted, integrity.

The collaborative approach adds several more principles to the evaluator's repertoire of guidelines:

Principle 13: Stakeholders must be given an opportunity to react to findings for both validational and ethical reasons, to satisfy the weak sense of the collaboration requirement.

Principle 14: The evaluator must involve all stakeholders (or their representatives) at all points in the evaluation process, soliciting and honoring their inputs even on what might be called the more technical decisions that must be made.

Principle 15: Stakeholders (or their representatives) must be engaged in a negotiation process to determine what course of action should be taken in light of their findings. This stakeholder group, not the evaluator alone, should act as judges in making recommendations. The evaluator rather acts as mediator of the process.

Principle 16: The evaluator must allow for the possibility of continuing disagreements among the stakeholders. The goal of the negotiation process is not so much consensus as understanding.

Principle 17: The evaluator should act as mediator and change agent in these negotiations, encouraging follow through in relation to whatever may be decided by the parties and acting as monitor to assess the extent to which follow-through occurs. The evaluator's role thus extends well beyond the point of reporting findings.

THE CHANGING MEANING OF EVALUATION

The evaluation guided by the concepts and principles outlined in the preceding section is clearly very different from more traditional forms. Indeed, we may point to eight distinctive features of this fourth-generation form, a version based not on measurement (first-generation), description (second-generation), or judgment (third-generation), but on negotiation.

1. *Evaluation is a social-political process.* As Cronbach's (1980: 13) 11th thesis asserts, "A theory of evaluation must be as much a theory of political interaction as it is a theory of how to determine facts." Because of its intimate involvement with value issues, evaluation inevitably serves a political agenda and becomes a tool of political advocacy. Consequently any individual or group with a stake in the evaluand (that is, put at risk by the evaluation) has a right to provide input based on its own value position, to have that input honored, and to be consulted in any decision making that results. Evaluation acts to produce change, and any given change may be construed as relatively more or less desirable by different stakeholders. Value differences that result in different constructions cannot be resolved on rational bases alone, but only through political negotiation. Failure to provide the opportunity for such negotiation is tantamount to disenfranchisement.

2. *Evaluation is a learning/teaching process.* No basis for negotiation can exist in the absence of information about the value positions held and judgments made by various stakeholding audiences. Evaluation must be conducted initially as a learning encounter, in which these different value positions and judgments are exposed. Later evaluation becomes a teaching encounter in which the positions of each of the audiences is clarified for and made more understandable to the others. Evaluation is not intended to capture an evaluand "as it really is," but rather to explore how it is constructed by many different groups. Evaluation teaches stakeholders not only about the positions of others but

also how to ask better questions of one another.

3. *Evaluation is a continuous, recursive, and divergent process.* Traditional evaluators have often treated evaluations as discrete, closed-ended, and convergent events, but the evolving conception of evaluation sees them as continuous, open-ended, and divergent. In this sense evaluations are never completed (although they may end for arbitrary reasons such as depletion of funds or time), but feed on themselves to yield ever-enlarging understandings. As the inputs from one audience are "taught" to another, questions emerge from the second audience that can profitably be put to the first. Thus the process is recursive as well. When the number of significant audiences numbers more than two or three (as is almost always the case), the number of recursions that can profitably be undertaken becomes quite large, usually greater than available time and resources will permit the evaluator to explore. The number of new questions enlarges in a virtually exponential ratio as compared to the number of old questions that have been answered.

4. *Evaluation is a process that creates "reality."* According to the evolving conception, reality does not exist in objective form, but is constructed by those persons who claim to "know" it. It is never the case that such constructions are either complete or immutable. The act of evaluation is an intervention that brings stakeholders face to face with their own constructions as well as those of others, and this intervention may lead to changes as stakeholders comprehend additional elements to consider, or as they revise their formulations in accordance with the apparently more sophisticated or informed constructions of others. Among the things that are constructed is the evaluand itself; the evaluand may *change* during the process of evaluation, as may the values brought to bear on it and the judgments made of it. Evaluation thus does not "discover" reality but fosters its creation.

5. *Evaluation is an emergent process.* Traditional evaluation approaches require that a design for an evaluation be specified beforehand and then, once accepted, be followed in undeviating form except for circumstances that are beyond the evaluator's

control, e.g., history, maturation, or mortality effects. But the evolving concept of evaluation suggests that evaluation designs *cannot* be very completely specified *a priori*, but must evolve as the evaluation proceeds. Since neither the constructions of stakeholders nor the value positions on which they are based are likely to be known beforehand, the opening phases of an evaluation must be devoted to learning about them. Further, these constructions cannot be known for all time, for the very act of evaluation is apt to change them. Structure emerges only as the evaluation unfolds; the "design" can be completely described only retrospectively.

6. *Evaluation is a process with unpredictable outcomes.* Traditional evaluation is predictable at least to the extent that one can say, depending on the model being followed, that the outcomes will be information about the extent of congruence of performance with objectives, information about decision alternative, information about effects, and the like. But the new evaluation cannot project even possible outcomes until at least stakeholders' claims, concerns, and issues have been explored, and even these may change as the process unfolds. There is no "correct" or "objective" outcome. Even when ended, evaluations represent at best constructions, values, and beliefs at some particular point in time and do not necessarily represent what the future state is likely to be or what the past state has been.

7. *Evaluation is a collaborative process.* Judgments remain an essential part of fourth-generation evaluations, but those judgments must not be made solely by the evaluator or the client. If different value postures can lead to quite different judgments even on the basis of the *same* evidence, then negotiation among the holders of those different values cannot be avoided if the evaluation is to be fair and nonexploitative. Further, the stakeholders must not be confronted with a fait accompli, in which only those options delineated by the evaluator or client remain open to choice. Finally, different stakeholders must be afforded the opportunity to provide inputs to the evaluation process at its every stage—and not only substantive or informational inputs but *methodological* ones as well. The stakeholders and the

evaluator must jointly—collaboratively—be in control of the *entire* procedure.[5] Negotiation based on options that emerge from activities controlled solely by the evaluator, or by the evaluator and the client, is patently unfair, as though the issues to be discussed by General Motors and the United Auto Workers were to be limited solely to those that General Motors elected to put on the table. The proper outcome of a collaborative evaluation is less a technical report than an *agenda for negotiation*.

8. *The agenda for negotiation is best displayed in a case-study format, with items requiring negotiation being spelled out in relation to the particulars of the case.* A case study can be explicit about contextual and value factors, and can provide each audience the opportunity to experience the evaluand from a variety of constructed viewpoints. Further, the development of the case can be handled in such a way as to explicate and clarify the items about which further negotiation is needed, as well as to spell out those items about which there seems to be substantial agreement. The case provides a basis for a discussion that the several audiences will recognize as authentic, representing as it must the emic views of each of them; it provide a "slice of life" with its fullest ramifications. It tends to force display of all elements rather than only selected ones, reducing the likelihood that information can be withheld, and, concomitantly, the fear that it has been.

The eight characteristics of fourth-generation evaluation—its social-political nature; its learning/teaching posture; its continuous, recursive form; its reality-creating dynamic; its unfolding design; the relative unpredictability of its outcomes; its collaborative quality; its case study reporting format—describe a kind of evaluation dramatically different from earlier-generation forms. And as a result, the role of the evaluator practicing this new form is also dramatically different.

THE CHANGING ROLE OF THE EVALUATOR

Traditional conceptions of evaluation gave rise, historically, to different definitions of the role of the evaluator, beginning with *technician* (first-generation measurement-oriented evaluation), moving through *describer* (second-generation objectives-oriented evaluation), and thence to *judge* (third-generation judgmentally-oriented evaluation). Fourth-generation evaluation retains all of these roles, albeit in markedly different form, and adds several others: *collaborator, learner/teacher, reality shaper* and *mediator and change agent.* Looking first at the retained but redefined role aspects:

1. The evaluator retains certain technician functions, but these are given a new form: the *human instrument and analyst.* The evaluator was traditionally seen as a person knowledgeable about the important variables that the profession was instrumentally capable of assessing, one who had a high level of familiarity with available standardized and normed instruments (paper-and-pencil and brass), one who knew the details of valid, reliable, and objective data collection and analysis (usually statistical), and one who was competent to write a technical report that would receive high marks from his or her professional peers. But in fourth-generation evaluation the focus of activity has shifted from objectives, decisions, effects, and other similar organizers to the claims, concerns, and issues raised by stakeholders, and these are often unpredictable a priori. Hence advance selection or development of instruments is largely impossible. Further, even when discovered, these claims, concerns, and issues may not be possible of assessment by existing instruments or by instruments that might be conventionally developed; they may, for example, be cultural or political in nature. While the fourth-generation evaluator should without doubt be well informed about conventional instruments, he or she must perceive the *self* as the most immediately available and useful form of instrumentation. If claims, concerns, and issues must be assessed before an evaluation can begin (in the usual sense), the assessment instrument must be highly adaptable and reprogrammable, so that it can ferret out the most salient and relevant matters (that is, salient and relevant with respect to the evaluand) and progressively focus on them through *continuous* data processing. If many of the claims, concerns, and issues do not deal simply with technical questions (e.g., "Will turning over ownership of prisons to profit-making

firms improve corrections in America?") but include social, political, religious, cultural, aesthetic, and other nontechnical matters (e.g., "Does workfare exploit the poor?"), then the evaluator may well find that the continued use of the self-as-instrument and the self-as-analyst is essential if these matters are to be usefully explored. Clearly "normal" designs, data collection devices, and data analytic techniques will not serve well.

2. The evaluator retains certain describing functions but exercises them all in an *illuminative and historical mode* rather than in an objective scientific mode. The evaluator describes (reconstructs) constructions and the value positions on which those constructions are based, recognizing that these have no objective reality and are subject to change on a moment-to-moment basis. Often these descriptions (reconstructions) have more value as history than as science, as Cronbach (1975) has pointed out. The purpose of these descriptions (reconstructions) is not to *fix* an image but to *illuminate* a scene, in such a way that the evaluator himself or herself, the client, and all other stakeholding audiences can come to a greater appreciation and better understanding of the constructions that are being entertained.

3. The evaluator understands the need for judgments in evaluation but eschews the role of judge; instead, the evaluator becomes the *mediator of the judgmental process*. This process is a *political* one. Value pluralism leads inevitably to judgmental pluralism. Action cannot be taken unless and until some compromise is reached among these variable judgments, or unless one or a few actors are sufficiently powerful that they can control the decision process—not an unusual but certainly an immoral state of affairs. The evaluator is in a position to serve as orchestrator because he or she has continuously interacted with the several stakeholder groups and, if the process has been carried out in terms of the earlier-described principles, has gained their trust. The fourth-generation evaluator is the agent most qualified and able to act as mediator.

Turning now to the emergent role aspects:

4. The evaluator conducts the evaluation from a *collaborative* rather than a controlling posture. We have noted the fact that unless stakeholders have the ability to provide inputs into all

aspects of an evaluation, they are in the end presented with nothing more than a fait accompli, a choice from only the options provided by those more privileged. Of course, to act collabora- tively the evaluator must necessarily *give up some of the control* that has not only been vouchsafed in traditional approaches but that has been insisted upon in the name of validity, reliability, and objectivity. Control is the essence in standard designs; without it the inquirer cannot guarantee, it is said, the integrity of the findings. Giving up control thus has farther-reaching consequen- ces than simply a reduction of personal autonomy and power; it seems to fly in the face of conventional principles for sound design. Yet without an extension of control to include stake- holders (or their representatives), the evaluation is an empty political vessel. Evaluations of the conventional sort are, not surprisingly, given short shrift in the political decision making arena.

5. The evaluator plays the roles of both *learner and teacher*. Initially the evaluator strikes a very open posture, soliciting information about constructions and values, as well as claims, concerns, and issues, that he or she does not yet comprehend, could not have predicted, nor about which he or she can ask very penetrating questions. That the evaluator is a learner is apparent to all. But after a time, as the learning leads to insights and understandings (that is, when the evaluator finds it possible to make some initial constructions of his or her own), the evaluator can share those not only with the audience from which they were derived (for the purpose, among others, of verifying their credibility), but with other audiences, whom he or she can now presume to *teach*. In practice, the learner/teacher roles are intertwined; at no stage does the evaluator stop learning, and he or she is in a position to do some teaching at every stage (for example, engaging in consciousness raising when dealing with an audience relatively unsophisticated about the evaluand).

6. The evaluator is part and parcel a *reality shaper*. While the constructions that emerge from various stakeholding groups may initially reflect only *their* values, the evaluator, in teaching those constructions to others, inevitably infuses them with his or her own reconstructions. Further, as we have noted, initial construc- tions of stakeholders are themselves subject to change as the audience interacts with the evaluator and, through the evaluator,

with other stakeholders. Thus evaluators and audiences literally produce the outcomes of the evaluation by their continuous interrelationship. Insofar as the responsibility of the evaluator extends to clarifying and refining the evaluand, such an outcome may be viewed as a major benefit of fourth-generation evaluation. More informed constructions that take the perspectives of other audiences into account are clearly preferable to partial, imperfectly informed constructions.

7. The evaluator is inevitably a *mediator and change agent*. It is the bane—and shame—of traditional evaluations that they are little used. That should not surprise us, for in conventional evaluations, many stakeholders will *not* find information that they consider germane to their own interests, while the information that *is* provided may represent a single value position that is repugnant to those of other persuasions. But when the output of an evaluation is not a technical report with a series of conclusions and recommendations that (tend to) represent the evaluator's judgments, but a case study that includes an *agenda for negotiation* to be mediated by the evaluator, then the evaluator becomes a change agent and the evaluation "findings" (constructions, value positions, and data relevant to stated claims, concerns, and issues) serve as a powerful means to agreeing on needed change.

We may end this section with a few observations about the characteristics that a fourth-generation evaluator must display to be effective. The new evaluator appreciates diversity, respects the rights of individuals to hold different values and to make different constructions, and welcomes the opportunity to air and to clarify these differences. The new evaluator must possess the personal qualities of honesty, respect, and courtesy, and like Caesar's wife, his or her integrity must be above suspicion. Without it the evaluator loses the one ingredient without which no fourth-generation evaluation can be conducted successfully: trust. Nor can there be any question of the new evaluator's professional competence; training and experience that include not only technical skills but social, political, and interpersonal skills must be clearly demonstrable. The new evaluator must have a high tolerance for ambiguity and a high frustration threshold. The new evaluation is a lonely activity, for one must remain sufficiently aloof to avoid charges of undue influence by one stakeholder group or another. The new evaluator must be aware of the possibility that he or she is being used by clients or other powerful groups, as well as of the fact that stakeholders may, individually or in groups, engage in lies, deceptions, fronts, and cover-ups. Finally, the new evaluator must be ready to be personally changed by the evaluative process, to revise his or her own constructions as understanding and sophistication increase. To be willing to change does not imply a loss of objectivity but a gain in fairness.

SOME CONSTRAINTS ON THE NEW EVALUATION

Throughout this paper we have taken the posture that fourth-generation evaluation represents an improvement over older forms. We have attempted to provide a warrant for that position. But it would be naive to assume that there do not presently exist, however temporarily, certain constraints that detract from the new evaluation's power and applicability. In this section we shall mention several of the more prominent.

1. *Lack of legitimation for the new approach.* In many circles fourth-generation evaluation (although hardly called by that name) is not accepted as a legitimate option on methodological grounds. It is viewed as too subjective, too open to cooptation, too unsystematic, too unreliable. Indeed, the approach rejects the usual tenets of scientific inquiry and hews to a new paradigm, which goes by various names such as qualitative, naturalistic, hermeneutic, phenomenological, or case study, a paradigm whose legitimacy is contested by the scientific community. We have made the case elsewhere (Guba and Lincoln, 1982b; Lincoln and Guba, 1985) that the new paradigm is not only legitimate but likely to replace positivism in all disciplines over the next decades. It also seems clear, on analysis, that the criteria by which the scientific community is judging the emergent or alternative paradigm are themselves rooted in the same assumptions that undergird positivism (Morgan, 1983), and hence are not fairly or

appropriately applied to it. We shall deal with the question of what criteria *are* appropriate in the following section. Here the point we wish to make is that we are still witnessing the struggle of the new paradigm to achieve recognition, and until that has occurred, as it surely will, efforts to work within the principles of fourth-generation evaluation will continue to be viewed by many with suspicion, however undeservedly.

2. *Political dysfunctionality of the new approach.* If one takes seriously the concept of a *collaborative* approach to evaluation, it is essential that the power figures in a situation to be willing to extend some of that power to less-powerful stakeholder groups. The history of man does not provide much support for the proposition that those who hold power will voluntarily give it up to those who do not. Evaluations, even conventional ones, are always disruptive of the prevailing political balance (Guba and Lincoln, 1981), a fact of life that is even more true of fourth-generation collaborative efforts. Moreover, the power that inheres in a situation is often held not only by formal gatekeepers, such as a superintendent of schools or a building principal, but also by informal ones who may treasure their power precisely because it is achieved and not ascribed. This difficulty does not have an easy solution, and we will not attempt to be glib about it here. It does seem to be the case that the development of the good will need to extend power is an important task for the fourth-generation evaluator; without at least some minimal success along this line evaluations will continue to be relatively meaningless. Of course power imbalances also characterize earlier generation forms of evaluation, so that perhaps the only additional decrement suffered by the new evaluation is to make those imbalances more obvious. But that may also be fourth-generation evaluation's strength; making a bad situation public is more likely to lead to remedy than is further complicity in its continuation.

3. *The human dysfunctionality of the new approach.* We have noted in other writing (Guba and Lincoln, 1981) that all evaluations are dysfunctional to human performance, creating anxieties and fears that are hard to combat. The more intense, personal experiences that members of stakeholding groups are likely to have in fourth-generation evaluations will exacerbate rather than inhibit this tendency. The building of trust is crucial and must, moreover, be attended to continuously. Trust is not something to

be achieved by some set of procedures and thereafter to be forever enjoyed. The building of trust is a developmental process that requires a good deal of time to carry out and that can be wrecked by one misstep. Scrupulous attendance to ethical principles is imperative. On the other hand, the intense personal involvement of stakeholders is also likely to result in much greater commitment to the evaluation process and its outcomes than is the case with more conventional evaluation.

4. *The time and context boundaries of the new approach.* Fourth-generation evaluation is closely tied to the time and context complex in which it is carried out. Evaluations can have meaning only for the particular time and context that yielded their findings, and certainly negotiated judgments will be honored only by the parties to the negotiation process. Fourth-generation evaluations are thus not generalizable; they must be repeated everywhere that the outcomes are expected to have utility. That is of course also true of conventional evaluations of worth (Guba and Lincoln, 1981), although that fact is, unfortunately, only rarely acknowledged.

5. *Inability to be design specific in applying the new approach.* It is an undisputed requirement of conventional evaluation models that there must be an evaluation design prior to the evaluation itself, for how can an evaluation that has not been planned be carried out? Fourth-generation evaluation flies in the face of this dictum by suggesting that designs are emergent, that they unfold, first, as claims, concerns, and issues are identified, and second, as information responsive to the most salient of these is collected.[6] But RFPs and other forms of solicitation are typically written with the conventional models in mind; thus they call for certain specifications that the fourth-generation evaluator finds it impossible to provide. This situation is well described by the phrase, contract-paradigm disjunctions. Unless and until funding agencies or other approving bodies alter their stance on what constitutes an appropriate solicitation, the fourth-generation evaluator will continue to be caught in this unfortunate disjunction. One can be optimistic, however, that as the features of fourth-generation evaluation become more widely appreciated, this disjunction will lessen markedly.

6. *The open-ended nature of the new approach.* Finally, we may point out again that since the new evaluation is divergent, it is

never possible to reach a logically self-evident point of closure. Fourth-generation evaluations end when time and money run out, and not when some full complement of questions has been answered. Answering any given question always raises several new ones. Clients and stakeholders are thus likely to be somewhat dissatisfied, perhaps even feeling that they are being exploited by the evaluator for his or her own ends. The inability to determine "the end" on logical grounds is another of the ambiguities that the fourth-generation evaluator must bear. On the other hand, logistics, funds, and timing continue to be powerful and useful determiners.

These six constraints are the most important and urgent that are likely to plague the new evaluator; others will no doubt emerge. Their existence contributes markedly to the ambiguity and frustration that the new evaluator will experience, and underscores the need for high personal thresholds for stress. It can be hoped, however, that these problems will be eliminated or reduced in the next few years as fourth-generation evaluation becomes better understood. They are by no means sufficiently debilitating, even in these early days, to be used as arguments against utilization of the new evaluation.

CRITERIA FOR THE NEW EVALUATION

Three separate issues emerge as one considers the question of how fourth-generation evaluation should itself be evaluated (metaevaluation). First there is the matter of technical adequacy—criteria that have traditionally been invoked such as validity, reliability, and objectivity. Second there is the matter of the extent to which existing standards, particularly those promulgated by the Joint Committee (1981) and the Evaluation Research Society (Rossi, 1982) are applicable. Finally, one may ask whether there are not some criteria that emerge because of the particular posture assumed by the new evaluation: Do new postures imply new criteria? We shall consider each issue in turn.

1. *Criteria of technical adequacy.* We have already observed

with Morgan (1983) that every inquiry paradigm carried within it the seeds for its appropriate criteria. Within the conventional scientific paradigm such criteria are usually given as internal validity, external validity (or generalizability), reliability, and objectivity. We have in other writing (Guba, 1981; Guba and Lincoln, 1982b; Lincoln and Guba, 1985) suggested that these criteria are inappropriate to inquiries (research, evaluation, or policy analysis) whose ontological and epistemological assumptions do not coincide with the normal scientific (positivist) paradigm, as those of fourth-generation evaluation certainly do not. Instead, we have proposed the substitution of four parallel or analogous criteria, which we have labeled credibility, transferability, dependability, and confirmability, and have suggested a variety of techniques whereby these criteria can be fulfilled and assessed. The interested reader is referred to these other sources for details.

2. *Criteria proposed by existing statements of standards.* Two sets of standards have been proposed recently: those developed by the so-called Joint Committee, (1981)[7] and those proposed by the Evaluation Research Society (Rossi, 1982). The Joint Committee standards are arranged in four categories, labeled utility standards, feasibility standards, propriety standards, and accuracy standards, and include 30 different prescriptions. While the language of these standards rather heavily favors conventional (first- through third-generation) evaluation concepts, the standards are written in language sufficiently flexible for fourth-generation evaluators to meet them at some reasonable level, and their use is recommended.

Those standards developed by the Evaluation Research Society, 55 in number, are arranged in six categories organized to reflect the "normal" progression of evaluation tasks: formulation and negotiation, structure and design, data collection and preparation, data analysis and interpretation, communication and disclosure, and utilization. As one of us has pointed out in a review of these standards (Lincoln, 1985), they fail to provide sufficient "wriggle room" for the fourth-generation evaluator on at least five counts: (1) the assumption of a straight-line systematic form for evaluation, in which the first communication an evaluator is likely to have with a client once the contract is written follows data analysis, when there are "findings" to be presented; (2) the demand that all worthy evaluations follow normal design specifications; (3) the emphasis on determination of cause and effect relationships to the virtual exclusion of description and characterization; (4) the implicit assumption that it is the client who has sole control of the evaluation to the disenfranchisement of other relevant parties; and (5) the failure of these standards to recognize the role that values play in evaluation efforts. Consequently, the use of these ERS standards for judging fourth-generation evaluations is unacceptable.

3. *Criteria suggested by the form of the new evaluation itself.* We propose five additional criteria that are applicable to fourth-generation evaluation on the grounds that they "fit" the new style: *openness, relevance, fairness, ethicality*, and *increased understanding*. By *openness* we mean two things: first, that the evaluator has solicited inputs from all legitimate stakeholders and can provide evidence of having heard and honored those inputs; and second, that the evaluator has displayed these separate inputs to all stakeholding groups, so that in the end there are no surprises that favor one group at the expense of another. All of the information is known to everyone. By *relevance* we mean that the information collected by the evaluator is responsive to the various claims, concerns, and issues that have been expressed by stakeholders; not all of them, of course, because there will never be sufficient time and resources to do that, but those judged by some open process to be most important or salient.

By *fairness* we mean that the positions of each stakeholding group or subgroup, as well as the value positions on which they are based, are presented in a balanced manner. The agenda for negotiation presented toward the end of the evaluation process leaves all options open to consideration; none are closed out by the arbitrary actions of the evaluator or the more powerful stakeholder groups. The best guarantee of fairness is open and continuous dialogue. By *ethicality* we mean that the evaluation is conducted in ways that put respondents at the lowest risk possible consistent with the agreed-upon purpose of the evaluation, and that every effort is made to protect privacy and confidentiality. We tend to agree with Cronbach's 46th thesis (Cronbach, 1980: 6) that "the crucial ethical problem appears to be freedom to communicate during and after the study, subject to legitimate concerns for privacy, national security, and faithfulness to contractual requirements," provided, we would add, that the contractual requirements do not close out any options. Finally, by *increased understanding* we mean that each audience will, by virtue of participation in the evaluation activity, be able to arrive at a more sophisticated and informed construction than before, while being better able to appreciate the constructions proposed by other stakeholders, even those in apparent conflict.

In short, on the matter of criteria for judging fourth-generation evaluations, we suggest that such evaluations should meet the technical criteria that have been proposed as relevant to the naturalistic (qualitative, case study, phenomenological, etc.) paradigm; that they should be in the main consistent with the metaevaluation standards proposed by the Joint Committee; and that they should in addition be able to satisfy requirements for openness, relevance, fairness, ethicality, and increased under-standing. We are confident that any evaluations that can meet that set of requirements will be more than adequate, and moreover *will be so judged by the several stakeholders*. Their confidence is, after all, the most important prize to seek.

POSTSCRIPT

The major purpose of this paper has been to suggest that a fourth-generation mode of evaluation is emerging whose hallmark is negotiation. We have identified certain concepts and principles that undergird this new mode, and have tried to show how the concept of evaluation, as well as the role of the evaluator, would change accordingly. Certain constraints that tend to inhibit the orderly development of these changes were identified. Finally, we have suggested a number of metacriteria that might be appropriate to judging exemplars of this evolving style of evaluation.

This article is *not* a call for an either-or allegiance. We have been accused of divisiveness (incorrectly, we think) in other matters, for example, in insisting on a clear choice between positivist and post-positivist paradigms to guide inquiry, while arguing that mix-and-match strategies or ecumenical embraces are not tenable (Guba and Lincoln, in preparation, a). But that is not the issue here. Fourth-generation evaluation is neither a competitor nor a replacement for earlier forms; instead, it subsumes them while moving the evaluation process to higher levels of sophistication and utility.

But fourth-generation evaluation cannot become a fully-functioning reality unless two conditions are met. It must first achieve acceptance and legitimation in the evaluation community. Clients cannot be expected to embrace it while it remains a dubious choice among evaluation "experts." Indeed, one can confidently assert that the lack of legitimation will be used by unscrupulous clients as a reason for rejecting it and the power sharing that it implies. Second, it must be implemented by the practitioners who are properly trained in its methods and socialized to its values. The evaluation training programs presently offered by the universities of this country are not adequate to this task. New programs must be developed and installed. That too requires a prior achievement of acceptance, for no university will offer a program that is treated derisively by the very faculty who must teach it. We beg the indulgence of our colleagues to examine this new evaluation, and if it is determined to have *both* merit and worth, to join us in working for its wide dissemination and implementation.

NOTES

1. We are aware that what is taken to be factual depends in part on the values of the apprehender. Science is not value free, and hence facts are themselves value laden. For an extended treatment of this topic see Lincoln and Guba, 1985.

2. The more traditional position is now frequently discounted as "naive realism"; post-positivists who continue in this tradition are more likely to label themselves "critical

realists." See Hesse, 1980, and Cook and Campbell, 1979.

3. The evaluator must also construct some view; that view may properly be termed *etic.*

4. The process described here should not be confused with transactional evaluation (Rippey, 1973), which focuses upon changes in the organization in which evaluation is taking place rather than on the evaluand and the findings regarding it per se.

5. The kind of control that can be asserted over an inquiry is discussed in detail in Guba and Lincoln, in preparation, b. It is only the positivist paradigm that insists on complete inquirer control as a precondition for disciplined inquiry.

6. What is taken as most salient may itself change as the evaluation unfolds. The evaluator must be alert to such shifts and engage in continuous redesign accordingly.

7. The organizations represented on the Joint Committee included the American Association of School Administrators, the American Educational Research Association, the American Federation of Teachers, the American Psychological Association, the American Personnel and Guidance Association, the Council for American Private Education, the Education Commission of the States, the National Association of Elementary School Principals, the National Council for Measurement in Education, the National Education Association, and the National School Boards Association.

REFERENCES

Boruch, R. F. (1974) Bibliography: Illustrated Randomized Field Experiments for Program Planning and Evaluation. Evaluation 2: 83-87.

Campbell, D. T. (1969) Reforms as Experiments. American Psychologist 24: 409-29.

Cook, T. D. and D. T. Campbell (1979) Quasi-Experimentation: Design and Analysis Issues for Field Settings. Chicago: Rand McNally.

Cronbach, L. J. (1975) Beyond the Two Disciplines of Scientific Psychology. American Psychologist 30: 116-127.

Cronbach, L. J. (1980) Toward Reform of Program Evaluation. San Francisco: Jossey-Bass.

Eisner, E. W. (1960) Instructional and Expressive Objectives: Their Formulation and Use in Curriculum. AERA Monograph Series in Curriculum Evaluation, No. 3. Chicago: Rand McNally.

Eisner, E. W. (1979) The Educational Imagination. New York: Macmillan.

Gronlund, N. E. (1985) Measurement and Evaluation in Teaching (5th ed.) New York: Macmillan.

Guba, E. G. (1981) Criteria for Assessing the Trustworthiness of Naturalistic Inquiries. Educational Communication and Technology Journal 29: 75-92.

Guba, E. G. and Y. S. Lincoln (1981) Effective Evaluation. San Francisco: Jossey-Bass.

Guba, E. G. and Y. S. Lincoln (1982a) "The Place of Values in Needs Assessment." Educational Evaluation and Policy Analysis 4: 311-320.

Guba, E. G. and Y. S. Lincoln (1982b) Epistemological and Methodological Bases of Naturalistic Inquiry. Educational Communication and Technology Journal 30: 233-252.

Guba, E. G. and Y. S. Lincoln (in preparation, a) Do Inquiry Paradigms Imply Inquiry Methodologies?

Guba, E. G. and Y. S. Lincoln (in preparation, b) Types of Inquiry Defined by Choice of an Insider or Outsider Stance and Inquirer or Respondent Control. (working title).

Hesse, M. (1980) Revolutions and Reconstructions in the Philosophy of Science. Bloomington: Indiana University Press.

House, E. R. (1978) Assumptions Underlying Evaluation Models. Educational Researcher 7: 4-12.

Joint Committee (1981) Standards for Evaluations of Educational Programs, Projects, and Materials. New York: McGraw-Hill.

Lincoln, Y. S. (1985) The ERS Standards for Program Evaluation: Guidance for a Fledgling Profession. Evaluation and Program Planning 8: 251-253.

Lincoln, Y. S. and E. G. Guba (1985) Naturalistic Inquiry. Newbury Park, CA: Sage.

Morgan, G. [ed.] (1983) Beyond Method: Strategies for Social Research. Newbury Park, CA: Sage.

Parlett, M. and D. Hamilton (1972) Evaluation as Illumination: A New Approach to the Study of Innovatory Programs. Edinburgh, Scotland: Occasional Paper No. 9, Centre for Research in the Educational Sciences, University of Edinburgh.

Patton, M. Q. (1978) Utilization-Focused Evaluation. Newbury Park, CA: Sage.

Pike, K. (1954) Language in Relation to a Unified Theory of the Structure of Human Behavior, vol. 1. Glendale, CA: Institute of Linguistics.

Provus, M. (1971) Discrepancy Evaluation. Berkeley, CA: McCutchan.

Rippey, Robert M. (1973) Studies in Transactional Evaluation. Berkeley, CA: McCutchan.

Rivlin, A. M. and P. M. Timpane [eds.] (1975) Planned Variation in Education. Washington, DC: Brookings Institution.

Rossi, P. H. and W. Williams [eds.] (1972) Evaluating Social Action Programs: Theory, Practice, and Politics. New York: Seminar.

Rossi, P. H. [ed.] (1982) Standards for Evaluation Practice 15, New Directions for Program Evaluation. San Francisco: Jossey-Bass.

Rowan, J. (1981) A Dialectical Paradigm for Research. Ch. 9 in P. Reason and J. Rowan (eds.) Human Inquiry: A Sourcebook of New Paradigm Research. New York: John Wiley.

Scriven, M. (1967) The Methodology of Evaluation. AERA Monograph Series in Curriculum Evaluation 1. Chicago: Rand McNally.

Scriven, M. (1973) "Goal-Free Evaluation," in House, E. R. (ed.) School Evaluation: The Politics and Process. Berkeley, CA: McCutchan.

Sims, D. (1981) "From Ethogeny to Endogeny: How Participants in Research Projects Can End up Doing Action Research on Their Own Awareness," Chapter 32 in Reason, P. and J. Rowan (eds.) Human Inquiry: A Sourcebook of New Paradigm Research, New York: John Wiley.

Smith, E. R. and R. W. Tyler (1942) Appraising and Recording Student Progress. New York: Harper & Row.

Stake, R. E. (1967) "The Countenance of Educational Evaluation." Teachers College Record 68: 523-540.

Stake, R. E. (1973) "Program Evaluation, Particularly Responsive Evaluation." Presented at the Conference on New Trends in Evaluation, Goteborg, Sweden.

Stake, R. E. (1975) Evaluating the Arts in Education. Columbus, OH: Merrill.

Stufflebeam, D. L. and W. J. Webster (1980) "An Analysis of Alternative Approaches to Evaluation." Educational Evaluation and Policy Analysis 2, 5-19.
Stufflebeam, D. L., et al. (1971) Educational Evaluation and Decision-Making. Itasca, IL: Peacock.
Torbert, W. R. (1981) "Why Educational Research Has Been So Uneducational: The Case for a New Model of Social Science Based on Collaborative Inquiry." Ch. 11 in P. Reason and J. Rowan (eds.) Human Inquiry: A Sourcebook of New Paradigm Research, New York: John Wiley.
Wolf, R. L. (1979) "The Use of Judicial Evaluation Methods in the Formulation of Educational Policy." Educational Evaluation and Policy Analysis 1: 19-28.
Worthen, B. R. and J. R. Sanders (1973) Educational Evaluation: Theory and Practice. Columbus, OH: Jones.

8

THE INFLUENCE OF THEORY
ON WHAT WE SEE

LAWRENCE A. SCAFF
University of California at Berkeley

HELEN M. INGRAM
University of Arizona

In the sciences it is no longer contestable to assert that the theories, frameworks, conceptual schemes, paradigms, or even commonsensical points of view that one adopts profoundly influence what one observes in the world. Since the classic studies of Hanson (1958) and Kuhn (1970), it has become commonplace to note that there is no such thing as a brute "fact" or a completely neutral "observation language" simply "there" in the world, existing independently of all conceptualization and serving as a definitive test of our theoretical generalizations. The "facts" composing the world of our observations are always "theory-laden" (Hanson, 1958: 19). In the sciences priority must be granted to those activities typically grouped under the heading *theory*.[1]

Given this starting point, the question that must be asked is not whether "theories" influence what we see, but rather *how* they influence our observations. We need to ask what the consequences are, practical as well as theoretical, of employing any given theoretical apparatus of concepts and generalizations in a context of alternative choices. The question is not whether we should adopt or should have a theory at all—inevitably we will, whether intentionally or not—but rather what theory should we embrace, for what purposes, with which intentions, as a result of what commitments, and in relation to which contexts of inquiry? Those are the questions we would like to pursue in this discussion. As we proceed it will become clear that certain inescapable "costs" are incurred in committing oneself to a specific theoretical position; part of our inquiry will be directed toward identifying some of these costs and clarifying their political meaning. It will also become evident that the practical consequences of such commitments can be not only intellectual but also political, ideological and oral. It could hardly be otherwise, especially with respect to public policy and the study of public policy, where the truly important issues are always a subject of political dispute and often a topic for ethical disagreement.

THEORY AND OBSERVATION
IN POLICY STUDIES

Scholars of policy have been aware of the need for "theory"—whether understood as a model, analytic framework, or conceptual scheme—to define, classify and explain the nature, formulation and effects of policy. In recent years such awareness has been evident in two tendencies that are not necessarily compatible: the search for middle-range generalizations suitable for the analysis of particular areas of policy, and the search for a comprehensive general theory applicable to the field of policy studies as a whole. If the latter attempt were to succeed and a truly comprehensive "theory" were to emerge, then all lower-level generalizations would necessarily become a subset of the victorious "theory." This outcome, however, has certainly not yet occurred—nor can we expect it to occur. We continue to operate with a variety of conceptualizations addressed to particular research problems and appropriate for answering a specific range of questions.

Consideration of the use of theory at the "middle-range" level has one distinct advantage: When tied to a specific context, theory can most readily be seen to have determinate effects on observation. We propose to develop this line of thought by considering two well-known and important examples: the case of studies of power, and the work on governmental decision processes during a crisis.

Studies of power are instructive for our purposes because they have a history that shows a pattern of interaction among theory, observation, and political concerns. Starting with the "community power" work of Dahl (1961), the modern social scientific "theory" of power has now moved through three distinct phases, in which the conceptualization of what power *is* has gone hand in hand with observational statements about how power is *used*—that is, not only "who gets what, when, and how," but also "who gets left out, and how" (Gaventa, 1980: 9)—and with political claims about how power *functions* in the context of inequality, deprivation and competing interests. In the first phase—the first "face" or "dimension" of power—power was thought of as "influence," as getting someone to do something he or she would not otherwise do. It was overt, visible, specific to a decision arena, and available to all with interests or grievances. In response to the omissions of the first phase, the second viewed power as covert manipulation, intended to control agenda, prevent certain issues from arising, and exclude potential participants. It was just as likely to come into play with "nondecisions" and "nonissues" as with its overt expressions. In the third phase, which developed in Lukes's analytic work (1974) as a criticism of inadequacies in the previous two views, power as influence or manipulation came to be seen as affecting the very way in which issues are conceived, the conceptual apparatus or "consciousness" of participants and nonparticipants alike (and especially the latter) through the operation of sociological or psychological forces. From this perspective power is used "to preempt manifest conflict . . . through the shaping of patterns of conceptions of nonconflict"

(Gaventa, 1980: 5-13); quiescence and powerlessness are alone sufficient to signify power's presence.

The development in Lukes's phrase of "three conceptual maps" (1974: 10) for understanding power catalogues a shift from a pluralist to a "radical" political perspective, or to a dimension of power that seems especially suited to investigating those hidden aspects of domination that work such pernicious effects upon the dispossessed. In Gaventa's words its mechanisms are by far "the least understood" in political science:

> Their identification, one suspects, involves specifying the means through which power influences, shapes or determines conceptions of the necessities, possibilities, and strategies of challenge in situations of latent conflict. This may include the study of social myths, language, and symbols, and how they are shaped or manipulated in power processes. It may involve the study of communication of information—both of what is communicated and how it is done. It may involve, in short, locating the power processes behind the social construction of meanings and patterns that serve to get B to act and believe in a manner in which B otherwise might not, to A's benefit and B's detriment [Gaventa, 1980: 15-16].

Moreover, these are not merely hypothetical generalizations about the processes of power, for "Such processes may take direct observable form" (Gaventa, 1980: 16). But it would be difficult, if not impossible, to make such observations at all, were it not for a theory that alerted the investigator to the "third face" of power. As Gaventa realizes in his application of Lukes' theoretical investigations, if the problem is to explain powerlessness and its causes, then one is hopelessly lost and misled until one sees the relevance of finding those third phase "processes behind the social construction of meaning and patterns that serve" power.

Quite similar conclusions about the tight fit between a "theory" and the observations it makes possible can be drawn from Allison's celebrated study (1971) of the Cuban missile crisis. In this analysis of governmental decision in a period of extreme stress, the author employs three "theories" or what he variously calls "models," "conceptual schemes or frameworks," or "analytic paradigms" (Allison, 1971: 4, 32)—"rational actor," "organizational process," and "governmental (bureaucratic) politics"—as lenses through which to view the same series of events. The use of three conceptual schemes is justified initially on the basis of a grouping of positions in the interpretive literature on decisions. The schemes do not emerge full blown from observational data, but instead come from the probing of a "complex theoretical substructure . . . which reflect[s] unrecognized assumptions about the character of puzzles, the categories in which problems should be considered, the types of evidence that are relevant, and the determinants of occurrences" (Allison, 1971: 4). Theoretical variety then becomes indispensable for explaining policy, both from the viewpoint of participants and from the perspective of outside observers.

The great advantage of Allison's study for our purposes is its clear demonstration that the choice of a particular conceptual scheme is never benign, but instead influences the collection and presentation of data and the inferences and conclusions drawn for policy. In his own words, "These conceptual models are much more than *simple* angles of vision or approaches. Each conceptual framework consists of a *cluster* of assumptions and categories that influence what the analyst finds puzzling, how he formulates his question, where he looks for evidence, and what he produces as an answer" (Allison, 1971: 245). It is not the case either that each of the three theories sees an identical factual world. On the contrary, the actual use of each theory for explaining events points toward "an apparent incompatibility" (Allison, 1971: 246) at the level of basic assumptions ranging from what counts as an adequate explanation to what counts as admissible evidence. In this regard Allison's findings run parallel to Kuhn's postulate of "incommensurability" among scientific paradigms, according to which "the proponents of competing paradigms practice their trades in different worlds" (Kuhn, 1970: 150). Or in Allison's phrasing, it is startling to realize that "while at one level these models produce different explanations of the same happening, at the second level the models produce different explanations of quite different occurrences. . . . different conceptual lenses lead analysts to different judgments about what is relevant and important"(1971: 251). In this case the study of policy shows that the "theories" we choose to employ not only conceptualize the world in different ways, they present to us altogether different "worlds" or "political realities."

This may appear to be a puzzling conclusion. Is there no realm of incontrovertible "facts" that can in itself, independently of any theory, act as a check against *all possible* interpretive generalizations? Of course there is a clear difference between Kuhn and the studies of power and decision making, for "incommensurability" in Kuhn's language demands a *choice* between competing paradigms—either A or B, but not A and B simultaneously—whereas the cases we have drawn from political science suggest the advisability of theoretical pluralism—work with A and B and C, regardless of their incompatibilities. The "metatheory" that can identify and incorporate all three is then to be preferred because it provides access to the widest range of potential observations. The choice among incompatibles is fully dependent upon one's research questions and cognitive goals. Thus one lesson to draw from our discussion is that problems of observation are best resolved not by appealing to a factual base, which cannot be grasped apart from *some* cognitive principle, but by searching for the widest possible range of "conceptual frameworks" or the most extensive "cognitive maps" consistent with a substantive question or program of research. In the initial phase of our investigations the more theoretical inventiveness we show, the better off we are.

THE INFLUENCE OF PUBLIC CHOICE THEORY

Having stated our general view about the relationship between theory and observation, we are now in a position to investigate the case of the "public choice" or "rational choice" approach that has been widely adopted and touted as a "comprehensive theory" in the field of policy studies. What are the leading assumptions of this approach? What are the consequences that follow from the application of it to policy studies?

Notwithstanding clear differences among those who work within the framework of public choice, there is a shared set of assumptions that can be regarded as "typical" for it. According to its formal and axiomatic propositions, borrowed mainly from microeconomics, political activity is conceived basically as an exchange activity among "self-interested" individuals acting in the setting of "market" transactions. The "exchange" is the basic unit of action and the "individual" the basic unit of analysis. Exchanges are said to have effects on third parties ("externalities"), and they are assumed to occur "rationally" according to rank-ordered preferences, despite imperfect information. The typical "political individual" becomes an efficient maximizer of individual utilities, modeled after *homo economicus* and engaging in strategic means-ends calculations of costs and benefits. Politics tends to be conceived as that activity in which aggregated utilities result in a choice concerning provisions of public goods, while policy is conceived as emerging from a combination of individual preferences.

For our purposes two assumptions from this brief summation should be highlighted. The first is found in a familiar "individualistic" premise, or the view that all statements about collectivities and collective action can be reduced to statements about a model individual without contextually substantial loss of meaning. With the "individual" as the unit of analysis, collectivities are conceived in terms of probabilities of individual choice and action. Methodological, conceptual (and some would say ideological) priority is granted this "individualistic" assumption.

The second major assumption has to do with a version of "rationality," which has probably become the most widely discussed aspect of the approach. For public choice the "individual" is assumed to be a purposive, self-interested and efficient maximizer of utilities. His "rationality" is assumed to consist of these qualities and of an ability in principle to put preferences in rank-order. All preference-orderings should be symmetrical, complete, and transitive, such that *utility* can be defined as a numerical representation of this "preference" (Sen, 1982: 88; Goodin, 1976: 10). This yields a particular specification of rationality: "A person's choices are considered 'rational'... if and only if these choices can *all* be explained in terms of some preference relations consistent with the revealed preference definition" (Sen, 1982: 89). Clearly this assumption is grounded in a metatheory of "human nature," in which the prudential, calculating, instrumental, and utilitarian dimensions of behavior are emphasized.

In addition to such assumptions one other feature of the public choice approach should be stressed, namely, its proclivity for entering a wide variety of research domains. As an analytic approach, not only is it well-established, but it has become a kind of metatheory or "paradigm," consisting of explanatory principles with confirming evidence and "compatible with, and open to, a variety of epistemologies" (Sproule-Jones, 1982: 800). This is to say that a significant number of proponents of public choice have championed its benefits as an overarching schema capable of seemingly limitless applications to substantive research areas in political science and public policy. This ambitious extension of public choice has certainly come to affect its self-understanding and to underscore the need for discussion of its limits as well as its potentialities.

What, then, are the important areas of controversy and criticism? Within political science and policy studies the critical questioning of public choice approaches has developed around three issues: (1) the logical status and clarity of the main concepts in public choice; (2) the relationship between the assumptions of the approach and the "real world" of politics; and (3) the problem of alleged "normative bias" in terms of both ideological distortion and a strong preference for "market" solutions to political controversies. Let us consider each of these areas of criticism.

Probably the most straightforward criticisms of the choice theoretic approach have been registered in the charge that "rationality" can have different and equally reasonable meanings (Machan, 1980) or that "self-interest" is too flexible to be a useful analytic tool (Bolembiewski, 1977). The response to such charges has typically proceeded through stipulation of precise and restrictive uses of terms. From the standpoint of logic the resort to stipulative definition has offered a successful strategy for counter-acting such objections. However, the problem that critics want to address here lies not so much with logic as with the implications of applying restrictive (if precise) definitions in certain contexts of inquiry. The question to ask is, What are the limits to applying such definitions in actual research?

The first kind of criticism then dovetails with the second, that is, with the question of the relationship between choice theory's analytic language on the one hand and the "political world" it purports to explain on the other. The *problem* of this relationship is itself open to interpretation in the philosophy of science (Moe, 1979), but perhaps the most widely accepted view of it postulates the relationship as "a trade-off between simplicity and realism" (Fiorina, 1975: 153). According to this language, the question of a "fit" between theoretical assumptions and "the facts" becomes a question of qualitative judgments about matters of *degree*. On the basis of such an assessment one can see that from Arrow's welfare paradox to Olson's paradox of collective action the formal "impossibility proofs" of public choice theory have been used not primarily as tests of "real events" but as ways of discovering independent variables and inventing explanations for certain classes of action.

To understand the objection to postulation of a "trade-off" requires an example. Consider Olson's formal "proof" that the rational, self-interested member of a large group will not voluntarily contribute to the provision of a collective good. As Kimber has shown, this proof is convincing "only under the somewhat unrealistic assumptions both that A has no information about the behavior of others and that he arbitrarily (and wrongly) assumes he is different from the others" (1981: 192). The result is an argument against provision of public goods in the absence of coercion or other inducements that "is not only intuitively odd, but also conflicts with much of our day-to-day experience," and when applied to actual events appears "absurd" and "whimsical" (Kimber, 1981: 196). Surprisingly, as "model" accounts of the way "rational" individuals act and choose, such formal proofs within public choice have rarely been abandoned. Their formalism as such has not led to their rejection as "hypothetical" or "unreal." This is the case because proponents hold that the "model," resting on explicit assumptions of rationality, can always in principle be defended as a "useful" device for reproducing and clarifying patterns of choice.

But in what sense can it be used this way? Significantly, some critics have insisted that the problems in this regard are not really a matter of degree, but are instead a matter of differences in *kind*. The basic assumptions of choice theory may belong to an idealized, "rational" order of behavior that exists at an enormous distance from the "social" order of action. Consider the concept of "revealed preference"; according to Sen it "essentially underestimates the fact that man is a social animal and his choices are not rigidly bound to his own preferences only." For humans an act of choice is "always a social act," and thus for the choosing individual "behavior is something more than a mere translation of his personal preference" (1982: 62). If this is the case, then the limits of "revealed preference" are determined by investigating the context of explanation in which the concept is employed. Whenever the assumption of transitivity of choice assumed by "revealed preference" is flatly mistaken for human actors in social contexts, the concept will not prove effective for suggesting explanations in that context, although it may still be fruitful in other (primarily microeconomic) domains.

One practical consequence, therefore, of its "idealized" conceptualizations is that public choice has difficulty acknowledging helpful insights developed through contrasting approaches. Even the notion of "choice" may itself become problematic. It is precisely this kind of difficulty that has led writers from a variety of fields to contend "that in its pure form (public choice) is only one useful, partial explanation of politics" (Weschler, 1982: 294). Noting that in public choice "considerable emphasis is placed upon paradoxes, proofs or demonstrations, robustness, generality, abstraction, and manufactured illustrations and problems," Mitchell underscores the conclusion that "much of the work ignores real world institutions and events" and "hardly involves governments, politicians, bureaucrats, and interest groups" (1982:

99). It is fair to say that one powerful source of resistance to public choice is disquiet over its application to political and social policy, where applications are often thought to yield "bizarre conclusions" or dysfunctional suggestions for the quality of public life (DeGregori, 1974; Miller, 1983).

As we have suggested, one reason for these apparently unsatisfactory outcomes is found in the assumptions internal to public choice. But there is another dimension to the problem that leads in the direction of bias or ideological distortion, the third main source of criticism. In this regard we have in mind a tendency that surfaces now and then within public choice either to denigrate "politics" as such for its alleged "inefficiencies" or to employ a public choice rationale in defense of certain approved causes. In a concise summation, one critique refers to the former tendency as "a technical objection to politics, which is seen as characteristically wasteful, ineffective, and subject to corruption," and as an expression of skepticism about government itself, which is "suspect as potentially and uniquely destructive of individual liberty or as inherently incompetent" (Lovrich and Neiman, 1984: 6-7). From this value-perspective public choice can then be expected to counteract governmental intervention and justify "market" solutions to public problems; the "rationality" of choice theory can rescue us from the "irrationalities" of politics.

In addition, one can speak of a "politics" of public choice. Some have characterized the choice approach as offering "an intellectual underpinning for the movement toward increased individualism in American politics" (Weschler, 1982: 188), while others have seen in it an overly prescriptive theory with "a consistent noninterventionist, antiadministration, and 'conservative' bent to it" (DeGregori, 1974: 211; also Baker, 1976; Furniss, 1978). The argument can be carried still further. Public choice has also been accused of concealing an implicit "normative" theory, and one so thoroughly entrenched in a utilitarian viewpoint as to be incapable of taking into account primary ethical issues or rights and duties having a "prima facie moral validity" (Kelman, 1982: 142; and Kelman, 1981). Whichever angle of criticism is emphasized, there can be no doubt that much of the sharp tone in the reaction against public choice is set by these kinds of suspicions concerning prescriptions, recommendations, and normative or ideological bias. At base the suspicion is that public choice, because of its "individualistic" assumptions, is peculiarly suited to advocate and justify a certain range of political choices and policies.

Whether or not such suspicions are well founded, one lesson to draw from this third kind of criticism is that the imposition of public choice prescriptions upon the political process as it is (as distinguished from the way it ought to be, according to reductionist assumptions) will be unlikely to lead to prescribed results such as increased "efficiency" in government (whatever that might mean in practice). Addressing political problems with nonpolitical or "technical" solutions is always a great temptation, but it never leads to the expected results. Stated in condensed form, "politics" always intervenes, introducing unanticipated conditions and leading to unintended results.

In sum, this survey of the leading assumptions and criticisms of rational choice suggests that when applied to political issues, choice theory tends to favor a certain *kind* of politics, one that fits well with the basic assumptions about individual "rationality," calculation of costs and benefits, and the maximization of "efficiency." What we tend to see through the lenses provided by public choice is policy in its most instrumental mode, where the language of direct costs, perceived individual benefits, efficient allocation of resources, and the like is descriptively plausible and satisfactory. Moreover, everything else—for example organizational constraints, bureaucratic forms of domination, and structural causes and effects—tends to be reduced to the very same set of terms, to the identical calculus of "rationality." It should come as no surprise, then, to find that starting from choice theory premises one will end by tending to favor "market" solutions over "planning," or "efficiency" over a competing value like "social justice." Politically, such preferences may be thoroughly defensible; yet they illustrate perfectly the "theory-laden" quality of even those judgments that are seemingly most practical and farthest removed from the influence of theory on what we see.

NOTE

1. In this discussion we propose to use "theory" loosely to mean any set of abstract generalizations for organizing, seeing and explaining the world. We do not attempt to distinguish theory from other closely related forms, such as "conceptual scheme," "framework," "model," and the like. For purposes of this discussion it is sufficient to think of "theory" as distinguished from "fact."

REFERENCES

Allison, Graham T. (1971) Essence of Decision, Explaining the Cuban Missile Crisis. Boston: Little, Brown.

Baker, Keith (1971) "Public Choice Theory: Some Important Assumptions and Public Policy Implications," pp. 42-60 in Robert T. Golembiewski et al. (eds.) Public Administration. (3rd ed.) Chicago: Rand McNally.

Dahl, Robert A. (1961) Who Governs? Democracy and Power in an American City. New Haven, CT: Yale Univ. Press.

DeGregori, Thomas R. (1974) "Caveat Emptor: A Critique of the Emerging Paradigm of Public Choice." Administration and Society 6.

Fiorina, Morris P. (1975) "Formal Models in Political Science," Amer. J. of Pol. Sci. 19: 133-159.

Furniss, Norman (1978) "The Political Implications of the Public Choice-Property Rights School." Amer. Pol. Sci. Rev. 72: 399-410.

Gaventa, John (1980) Power and Powerlessness, Quiescence and Rebellion in an Appalachian Valley. Oxford: Clarendon.

Golembiewski, Robert T. (1977) "A Critique of Democratic Administration and Its Supporting Ideation." Amer. Pol. Sci. Rev. 71: 1488-1507.

Goodin, Robert E. (1976) The Politics of Rational Man. London: John Wiley.

Hanson, Norwood R. (1958) Patterns of Discovery. Cambridge: Cambridge Univ. Press.

Kelman, Steven (1981) What Price Incentives? Economists and the Environment. Boston: Auburn House.

Kelman, Steven (1982) "Cost-Benefit Analysis and Environmental Safety, and Health Regulation: Ethical and Philosophical Considerations," in Daniel Swartzman et al. (eds.) Cost-Benefit Analysis and Environmental Regulations: Politics, Ethics, and Methods. Washington, DC: Conservative Foundation.

Kimber, R. (1981) "Collective Action and the Fallacy of the Liberal Fallacy." World Politics 34.

Kuhn, Thomas S. (1970) The Structure of Scientific Revolutions (2nd ed.) Chicago: Univ. of Chicago Press.

Lovrich, Nicholas P. and Max Neiman (1984) Public Choice Theory in Public Administration, an Annotated Bibliography. New York: Garland.

Lukes, Steven (1974) Power: a Radical View. London: Macmillan.

Machan, Tibor R. (1980) "Rational Choice and Public Affairs." Theory and Decision 12: 229-258.

Miller, Nicholas R. (1983) "Pluralism and Social Choice." Amer. Pol. Sci. Rev. 77: 734-47.
Mitchell, William C. (1982) "Textbook Public Choice: a Review Essay." Public Choice 28:
    97-112.
Moe, Terry M. (1979) "On the Scientific Status of Rational Models," Amer. J. of Pol. Sci.
    23: 215-243.
Sen, Amartya K. (1982) "Rational Fools: a Critique of the Behavioral Foundations of
    Economic Theory," in Choice, Welfare and Measurement. Oxford: Blackwell.
Sproule-Jones, Mark (1982) "Public Choice Theory and Natural Resources: Methodolog-
    ical Explication and Critique." Amer. Pol. Sci. Rev. 76: 790-804.
Weschler, Louis F. (1982) "Public Choice: Methodological Individualism in Politics,"
    Public Administration Rev. 42: 288-294.

9

THE POLITICAL USES OF EVALUATION RESEARCH: COST-BENEFIT ANALYSIS AND THE COTTON DUST STANDARD

S U S A N J. T O L C H I N
George Washington University

CHANGES IN THE REGULATORY ENVIRONMENT: THE ELEVATION OF COST-BENEFIT ANALYSIS AS A VEHICLE FOR PRESIDENTIAL POWER

This didn't happen overnight. The rush to deregulate was industry's answer to double-digit inflation, and its leaders convinced the leaders of both political parties, in the White House and in Congress, that they had a simple way of reducing product costs: reduce the onerous regulations that were often confusing and duplicative, and trust the free market to regulate itself. In the process, the country's leadership forgot that the social regulatory agencies were created in the first place because the free market had failed to provide the necessary safeguards for clean air and water, worker safety and consumer protection.[1]

The "sea change" in regulatory power came about through the efforts of Presidents Jimmy Carter and Ronald Reagan, who both attempted to increase the hegemony of the president over the regulatory agencies in the executive branch. Carter designed the blueprint, while Reagan followed through with an intense commitment to accelerating presidential domination and providing regulatory relief to industry. Shortly after he came to office, President Reagan issued an executive order (EO 12291), modeled after President Carter's EO 12044, granting the Office of Management and Budget (OMB) superagency status over regulations, and mandating economic analysis from the executive branch agencies. It was not a bad idea on paper, but the implementation of the order resulted in vast numbers of regulations being blocked, quashed, or put on permanent hold. The order also had a chilling effect on regulation writing, leaving agencies fearful of issuing new regulations or of introducing too many regulatory initiatives—whether they were needed or not (Tolchin and Tolchin, 1985: Chs. 2 and 3).

Not surprisingly, all too many of the regulations that disappear into what some call the "black hole at OMB" involve public protection—environment, worker safety, and pure food and drugs. In the fall of 1983, for example, OMB temporarily withheld an OSHA regulation restricting worker exposure to the pesticide ethylene dibromide (EDB) (S. Tolchin, 1983: A22). Congressional testimony and court cases have revealed that OMB does much of its regulatory oversight work behind closed doors, meeting privately with industry representatives, and then quietly killing—or forcing the agencies to kill—offending regulations.

OMB's regulatory oversight role remains virtually unknown to the general public, insulating the agency from the kind of political pressure that would moderate its activities. Since many also forget that OMB represents the White House, the president also remains insulated from public accountability for policies—like EDB—that result from presidential efforts to force social deregulation.

OMB justifies its position as superregulator in terms of its primary mission: budgetary constraint and fiscal austerity. Almost any social policy running this gauntlet is bound to reach a preordained outcome, and regulatory policy is no exception. But now there is a respectable methodological rationale: cost-benefit analysis. Reagan's executive order placed heavy reliance on cost-benefit analysis, with informational requirements spelled out in great detail. Agencies were directed, for example, to develop new regulations involving the "least net cost to society," and discouraged from taking regulatory action at all unless the "potential benefits to society. . . . outweigh the potential costs to society." Additional requirements mandated that if an agency wished to issue regulations it had to submit impact analyses showing that the benefits exceeded the costs.

As a tool to rationalize regulatory policy, cost-benefit analysis gave the appearance of neutrality. In reality, the method reflected its masters; a study issued by the Congressional Research Service concluded that the single most important factor determining the outcome of a cost-benefit study was its author (M. Tolchin, 1983). When the authors are also political appointees, the results become even more predictable.

As the primary practitioners of cost-benefit analysis, OMB analysts used cost-benefit analysis to impose an economic grid on social policy, often an impossible task when it came down to the hard decisions involving life, community health and regional stability. It was not the theory itself that created distortions, but the way in which it was subjected to political manipulation. The method was window dressing to the deregulation of social protections, a policy that acquired great credence in the middle 1970s, and continues to enjoy substantial acceptance to this date. The net effect of the wholesale application of cost-benefit analysis to regulatory policy led to the reordering of national priorities away from clean air and water, safe workplaces, and consumer protection to the more politically immediate values of the marketplace. It also marked the ascendance of economists in the policy process, who conducted a form of regulatory oversight that habitually subordinated the technical and legal judgment of the agencies to a different perspective.

THE COTTON DUST CASE

The cotton dust regulations represented only one of many health and safety issues subjected to the standards of cost-benefit analysis, and its history reflects the unique involvement of the three branches of government. Sadly, for the vast majority of regulatory issues, there is little likelihood of the kind of public debate that opened up the regulatory issue to public scrutiny.

The landmark 1981 U.S. Supreme Court cotton dust case (*American Textile Manufacturers Institute v. Donovan*) came as a shock to the yet unchallenged regulatory "reform" movement, which by that time had become almost synonymous with the imposition of cost-benefit analysis to social regulation. By refocusing attention to the requirements of the statute, the Supreme Court forced decision makers from their economic gridlock back to legal basics. For even though the economists who rose to dominance in the Carter and Reagan administrations paid lip service to the phrase "unless specifically prohibited by law," they tended to pressure agencies to utilize cost-benefit analysis regardless of the legal constraints, often disregarding the clear intent of the Congress. (In fact, in hearings before a House of Representatives subcommittee investigating EO 12291, two White House officials in charge of regulatory reform were unable to identify legislation that either prohibited or allowed cost-benefit analysis.)[2]

The cotton dust rules first came under siege during the Nixon administration, when OSHA Administrator George Guenther sent a memo urging his GOP bosses in the White House to use the threat of a "Democratic-imposed cotton-dust standard" as a means of raising contributions for President Nixon's reelection campaign (Regulation, 1981: 5). The pattern of presidential intervention continued for the next decade; the clout of three presidents a formidable obstacle in the path of resolving the issue. Not as crass, but just as political, officials in the Carter administration also tried to use the cotton dust rules to curry favor with the textile companies. This set them on a collision course with the administrator of OSHA, Dr. Eula Bingham, whose personal commitment and professional background in public health enabled her eventually to prevail over White House economic advisers who regarded the cotton dust standards as inflationary. Secretary of Labor Ray Marshall was also instrumental in convincing the President to withdraw his opposition to the cotton dust rules. In the meantime, Carter's attempt to intervene to modify the standards in favor of the textile industry created an unexpectedly intense reaction from labor unions and public interest groups. From that time on, Carter was careful to cover his tracks when he intervened in a regulatory decision (S. Tolchin, 1979: 45).

Carter's advisers argued that the proposed engineering standards were too costly and the health benefits too low to justify the regulations. They favored regulations that set broad performance standards, allowing industry to decide how to address the problem rather than defining the specific actions to be taken. The results would be the same, and the costs would be considerably less, they argued. Instead of forcing industry to install expensive engineering systems, companies would be allowed to formulate their own methods. The textile industry favored techniques requiring workers to wear respirators to reduce exposure to cotton dust in the work place.

OSHA rejected the respirator idea, arguing that respirators caused severe physical discomfort as well as safety problems of their own. Workers already afflicted with lung disease were unable to wear respirators at all (Federal Register, 1978). Besides, the agency added, it was unfair to put the burden of compliance on the workers, who were not responsible for the poor quality of their work environment.

A compromise was finally struck between OSHA and the White House, and the regulations went forward in 1978. Nobody was happy with the compromise, neither the textile industry nor the labor unions, and both groups took their objections to court. In fact, the industry based its entire case on cost-benefit analysis, claiming that OSHA's standards were invalid because the agency had not shown that the costs of compliance ($656.5 million by OSHA's estimates) were justified by the benefits. This meant that "permissible exposure levels for different segments of the industry be structured according to cost-effectiveness considerations . . . OSHA had agreed to prescribe levels that varied from 0.2 to 0.75 milligrams to different stages of cotton processing" (Regulation, 1981: 5).

The struggle illuminated the deficiencies of the implementation of the cost-benefit standard as the sole criterion for regulating decision making. White House economists, for example, in weighing costs against benefits invariably tipped the scales in favor of costs, ignoring other forms of analysis—political, demographic, scientific—in their scheme. They also neglected in the process to factor in the costs of inaction: increased illness, for example, would surely lead to lowered productivity and increased medical expenses over the long term.

In any case, the limitations of the cost-benefit standard became even clearer when the data gaps emerged. On the health risks, for example, widely disparate views appeared on both sides. The textile industry claimed that byssinosis—or brown lung disease— wasn't all that serious; that only 2% of the workers were affected by cotton dust; and that the disease was easily treatable if caught in its early stages.

OSHA disagreed. The agency's studies showed that brown lung disease was common among textile workers, and in its most disabling form had afflicted at least 35,000 employed and retired cotton workers. More than 100,000 more still suffer from less severe forms of the disease, while one-quarter of the 864,000 people currently employed in cotton production are exposed to cotton dust.

One year later, the United States Court of Appeals for the District of Columbia upheld the regulations, with Chief Judge David L. Bazelon writing the opinion. Citing medical journals, government studies and legislative testimony, Judge Bazelon bridged the data gap. "Byssinosis," he wrote, "is the most serious health hazard for cotton workers. . . . when byssinosis reaches its advanced stage, the worker exhibits the symptoms of emphysema and chronic bronchitis. Ultimately, irreversible lung damage results" (AFL-CIO v. Marshall, 1979).

While the case was pending before the Supreme Court, the Reagan administration took office. The time was ripe for another presidential intervention in the name of cost-benefit analysis. The Reagan administration, unencumbered by obligations to labor unions, OSHA officials, and public interest groups committed to the cotton dust standards, asked the Supreme Court not to review the case, but to send it back to the Department of Labor for reconsideration in light of the President's regulatory reform policy. In effect, the executive branch in an unprecedented action, was asking the court to withdraw its exercise of judicial review in favor of a presidential policy—in which the Supreme Court struck down OSHA's standards regulating the chemical benzene—and expected to reap the benefits of that precedent (Industrial Union Department v. American Petroleum Institute, 1980). In the benzene decision, the court held that OSHA had not justified the new standards by showing that there was a significant health risk, nor had it demonstrated that the standards were feasible technologically as well as economically.

The Supreme Court rejected Reagan's request and upheld Judge Bazelon's decision. The OSHA statute, wrote Justice William Brennan for the majority, allowed the agency to protect the public against health risks "restricted only by technological and economic feasibility," a more flexible criterion than cost-benefit analysis, as interpreted by the political leadership (AFL-CIO v. Marshall: ii).

Justice Brennan's reminder that "Congress itself defined the basic relationship between costs and benefits, by placing the 'benefit' of the worker's health above all other considerations save those making attainment of this 'benefit' unachievable" restored some of the balance between Congress and the president in the implementation of legislation. The application of cost-benefit analysis to increase the discretionary power of the executive branch in this case—as in many other instances of regulatory power—distorted the intention of the Congress, as well as the equilibrium between the two branches. Drawing heavily from the Act's legislative history, Brennan's decision made the subordination of cost-benefit analysis to legislative intent very clear: "Any standard based on a balancing of cost and benefits by the Secretary (of Labor) that strikes a different balance would be inconsistent with the command set forth in the statute" (AFL-CIO v. Marshall: ii).

THE FEASIBILITY STANDARD
AS AN ALTERNATIVE

The concept of feasibility enabled the court to reject industry's claims in much the same way OSHA had earlier rejected the union's proposal for more stringent standards on the grounds that the proposal was not within the "technological capabilities of the industry." Feasible meant capable of being done, executed, or effected (American Textile: 16-17). OSHA was not under any obligation to consider the ratio of costs and benefits while it was still feasible to reduce health risks, said the Court.

Interestingly, the textile industry never really argued that reducing the risks from cotton dust was not feasible, only that it was expensive. Indeed, it did not appear that any of the petitioners feared going out of business as a result of cleaning up their workplace. What they feared was a future without the cost-benefit criterion, or a "serious misallocation of the finite resources that are available for the protection of worker safety and health" (American Textile: 17).

How finite? To some extent, Congress and the courts agreed with the textile industry. The workers would not be protected if their employees were put out of business. Where Congress and the courts diverged from the White House was in their broader interpretation of degree: Some businesses would suffer economically from the imposition of cotton dust standards, but that was to be the price of reducing risk. "Standards do not become infeasible simply because they may impose substantial costs on an industry..." wrote Judge Bazelon, "otherwise the Act's commitment to protect workers might be forever frustrated" (AFL-CIO v. Marshall: 36).

Or any Act's commitment, for that matter. What is there to prevent a president from subverting the intent of any piece of legislation with which he disagreed merely by imposing criteria that create obstacles in the path of statutory goals? Ultimately, the feasibility standard resulted in a more humane calculus than the cost-benefit ratio, which too often locks decision makers into the position of trying to quantify the impossible. The Secretary of

Labor recognized this, said the Supreme Court, in "realizing that any meaningful balance between costs and benefits involved placing a dollar value on human life and freedom from suffering."

In the final analysis, the Court did not decide among competing theories of policy making, but among competing interpretations of the role of OSHA. The power of the Court is derivative, superseded by the intent and the laws of Congress. But because neither the intent nor the laws are crystal clear, the court serves an important function in reconciling the actions of the executive branch with the policy directions set by Congress.

What was significant about the cotton dust decision was not that the Court rejected cost-benefit analysis (it did not) but that it raised questions about the legitimacy of its application in all areas of regulation. "When Congress intended that an agency engage in cost-benefit analysis, it has clearly indicated such intent on the face of the statute," wrote Justice Brennan (American Textile: 17-18). The implications of the Court's decision were both far-reaching and, to a certain extent, confusing. Did the decision intend that when Congress meant cost-benefit analysis to be used as a decision making tool it would have to be stated clearly in the statute or it would be prohibited? Or would the prohibition also have to be clearly stated? What impact would this have on the executive orders of Presidents Carter and Reagan—neither of which has been put to a comprehensive judicial test—which superimposed cost-benefit analysis on agencies except where specifically prohibited?

What was left unanswered by both the Court's decisions and the legislation is what would happen if the choices were harder; if they were presented in the form of their logical extremes? What if the textile industry were so marginal that the imposition of the cotton dust standards would bring about its extinction? At what point, if any, is it worth sacrificing the health of a certain percentage of the workers to the health of the industry? What if it wee not 'feasible' to protect the health of the worker and the health of the companies? What then? Who sacrifices: the worker or the industry?

Neither the feasibility nor the cost-benefit guidelines provide an answer to those questions, and the Court enjoyed the luxury of deciding the case with the comfortable assurance that "although some marginal employers may shut down rather than comply, the industry as a whole [would] not be threatened by the capital requirements of the regulation" (American Textile: 33). In that sense, perhaps even cost-benefit analysis, with the benefits properly quantified, would have led to a decision to uphold the cotton dust standards, especially when the healthy costs of not regulating became sufficiently apparent to establish their correct weight in the equation.

HOW THEORY DRIVES POLICY: THE POLITICAL DOMINATION OF COST FACTORS

In spite of its impact at the time, the Supreme Court decision on cotton dust appears to have had little impact on patterns of regulatory decision making under the Reagan administration, which continued inexorably to rely heavily on the cost-benefit analysis calculus to deregulate the social environment.[3] Congress, for example, has changed considerably from the heady days of the early 1970, when a favorable social and economic climate made it possible for progressive social goals to be written into law. Indeed, Congress's commitment to cost-benefit analysis is regularly expressed in drafts of regulatory reform legislation, submitted each year since 1978, which virtually replicate President Reagan's executive order. All versions of the proposed legislation mandate a series of complicated steps of requiring agencies to do extensive and detailed cost-benefit analysis before issuing regulations. Adding these steps to agency procedures creates obstacles that virtually guarantee a dignified burial for many new regulatory policies, and contribute to the already weakened state of the Federal agencies.

Add to the congressional legitimization of cost-benefit analysis the clout of two Presidents and their executive orders, and the theory's hegemony over the policy process becomes almost complete. All told, it spells an era of minimal regulation, even when the law clearly states otherwise. And, indeed, even when the courts rules otherwise, executive power countermanded the decision. Within weeks after the Supreme Court handed down its decision on cotton dust, the Reagan administration's OSHA director, Thorne Auchter, ordered the withdrawal from circulation of two publications and a poster warning workers of the health hazards of cotton dust. His reason: The literature no longer represented agency policy.

The President and Congress reflected the political power of groups that brought cost-benefit analysis to the forefront of the policy process, once again affirming the axiom that those who dominate the formulation of an issue also dominate the end product. The groups that promoted cost-benefit theory determined how it would be applied; they also formed the nucleus of a political leadership that successfully compressed the issue of social regulation into an artificial set of guidelines, as restrictive in their own way as the regulations they sought to reduce. In so doing, they were able to construct a scheme that looked neat, appeared to factor in all the options, and seemed neutral to the naked eye. Reducing policy to numbers made people feel comfortable; the process gave a sense of clarity to issues that had heretofore defied easy definition.

Despite rare challenges like the cotton dust case, current trends indicate the growing respectability and receptivity to cost-benefit analysis as a dominant regulatory tool. This is largely due to the substantial political power of its proponents, which far exceeds that of its critics, so that the advantages and disadvantages of cost-benefit analysis are never fully aired. Moreover, the vagaries of the economy convey an immediacy that renders short-term cost factors more acceptable and more urgent in the policy arena than long-term health and safety risks, and narrows the criteria for public intervention to the framework of cost-benefit analysis. In its application, the method has become even more circumscribed than when the public sector enjoyed the dividends of a buoyant economy.

In fact, when transposed to the public sector, cost-benefit analysis often turns out to be nothing more than cost analysis, a simple accounting of the costs of doing business. This form of analysis basically derives from the profit and loss ledgers of the private sector, where costs and profits are balanced each year to determine the fiscal health of a company. The benefit side of the equation, the firm's profits, are easily measurable, unlike the benefit side of public policy. In the private sector a firm's obligations rest primarily with its own well-being, and only secondarily with society or the well-being of its employees.

Worrying about what happens when the firm's efforts to maximize profits result in harm to society is the job of the public sector. The government is there to restrict the firm's freedom when the effects of doing business "spill over" into polluting the environment or creating hazards in the work place. In that context, the government quite legitimately puts its emphasis on the social costs of industrial practices in its efforts to regulate the private sector.

The problem is that on the government side, clear-cut statements of profit (benefits) and loss (costs) are extremely difficult to quantify. And so the calculations simply do not get done. Or they are done in a biased fashion that justifies what the policy makers wanted to do in the first place, namely, deregulate social protections. At that point it becomes easier, as factors conducive to measurement become weighted more heavily than those that elude the calculator. Recent applications of cost-benefit analysis to the public sector reveal their private sector limitations: Benefits are rarely factored fully or accurately into the equation, and costs are more often than not calculated for the short term, neglecting long-term productivity and health costs.

COST-BENEFIT FOR WHOM?
THE LOSERS IN SOCIAL DEREGULATION

In the debate over regulatory choices, the political protagonists argued that since benefits could not be measured accurately, they should be downgraded in the policy equation. Since evidence of benefits is needed to justify costs, it is easy to see how the cost advocates quickly prevailed over fellow analysts in scaling down the regulatory process.

Before benefits can be measured, they must be identified—a task that has been shunted aside with the same alacrity as their measurement. The genuine identification of benefits moves closer to the crux of the political problem: the struggle over which funds are expected and for whom.

The most common pattern, when benefits cannot be easily measured, is to discard or to trivialize them. "How do you put a value on the view over the Grand Canyon?" asked vice presidential aide Boyden Gray when queried about the methodology in which his administration had vested so much of its resources. It can't be done, but, at the same time, the answer masks the real issues. On the surface, it is easy to agree that it is not really worth the expenditure of billions of dollars to preserve the view over the Grand Canyon for the benefit of tourists and their visual pleasure. Putting the question another way, however, lends a less frivolous cast to the issue. What is it worth to maintain air purity in the southwest? After all, the air mass over the Grand Canyon does not stop at the boundaries of that giant crevice; it moves with the wind currents, and affects vast numbers of people, most of whom are not out enjoying their holidays.

Benefits like the view over the Grand Canyon often elude cost-benefit practitioners even when they are not trivialized by decision makers like Boyden Gray. These benefits elude measurement because they are often indivisible: If one person benefits, all benefit. How can one measure benefits like clean air and water, good health, a minimum of pain, economic stability, wilderness preservation, and national defense? Because of the difficulties of measurement, very few researchers have attempted to measure benefits. A notable example is Nicholas A. Ashford (1981), of the Massachusetts Institute of Technology. In a valuable study prepared for the Senate Governmental Affairs Committee, Ashford concluded that "the American people save billions of dollars each year as a direct result of federal regulation in the areas of health, safety and the environment" (U.S. Senate Governmental Affairs Committee, 1980).

The benefits in question are referred to as "public goods;" they are non-purchasable, and for that reason no single group can enjoy their special protection.[4] For that reason they also lack defenders, a political problem that recurs continually in the regulatory arena.

The trend toward downgrading benefits also leads to the question of cost benefit for whom? Who are the true beneficiaries of public policy tilted toward the cost side of the cost-benefit equation? The polluters are the definite victors in the battle to dismantle EPA: They have increased their short-term profits and decreased their capital expenditures for antipollution equipment. The strip miners in Appalachia have emerged the winners in the recent reorganization of the Office of Surface Mining, a bureau now less inclined to enforce federal legislation preventing the gutting of the land. And if the court had not stepped in, the textile industry would have been counted among the victors in the battle over their notion of benefits, namely, profits versus the health of their employees.

In one of its more enlightened periods, Congress recognized the political conundrums of social regulation, among with the fallacies of cost-benefit analysis. With specific recognition of its inadequacies in providing equal weight to benefits, Congress prohibited the calculation of costs in certain pieces of legislation. In addition to the legislation creating OSHA, Congress also required 'unbalanced' decisions in the Clean Air and Water Acts, as well as other legislation in the social regulatory area. In that way, Congress protected the agencies from succumbing to the familiar pattern of the "captive agencies," those economic regulatory agencies whose officials often became too closely tied to the industries they were responsible for regulating. Implicitly, Congress was also recognizing the different time horizons distinguishing the public and private sectors, with government more willing to build in protections for future generations.

REBUILDING THE EQUATION

In lieu of costs and benefits, there are other questions that are rarely asked by the current practitioners of regulatory policy. Judge David Bazelon (1981: 7-8) whose decisions have consistently stood well ahead of his time, addressed some of them. "The efficiency label," he wrote, "may frequently mask special benefits for special interests. The real questions should be more qualitative ones. Who will be affected? In what ways? On what bases are these predictions made?"

Invariably, those who ask the questions get first crack at making the choices. With cost-benefit analysis the marketplace essentially makes the regulatory choices, since it is business's needs that are most often addressed and given priority, and business's information that form the basis for decisions. Time after time, the costs are exaggerated, and the risks minimized, even though both categories often fall in the realm of the unknown. In the cotton dust case, industry argued that brown lung disease was reversible, that it affected an infinitesimal percentage of the workers, and that controlling it would place an unfair burden upon their companies. It took two outside consulting firms, employed by OSHA, as well as the separate evaluation of that evidence by two levels of federal courts to refute industry's contention.

Not every regulatory decision gets the benefit of that kind of scrutiny; more often, industry data are the only game in town, and heavy reliance is placed upon their findings. Even when the data are essentially correct, the interpretation of them can distort the conclusions. Chrysler makes a good case against the burdens of regulation, for example, that is shared by the other major auto companies, namely, that energy regulation, safety rules, and environmental standards have made them less competitive than Japanese auto makers (Clarkson et al., 1979: 44-51). Omitted from that argument is the fact that the Japanese companies are subject to the same regulations if their cars are to be sold on the American market; they must install the same catalytic converters, safety belts, and other devices mandated by the government as the

American companies. Also omitted are other key factors—such as government support, management, and investment strategies—that enabled the Japanese to pull ahead of their American competitors while adhering to similar regulatory ground rules.

Not only are there gaps in the available data, but there are vast realms in which the data needed for intelligent regulatory decisions simply do not exist. Cutting the EPA research budget in half, as President Reagan did in his first year in office, merely exacerbates the problem of the data gap: it will ensure less regulation, because the agency cannot regulate without research. Meanwhile, over 60,000 chemicals have now been identified, with an additional 1,000 added each year. Few of these have been adequately researched—their effects are often unknown until years later. Still, the public risks their release into the environment with uneven protection from the public sector. The effects of the synthetic hormone DES (diethylstilbestrol), given to pregnant women to prevent miscarriage, were not known until 20 years after their prescription; the drug failed to prevent miscarriage, but has since been related to cancer in the offspring of those who unwittingly took the drug. In this case, the drug companies did not know the effects, since no benefit or risk data were available.

The tendency to ignore the unmeasurable in the cost-benefit calculus shifts many of these regulatory decisions to the courts, where the limits of the law parallel those of science. "The role of the court," said Judge Bazelon in an interview with the author,

is to ensure that proper procedures have been followed and that the agencies utilize the best available data before issuing regulations. Agencies should announce in words of one syllable what they've done, and why they're doing it. The problem is that there are deep uncertainties. In Vermont Yankee (a case involving nuclear waste), the Nuclear Regulatory Commission gave us only in-house experts. They said, in 100 years we'll have the answer. I said their procedures were inadequate. There was no cross-examination, for example. I was reversed. There weren't enough smart people around in 1973 to know disposal would be a problem. The record was inadequate because there were inadequate opinions.[5]

Facing the unknown also leads the more extreme among the free market advocates to argue for less regulation on the grounds that liability laws will protect the public from irresponsible corporate behavior. Given the condition of uncertainty surrounding this body of law, their assessment is unfair from the public and private sector's points of view. "Such uncertainty makes a finding of negligence liability unlikely, inappropriate, and therefore ineffective in protecting society from these dangers," argued Judge Bazelon (1981: 7-8).

For liability laws to have some effect, blame must be attached to an individual or to a company. Very often it is impossible to trace a pollutant to its source; more often, its effects may not be felt for years. Even if the source can be determined and blame properly affixed, the company may long since have gone out of business and be unable to pay damages. In addition, a company may also have fully protected itself from subsequent legal damages, as did the Hooker Chemical Company when it turned over the Love Canal property to the local school board, which was duly warned of the health hazards. Witness also the decision by the Manville Corporation, the nation's largest asbestos producer, to file for bankruptcy protection to avoid 17,000 asbestos-related damage suits.

Who pays for the consequences of these acts? In the case of Love Canal, the government of New York State, aided by the federal coffer, paid the damages for the private sector. In the case of the asbestos manufacturers, the jury is still out, but discussions among members of Congress involving the creation of worker compensation funds indicate that the government once again will probably step in to pick up the tab.

To be fair, companies may innocently produce products whose toxicity may be uncovered at a much later date. If they remove these products from the market immediately after their hazards are revealed, as Proctor and Gamble did following reports linking the Rely tampon to toxic shock syndrome, should the company then be liable for damages in the thousands of legal suits that now plague them? No one really knows the answer, but recent evidence shows that juries are more sympathetic to the plaintiffs, spelling potential financial disaster for many manufacturers.

What of the less responsible companies—the fly-by-night operations polluting the air and water—who are as elusive to prosecutors as the chemicals they leave for society to clean up? The midnight dumpers, who leave toxic wastes in dump sites of their own choosing, are as difficult to apprehend as they are to identify. How do liability laws protect the public against them? Once again, the government ends up paying for the cleanup, but should this be included as a cost of regulation? Any cost analysis would show that careful regulation and enforcement at an early stage are much cheaper than cleanup costs later on. Not to mention the health costs, which are rarely factored into the equation.

In the final analysis, the dominance of cost-benefit analysis over regulatory policy shunts aside the management of risk and negates the government's role in managing risk. Although we cannot achieve a risk-free society, government is the only agent with the capacity to protect the public against untoward risk, and it remains the only agent whose purpose is to protect the public. Industry cannot be trusted to make these determinations, and should not be accorded the legitimacy to make those decisions. The task of a firm is to make profits, not public policy, and there is no justification to fault its social consciousness if it neglects to weigh considerations other than self-promotion. It is up to the regulatory system, with guidance from Congress, to make policy decisions and to provide the constraints necessary to preserve the public's interests. Moreover, the political system, unlike the private sector, makes its policy in the open; its deliberations are guaranteed by law to be open to public debate and to public view. Though often flawed, its policies are also open to change, when change is warranted.

Although cost-benefit analysis can be useful in determining the most cost-effective alternative among competing regulatory devices, it should be removed as a dominant policy tool for being inadequate, inequitable, and subject to excessive political distortion in its application. In the private sector, it has led to discussions and decisions of chilling proportions, such as the decision to market the Pinto, which weighed profits against safety in designing an automobile.

It is, indeed, surprising that decision making of this kind has achieved the level of respectability it enjoys today. Ultimately, it omits the human factor, with unfortunate results for those who count on government protection. As a victim of industrial lung disease testified: "Dying is a tough way to make a living."

NOTES

1. Much of the material for this article was drawn from *Dismantling America—The Rush to Deregulate* (Tolchin and Tolchin, 1983). See Chapter 4.

2. During the congressional hearings on the Reagan regulatory reform program, specifically Executive Order 12291, two of the order's principal architects occasionally demonstrated ignorance of which statutes required cost-benefit analysis and which specifically prohibited it. A few extracts from the hearings indicate the embarrassing result:

> DINGELL: Can you tell us . . . whether you did any research to find out which of these (acts) were subject to this cost-benefit analysis and which were not, before the orders were issued:

> MILLER: The answer is no.

> DINGELL: Well, you seem to be in the rather anomalous position of having an order which you defend vigorously but not being able to tell us who might think on the basis of their own research that it applies to them.

At the same hearing, which followed the Supreme Court decision, the Reagan appointees still insisted with total disregard of the court decision that cost-benefit analysis would be applied to OSHA regulations.

> GORE: Are you going to insist that OSHA apply a cost-benefit test to new regulation issued pursuant to section 6 (b) of OSHA?

> MILLER: Yes . . . in the following sense: first, to the degree that the decision is relevant . . . and, second, the executive order requires certain analyses be done with respect to the lowest-cost way of meeting any given objective. [House Subcommittee on Oversight and Investigations, 1981].

3. Throughout this article cost-benefit analysis is referred to as both a method and a theory, where appropriate. To be sure, it is utilized in both contexts. As a theory it can be distinguished from classical models of politics, where consensus prevails as the decision rule. Instead, cost-benefit analysis substitutes economic efficiency as the rule (in maximizing the net present value of the benefits); and as such it tilts the normative preference to efficiency. In addition, the logic and normative biases of cost-benefit analysis as a theory inexorably lead to a methodological framework, which includes (1) objective

function, (2) choice set, (3) constraints, (4) classification of subjects and costs, (5) their valuation with prices, (6) discounting of present values, and (7) summation as a ratio of net benefit. (For several excellent references on this issue, see Haveman and Margolis, 1977; U.S. Congress, Joint Economic Committee, 1969; Burkhead and Miner, 1971; and Mishan, 1971).

4. A body of literature in economics and political science has developed around the theory of public goods. Olson, (1965) points out that people are not inclined to actively promote the securing of public goods; nor do they avoid public bads. See also Hardin's work (1968: 1243-1248) on the "commons," a metaphor of a medieval English village in which cattle owners, by overgrazing their cows on the "common," ruined the pasture for everyone.

5 Bazelon's decision, subsequently overturned and remanded by the Supreme Court, faulted the NRC for failing to "come to grips with the limits of its knowledge" and giving "no serious response to criticisms brought to its attention. No technical oversight within the agency was demonstrated, and no peer review by the expert community at large was possible."

REFERENCES

43 Federal Register 27, 384 (1978).

AFL-CIO v. Marshall (1979) 617 F. 2d 636.

Allen, Julius (1978) "Costs and Benefits of Federal Regulation: An Overview." Congressional Research Service, LOC Report 78-152 E, July 19: 16-17.

American Textile Manufacturers Institute v. Donovan (1981) 101 U.S. 2478

Ashford, Nicholas A. (1981) "Alternatives to Cost-Benefit Analysis in Regulatory Decisions." Annals of the New York Academy of Science 363 (April): 129-138.

Brazelon, David L. (1979) "Risk and Democracy." Presented at the National Academy of Engineering, Washington, DC, November 1.

Bazelon, David L. (1981). "Science and Uncertainty: The Regulation of Health Risks." Presented at the Health Policy Forum, Harvard School of Public Health, May 4: 7-8.

Burkhead, Jesse and Jerry Miner (1971). Public Expenditure, Chicago: Aldine Atherton.

Clarkson, Kenneth W., Charles W. Kadlec, and Arthur B. Laffer (1979). "Regulating Chrysler Out of Business," Regulation (September/October): 44-51.

Hardin, Garrett (1968) "The Tragedy of the Commons." Science (December 13): 1243-1248.

Haveman, Robert H., and Julius Margolis [eds.] (1977) Public Expenditure and Policy Analysis. Chicago: Rand McNally.

Industrial Union Department v. American Petroleum Institute (1980) 440 U.S. S. Ct. 2844, 65 L. Ed. 2d 1010.

Mishan, E. J. (1971) Cost Benefit Analysis, New York: Praeger.

National Resources Defense Council, Inc., and Consolidated National Intervenors, Petitioners, v. United States of America, Respondents, Baltimore Gas and Electric Co., et al., Intervenors (1976) 547 F 2d 633.

Olson, Mancur (1965) The Logic of Collective Action, Cambridge, MA: Harvard Univ. Press.

Regulation (1981) "Perspectives on Current Development: The Cotton Dust Case." (January/February): 5.

Tolchin, Martin (1983) "Regulations and the Economist." New York Times, November 20.

Tolchin, Susan J. (1979). "Presidential Power and the Politics of RARG." Regulation (July/August): 45.

Tolchin, Susan J. (1983) "The Damage OMB is Doing." Washington Post (November 28): A22.

Tolchin, Susan J. and Martin Tolchin (1985) Dismantling America—The Rush to Deregulate. New York: Oxford Univ. Press.

U.S. Congress, Joint Economic Committee (1969) The PPB System, 91st Congress, First Session.

U.S. House Subcommittee on Oversight and Investigations, Committee on Energy and Commerce (1981) "OMB: The Role of the Office of Management and Budget in Regulation." (June 19): 149-50:"

U.S. Senate Committee on Governmental Affairs (1980) "Benefits of Environmental, Health and Safety Regulation." 96th Congress, second session. (March 25) Washington, DC: Government Printing Office.

Vermont Yankee Nuclear Power Corp. v. NRDC (1978) 435 U.S. 519 and NRDC, 685 F. 2d 459 (1982).

10

THE POLITICS OF MEANING
AND POLICY INQUIRY

R I T A M A E K E L L Y

Arizona State University

Policy inquiry is like science in that it is never truly existential, but rather must be grounded in terms of the cognitive reality of models and working hypotheses. As a consequence, researchers typically depend on theories, ideologies, and politics for their interpretations of the meaning to be ascribed to these. When neither theory nor ideology is available to determine the meaning of human acts and actions, then a politics of meaning necessarily arises. In evaluation research the necessity to conduct inquiry from within an abstracted conceptual framework means that the reality depicted and evaluated often does not reflect the actuality that is lived and perceived by those close to the program, the agency being evaluated, or the people being served unless special efforts are made to make it do so.

In evaluation and applied social science research, difficulties exist in establishing correspondence between empirical behavior and the meanings such behavior, acts, or data have for those participating in the acts. In policy inquiry the absence of a body of disciplinary theory from which meanings can be independently derived facilitates wide-ranging negotiations and power plays over the meanings given to goals and the content of performance measurement and monitoring systems, official records, and success indicators.

In this article I first highlight how a politics of meaning is involved in various stages of the evaluation process. Second, I examine the development of the applied social science approach to policy inquiry and point out some of the elements embedded in the logic of this approach that contribute to the use of politics to define our meanings and conceptual frameworks. Third, I present an analysis of how our liberal philosophical heritage supports a particular kind of politics of meaning. Fourth, I examine selected postpositivist efforts to address the contradictions within the liberal world view and assess commonalities among them. And finally, I explore how an alternative conception of the meaning of politics might help make sense out of recent developments in the logic of policy inquiry and postpositivist methodology and facilitate the advancement of the policy sciences.

THE POLITICS OF MEANING
IN THE EVALUATION PROCESS

Politics has been defined in numerous ways. Easton (1953), for example, equated it with "the authoritative allocation of values." Hart (1961) emphasized persuasion and the activities surrounding the bending and ignoring of rules. Frohock (1978) has explored politics as a cluster concept with structure. In this article politics refers primarily to "bargaining transactions, maximizing actions, criteria-establishing negotiations" (Frohock, 1978: 859), but also encompasses rule-permissiveness and disputes over the allocation of values and substance.

"Meaning" is used in a straightforward manner, to denote the idea conveyed to the mind, the interpretation given a term and its empirical referent. A "politics of meaning" exists when bargaining and negotiating over the specification of concepts and particular indicators takes place. It also exists when an authoritative decision from an elected or appointed official determines substantive content, or makes decisions that give that right to a specific person or group.

THE GOAL-SETTING STAGE

Evaluators often assert that programs with clearly stated goals are essential in order to conduct evaluations. Embedded within this assertion is an assumption that one or more selected groups' meanings and values ought to be used to hold a program or agency accountable. Agreement on goals is most probable in economic and physically concrete areas, for example, dollars expended and services provided. But psychological aspects of program performance such as client satisfaction and political ones such as the impact of the program on the distribution of power in the community are more nebulous (Kelly, 1980).

Client-centered organizations generally have more difficulty defining clearly stated goals than hierarchical, management oriented ones. Windle and Keppler-Seid (1984: 12) confirm that "This greater compatibility of measurement approaches with hierarchical structures leads to evaluations being oriented toward and accepting the structural constraints of the system being evaluated." Working within the hierarchy makes for a more efficient research operation. It also conceals the fact that a decision with political implications has been made as to whose values and interpretations of goals will guide the evaluation. When the goals of the program managers alone are considered by evaluators, political preference has been given to those managing the program. Similarly, if preference is given to the goals of the oversight agency, then the evaluators have in effect accepted the assumption that the values and interpretations of that agency are better for the public's and the program's well-being than are the values and interpretations of those managing the program or of the clients themselves.

Evaluations that are conducted from a goal-free basis or from the perspective of citizens, clients, or multiple stakeholders, such as program staff, taxpayers, and program competitors usually require a systems perspective. In such circumstances the specification of goals and meaning given to indicators and measures often becomes both more difficult and, if done inadequately, more obviously political. When done well, such evaluations tend to be more comprehensive, including unintended consequences and a broad range of values. In such circumstances preliminary ethnographic studies of the meanings that key concepts and goals have for various stakeholders are needed.

POLITICS OF MEANING
AND OFFICIAL RECORDS

The basic data used in many evaluations come from the official records of the program being evaluated. While this usage is cost-efficient, it introduces politics into the meaning given to measures. As Campbell (1979: 85) has noted, "The more any quantitative social indicator is used for social decision making, the more subject it will be to corruption pressures and the more apt it will be to distort and corrupt the social processes it is intended to monitor."

Information is power—a major instrument in power struggles. Within organizations those persons who control the sources of information and who can manipulate its meaning typically wield substantial influence. In times of great competition the communication of information can cause a loss of power and money. Quantitative information that can be used to monitor agencies and programs tend to reduce the freedom of the managers within those agencies and programs by facilitating accountability. If particular indicators are linked to funding, the concern of managers for the interpretation given those key indicators rises. Hence, managers have a strong interest in determining the meaning that any indicator or statistic might have. Interorganizational battles over definitions typically occur when the party receiving the information might be given added ability to control the agency.

Self-reporting by programs and agencies can also lead to propagandistic and other types of self-serving statements that distort the meaning of data. Records are produced within given social contexts by particular individuals who typically have a vested interest in them. McCleary (1984: 23) asserts that "Where possible, the worker will use a statistic not as a statistic but, rather, as an instrument to reduce the workload."

Ginsberg (1984) has enumerated the many ways official records can be manipulated to accomplish one objective while the defined meaning the records are supposed to have is obfuscated. For example, therapists often record an hour of therapy when only a half hour has been given so that a client's insurance will cover the total cost. Hospital patients with no or poor health insurance are declared "well" several days before patients with excellent health insurance, and so forth. As Ginsberg notes, evaluators examining the raw data on length of hospitalization in different hospitals and for different patients might well misinterpret the meaning of the data. Rather than signifying anything about the patients or their illness or even the quality of treatment received, the data "describe only administrative convenience in the face of regulatory restraint and third-party coverage" (Ginsberg, 1984: 68). Such behavior is part of the politics of implementing regulations, acceptable for political and administrative reasons even though the meaning of the data has been distorted.

POLITICS OF MEANING
IN PERFORMANCE MEASUREMENT SYSTEMS

Recent studies of performance measurement and monitoring (PMM) systems (see Windle, 1984, for several summaries of such studies) reveal that politics is intimately interwoven into these systems. Politics is particularly evident in those stages where meaning is to be given to specific indicators. Kimmel (1984: 108-116) completed a comparative study of state mental health program performance measurement systems from three states— Pennsylvania, Colorado, and Tennessee. His findings led him to conclude that value judgments and political trade-offs were integral parts of the PMM systems. To keep the PMM systems responsive "to changing politico-bureaucratic conditions and evolving service philosophy and ideology are important" (Kimmel, 1984: 112). He found that "fudge factors" and qualitative judgments were needed to adjust the data reported to the system so that "artifacts and radical changes in indicator scores that might result in arbitrary and undesirable intercounty comparisons" could be removed. Kimmel emphasizes:

Data do not speak for themselves. They must be *interpreted*, with all the value-screening, variable inference and supplementary knowledge that normally go into interpretation. PMM systems are *intended* to generate information to induce changes. All PMM systems are thus "political" if only in the small "p" sense of the word.

All PMM systems are amenable to "gaming" by those who supply information on which their own performance is to be gauged. Once the logic (rules) of a system (game) is known, informed judgment (well short of blatant cheating) can be and often is used to generate favorable indicator results [Kimmel, 1984: 115].

Kimmel also reminds us that *"measurability is no index of importance,"* hence, what is left out of such systems is as important—and as political potentially—as what is included.

One way program managers deal with the politics of external demands is by giving reluctant cooperation in establishing management information systems that can be used for external control. More active support for such systems typically occurs when internal information requirements are also met, and when the program manager has substantial control over the system's development (Attkisson and Broskowski, 1984).

THE POLITICS OF MEANING IN SPECIFYING INDICATORS

The standard procedure within the positivist social science tradition for bridging the gap between concepts with theoretical significance and empirical import is to operationally define concepts and meanings so that empirical measures can be used. Within the early applied social science approach and the Lasswellian framework for policy inquiry of the 1950s and 1960s such a procedure for obtaining indicators was at least logically feasible (Kelly, 1986). However, in the 1970s and 1980s the logic undergirding the applied science approach to policy inquiry changed. The change led to downplaying the role of disciplinary and social change theories and models and to enhancing the role of politics in specifying indicators and interpreting their meaning.

Miller (1984) and Lincoln and Guba (1985) among others have

argued that the applied social science approach to policy inquiry has failed. Central to their argument is the assertion that the units of analysis of interest (e.g., cities, HUD programs, agencies) are not comparable across time and space. A substantial portion of the lack of comparability in these units of analysis stem from the impact of politics on the indicators chosen and the meaning given them. For example, in HUD programs political choices made in various localities can determine how benefits will be defined and measured. In one locality a dollar benefit might be the replacement value of particular units. In another the dollar benefit might be defined as the actual cost of the benefit. In other localities economic benefits might have less weight than an indicator of the impact of the housing program on racial integration (Elmer, 1984: 90; see also Sechrest, 1985).

Smith (1984, p. 14) has provided an excellent illustration of how altruistic program officers responding to a survey can corrupt the meaning of an indicator, making it useless for obtaining accurate and comparable information but nonetheless furthering the political goal of obtaining higher funding levels. Agency workers in Colorado apparently believed that adding to the number and severity of cases would bring more money and services to children with learning disabilities. A separate study to verify the agency responses revealed that less than half of the population declared disabled were in fact able to meet minimum standards of disability. Smith (1984: 14) concludes, as Ginsberg (1984) had earlier, "As these categories become corrupted, the possibility of conducting sensible research on the characteristics and origin of learning disabilities or on the efficacy of treatments diminish. In this way . . . bureaucracy is served at the cost of knowledge."

A politics of silence with regard to the meaning of indicators also exists. For example, using housing again, if dollar benefits and number of housing units produced are the main indicators, silence can prevail over how a housing project for the elderly poor was used as a way of avoiding housing for racial minorities.

The implications of the politics of meaning for developing

indicators are substantial. For one thing a better understanding of the way meaning is given to values, goals, and indicators can help clarify why our units of analysis in policy research often are not comparable. The source of the noncomparability might well be due to the politics of meaning rather than to the quality or utility of the logic of social science inquiry underlying the research effort.

The critical importance of politics and intersubjective understandings for the meanings we give to concepts and indicators can be seen from the data gathered by Lipsey et al. (1985: 7-28) on evidence provided on the reliability and validity of program performance and success measures in 122 evaluations conducted between 1978-1980. They found that 70% of the evaluation studies did not mention reliability of the measures; 81% did not discuss validity, and "93% made no mention of the sensitivity of the measures to the expected program effects" (Lipsey et al., 1985: 16). As many as 40% of the success measures were selected ad hoc, with no reference to previous evaluations, a body of theory, or methodological concerns for pretesting or validation. Obviously considerable room exists for political maneuver in the specifying of indicators.

APPLIED SOCIAL SCIENCE
AND THE POLITICS OF MEANING

The prevalence of a politics of meaning in evaluation research and, indeed, in policy inquiry in general is directly related to developments in the logic of inquiry undergirding the applied social science approach to policy analysis and evaluation research. The positivist efforts to separate and compartmentalize values and the more recent effort to make them the heart of the policy inquiry enterprise have led to political rather than theoretical, rational ideological, or empirical determination of meaning for concepts and indicators. The debates over the most appropriate logic of inquiry for evaluation and policy reflect the inability of philosophers and methodologists to address the problems—and the politics—of establishing meanings.

The policy sciences are often viewed as applied social sciences, that is, as forms of social engineering. At its simplest, the applied social science approach has been interpreted to refer to the idea that knowledge accumulated in the various disciplines will be used to improve social programs and policies. Researchers will remain within the disciplinary framework to build theory, test hypotheses, and expand explanatory and predictive power. Applied social scientists can cull through the resulting body of knowledge for ideas and theories applicable to real world problems. This understanding of the relationship of social science to policy is obviously restrictive; it makes the policy analyst dependent on the disciplinary researcher. Applying social science knowledge to the world of action is necessarily slow; the concern for "truth" and the advancement of theory overrides the concern for providing a decision maker the best information possible at a given point in time. The meaning given to terms, referents, and concepts is driven by the developments in the established disciplines.

Harold Lasswell, the founding father of the policy sciences, rejected a narrow instrumental relationship between the social sciences and policy research (Lasswell, 1951). He defined the policy sciences as "The disciplines concerned with explaining the policy-making and policy-executing process, and with locating data and providing interpretations that are relevant to the policy problems of a given period" (1951: 14). He emphasized that pursuing a policy orientation does *not* mean dissipating energy on a variety of topical issues. Rather the policy scientist is to study "fundamental and often neglected problems that arise in the adjustment of man in society" and develop a policy science of democracy. Lasswell argues that having a policy orientation does not mean abandoning objectivity. Nor does it mean reducing an emphasis on theory and model building. According to Lasswell:

> The policy frame of reference makes it necessary to take into account the entire context of significant events (past, present, and prospective) in which the scientist is living. This calls for the use of speculative models of the world revolutionary process of the

epoch, and puts the techniques of quantification in a respected though subordinate place [1951: 14-15].

Meaning is still derived from theory, rationally articulated visions of "the good society," and creative efforts to expand on existing knowledge.

While Lasswell and others (e.g., Dror, 1984) were advancing a broad view of policy inquiry, others in the positivist, behavioral tradition were articulating a more modest but nonetheless major role for the social sciences. Donald Campbell (1971) and James Coleman (1972) were instrumental in linking the social sciences (economics, sociology, psychology, and political science in particular) to the notion of an experimenting society. This society would be scientific not in that it would be based on social science theory, but rather in that it would rely on scientific methods as its evolutionary mechanism. "The relation of the policy sciences to such a society is a relation in which social science theory plays a small and secondary part, but methods of the social sciences play a central part" (Coleman, 1972: 2).

According to Coleman, policy researchers live in two worlds: One is their discipline and the other is the world of action. Their job is to interact between the two, realizing that action-oriented research has a different philosophical base than disciplinary research. The major properties distinguishing policy research from disciplinary research are its concern for timeliness, action, and the use of everyday language and concepts, the ever present involvement of special interests, conflict, and struggle over resources, and a need for redundancy rather than economy of information.

Coleman's (1972) resolution of these differences are all method-ologically and procedurally based. In contrast to Lasswell's (1951) call for more speculative models encompassing entire epochs, Coleman emphasizes statistical models and research design. Moreover, "Models used as the basis for analysis should be relatively simple and robust under conditions of only partially-met assumptions" (1972: 5). He also writes that we must be concerned with policy variables that can be manipulated and to distinguish them from situational variables that may be causally related to outcomes but not manipulable. The general principle being stressed is "For policy research, the ultimate product is not a 'contribution to existing knowledge' in the literature, but a social policy modified by the research results" (1972: 6).

Coleman's emphasis on the scientific method, statistical models and research designs seemed appropriate largely because of the acceptance of the correspondence theory of truth undergirding positivism and assumptions made about reality within the behaviorist framework. In brief, these assumptions were that reality is tangible, separate from the observer, stable over time and space, and fragmentable, with the whole being the sum of its parts. With proper designs, appropriate operational definitions, measuring instruments, and research techniques, reality could be apprehended and linked to extant theories. Reality is viewed as being objective, discernible to skilled researchers, and capable of being interpreted correctly in sentences exhibiting isomorphism between the empirical world and theories about the world. Methodology would protect the researcher from political efforts to distort meaning. Operational definitions would clarify what reality actually is regardless of political intrusions. Value neutrality could be maintained. The policy researcher envisioned by Coleman in the 1970s was self-consciously aware of values but did not necessarily analyze or advance them.

Coleman's approach to policy inquiry was a logical derivation of the liberal epistemological and political tradition. Because it was, over time this approach has contributed greatly to the realization that the liberal world view contains basic contradictions that make the applied social science methodological approach to policy inquiry ethically and intellectually questionable.

THE LIBERAL POSITIVIST WORLD VIEW

Liberalism is a mind-set, a weltanschauung that has developed incrementally as a result of three centuries of reflection and action based on a few original thinkers, among them Hobbes, Locke, Smith, and Hume. These thinkers laid the foundations for many of the contradictions in liberal epistemology affecting policy inquiry in the 1980s. The basic epistemological contradictions influencing policy inquiry, particularly the applied social science methodological approach, are those existing (1) between theory and fact (arising from modern ideas about science and nature), (2) between reason and desire (representing the core of liberal psychology), and (3) between rules and values (on which liberal political structures are built). The basic political contradiction facing policy researchers is that the Hobbesian notions of freedom and sovereignty are inherently undemocratic.

THE CONTRADICTION
BETWEEN THEORY AND FACT

Evaluation research began as an applied form of social science developed within the positivist empirical tradition. Empirical science from this perspective needs to make the assumption that an order of real things exists that is independent of the mind and capable of objective assessment, regardless of an observer's biases. Yet the liberal philosophical tradition also requires that all facts be mediated through theory. Though theories are to be tested by determining what is empirically true, theories can never be proven to be true. They can be falsified only after numerous replications showing repeated nonconformance between fact and theory. However, since communication among scientists requires consistency of concepts and relative comparability among measures that must come from the theory, the theoretical reference continually structures and shapes the order of real things that we study, those very empirical entities that we use to confirm the objectivity of our conclusions. A major element of the liberal epistemological world view is the Kantian assumption that there is "an all-embracing ahistorical context in which every other species of discourse could be assigned its proper place and rank" (Rorty, 1982: 161). Put simply, fact has no existence separate from theory in liberal epistemology. Therefore, to deny a significant role for theory in policy research (as is the current mode) means denying a basic premise of the liberal world view.

To be logically consistent in such a denial and to also retain a viable logic of inquiry one would need to construct an alternative justification and understanding of "fact" and how facts can be related to knowledge and the use of generalizations and projections to the future. (Lincoln and Guba in *Naturalistic Inquiry* (1985) appear to be attempting to do this.)

Coleman did not construct an alternative justification. He merely assumed that methodological rigor along with the constancy of nature itself (part of the correspondence theory of truth) would suffice. By the 1980s many of the assumptions undergirding Coleman's approach had been rejected. Cronbach (1982) and Miller (1984), among others, pointed out that generalizations have not held over time and space; and that the large-scale, highly funded studies that were supposed to produce solutions to society's problems by means of large sample sizes, sophisticated methodologies, and the inclusion of large numbers of variables simply did not do so. Campbell (1984: 35, italics in the original) bemoaned the "*gross overvaluing of, and financial investments in, external validity*, in the sense of representative samples at the nationwide level" and he condemned even more strongly definitional operationalism calling it "positivism's worst gift to the social sciences" (Campbell, 1984: 27). There is no longer the same confidence that behavioral methods can ensure objectivity and enable the observer to assess reality reliably and validly, thereby making generalizations and linkage with theories possible.

In the 1980s the philosophical foundations for determining what is objective reality have become fuzzy. Donald Campbell (1984: 27) describes the current situation as follows:

> This rejection (of logical positivism), in which I have participated, has left our theory of science in disarray. Under some interpretations it has undermined our determination to be scientific and our faith that validity and truth are rational and reasonable goals.

THE ANTINOMY OF REASON AND DESIRE

The liberal view of the relationship between reason and desire is based on three principles: that reason and desire are separate, that desires are arbitrary, and that knowledge is acquired by the combination of elementary sensations and ideas (Unger, 1975: 30). Within the liberal world view what distinguishes humans from each other is not that they understand the world differently, but that they desire different things even when they share a common understanding of the world. From this perspective our choices are arbitrary, that is, unable to be discerned or controlled by the dictates of reason. Reason is only instrumental, serving to select among a myriad of choices those ones that advance individual desires and goals. Within the positivist and even the postpositivist logic of policy inquiry the role of the analyst or researcher is to use rational criteria to select the most efficient means to a predetermined desired end.

This liberal contradiction of reason and desire has been the source of the emphasis on efficiency and rationality as the central thrust of policy inquiry. The rejection of the value neutral approach rests on a rejection of this instrumental means-end relationship between reason and desire (interests and values). Much of the controversy over which logic of inquiry is best is linked to the search for a more just, more equitable, and more fair democratic society. Most of the recent approaches insist that reason can assess and determine which value is superior in particular contexts—equity or efficiency, freedom or order, responsiveness or control, representativeness or merit, meeting changing human needs or protecting established programs and agencies.

THE ANTINOMY OF RULES AND VALUES

Within Liberalism, values are simply the visible, public side of desire. Self-interest dominates. Rules are separate from values. We may value what we will, but we must obey the law, those rules that facilitate the social order. Thus though there is nothing in principle that can make one person's or group's values worthier than others, the expectation, the norm, that the law will be followed, weights both liberal thought and liberal political systems—and discipline and policy paradigms developed within the liberal philosophical tradition—in favor of "the Establishment" and in favor of those who got there first.

The effort to separate and compartmentalize values in the policy inquiry enterprise has, as Scriven (1984) has noted, promoted a managerial and relativist ideology. These ideologies are most compatible with the value neutrality notions of logical positivism. In evaluations, for example, the goal-achievement evaluation model permits passing value judgments back to program managers and governmental policymakers who in turn can pass responsibility back to legislators. By focusing on the effectiveness of the means to attain ends specified by others, researchers are able to convince themselves that they are maintaining their value neutrality (Scriven, 1984). In the late 1960s and the early 1970s such value neutrality was considered an appropriate professional norm. By the 1980s this positivistic position had come to be roundly condemned by many not only as an unethical abdication of moral responsibility by social scientists, but also as illogical and philosophically wrong (Scriven, 1984).

THE POLITICAL CONTRADICTION

The basic contradictions within liberal epistemology along with the efforts to resolve them reveal the political contradictions of Hobbesian liberalism. Hobbes posited numerous positions that undergird assumptions made by policy analysts and evaluation researchers about the nature of politics and how truth and power are interrelated.

Hobbes' assumption that individuals enter the world alone and are inherently separate from each other lays the groundwork for theories of egoism, interest group politics, and pluralism. From the Hobbesian perspective, free persons are estranged from each other. A basic political problem for Hobbes is how to bridge individualities (Hummel, 1985), how to bring peace and order among hostile beings who have no "natural" way of determining whose values should dominate. Hobbes' solution was to establish a government based on a social contract that specifies the processes by which the rulers and the ruled will be determined.

A central problem facing democratic societies attempting to function within the Hobbesian liberal framework is that problems quickly come to be defined and analyzed from the standpoint and perspective primarily of those who dominate, of those who are most capable of getting what they want when, where, and how they want it. The ontological assumptions of separate individuals along with liberal positivist epistemology and emphasis on methodological individualism permit the elite and their representatives to claim they can define reality and to defend the assertion that their definitions of reality are accurate and valid; that they are *truth*. The politics of meaning so evident in evaluation research seems appropriate from this Hobbesian perspective.

Hobbesian liberalism leads to the idea that freedom and rational choice can be equated with the power to dictate and command. As Hannah Arendt (1968) has noted, it leads to the notion that freedom can be reduced to sovereignty. Those with sovereignty are free; those without it are not. Sovereigns can delegate their authority to those who will do their bidding. As the chain of progression develops, delegated decision making by bureaucrats and political appointees replaces political dialogue not only by citizens as sovereigns but also by elected representatives as sovereigns. Policy analysts and researchers come to see themselves as instruments of the powerful, skilled in the methods that will identify the rational way to attain the goals set by the powerful. The managerial and relativist ideologies become ways of avoiding the epistemological contradictions of liberalism. They cannot, however, avoid the political contradiction that such assumptions are inherently undemocratic and ultimately reduce the freedom and potential for rational choice of the citizenry.

POSTPOSITIVIST EFFORTS TO ADDRESS THE CONTRADICTIONS OF LIBERALISM

The responses to the crisis in the applied social science approach to policy inquiry have varied. Some, such as Majchrzak (1984), have tried to retain the essence of the approach by recognizing that policy inquiry is part craft lore and art as well as an applied science. According to Majchrzak, policy research is distinctive in that it is multidimensional in focus, uses an empirico-inductive research orientation rather than a hypothesis testing approach, incorporates the future as well as the past, responds to study users, and explicitly incorporates values into the research process. No disciplinary theory or ideology about the relationship of cause and effect guides applied policy research. "Instead, the researcher engages in an iterative process whereby information and model building are constantly interchanged. This type of research approach has been termed by some as the "grounded theory" approach to research (Majchrzak, 1984: 19). Tangible reality is still accessible to the appropriately trained researcher, but value neutrality and the application of time- and context-free generalizations from a body of substantive theory are less frequently and less strongly asserted.

MULTIPLISM

The attack on positivism and the lessons of research conducted on Lyndon Johnson's Great Society programs have led Cook (1985) to multiplism to justify and guide the applied social science approach to policy inquiry. "The fundamental postulate of multiplism is that when it is not clear which of several options for question generation or method choice is 'correct,' all of them should be selected so as to 'triangulate' on the most useful or the most likely to be true" (Cook, 1985: 38). Multiple measures allow examining the comparability of findings from several different measures and modes of measurements (e.g., using pen-and-paper tests, personal interviews, or unobtrusive measures). If the multiple measures produce similar results, replication is demonstrated and alternative interpretations can be eliminated. Multiplism rests on the notion that the reality being studied can be perceived in multiple ways. While reality is tangible and observable, what is measured is perceived reality.

According to Cook, multiplism also helps specify causal contingencies, enabling the researcher to identify time and space limitations of relationships. Cook (1985: 40-41) recognizes that

"Although realist, the operational ontology of most social scientists differs from the positivist's world of parsimonious, deterministic, ahistorical, and nonmentalist forces. . . . Statistical main effects will not describe this world as well as higher-order statistical interactions. . . . Postpositivist social science cares more than its predecessors for heterogeneous sampling and data analyses that examine the degree of dependability achieved across subpopulations." Because the resources are not always available to do this multiple sampling and analyses required by multiplism, literature reviews and metaanalyses of several studies are recommended. No one single study, even carefully designed true experiments, can claim to have found truth. Returning to a Lasswellian notion, Cook (1985: 44) justifies using qualitative data from multiple stakeholders as a way of advancing a pluralist democracy.

Cook (1985: 42) also revises the positivist notion of the purpose of testing causal models. "With causal explanatory models, the advocacy is to pit multiple models in competition with each other rather than to test the goodness of fit of a single model. . . . When multiple explanatory models are explicitly pitted against each other, the aim is to see which one is superior rather than which one is necessarily 'true'."

Multiplism is clearly an advance over earlier methodology. It places multiple causal models in competition with each other. It uses multiple constructs, multiple measures of each construct, multiple types of constructs—mentalist and historical as well as empirical—and examines the fit of the models to the data and interpretations multiple times. In addition, qualitative data are systematically gathered to help set research priorities, describe, discover, explain, and communicate the study's results and to provide the context for interpreting the information, that is, to ground the knowledge.

Multiplism is postpositivist. It breaks away from the correspondence theory of truth and moves to a consensus theory of truth. Cook (1985: 45) readily admits to the change. "Social science is concerned, not with guaranteeing truth or utility, but with offering defensible interpretations of what is in the outside world." Given this ambiguity, democracy requires that multiple investigators conduct analyses of the data so that rival plausible interpretations will be disclosed. Research on critical national policy issues requires multiple value perspectives and multiple metaanalyses "to identify commonalities of findings and interpretation through processes that rigorously attempt to falsify all the claims made about knowledge and utility" (Cook, 1985: 46).

The movement away from the correspondence theory of truth is linked to changing perceptions of reality. Lasswell's policy science and Coleman's applied science approach to policy inquiry assume a tangible reality existing separate from humans. Cook's multiplism reflects a sharp drop in confidence in these assumptions, and from other logic of inquiry perspectives even this concern for realism is not meaningful.

THE RATIONAL IDEOLOGY APPROACH

Paris and Reynolds (1983) present a more dramatic alternative to the applied social science approach. They put "rational ideologies" at the heart of policy inquiry. The policy argument, the "reasons for the adoption of a policy" (1983: 3), determine the shape and course of policy inquiry. Analysis from this rational ideology perspective does not focus on cause-effect relationships so much as it focuses on exploring the premises of the policy argument.

From the rational ideology stance of Paris and Reynolds (1983), the positivist concern for a stable, constant, empirical reality that is external from the observer is of no great significance. A perception of truth as being eternal and objective has little significance in their logic of policy inquiry. The truth sought within the rational ideological perspective also relies on a consensus theory of truth. With the rational ideology approach empirical legitimacy comes from rating alternative policy arguments. Truth resides in the eye of the beholder as much as it resides in the argument or findings themselves. This methodology is also similar in basic ways to philology or hermeneutics in the humanities, in which scholars persistently explore the meaning of a phrase or text for a particular period of time (Campbell, 1984). Consensus on meaning rather than agreement about objective truth is the goal.

Miller's (1984) design science and Lincoln and Guba's (1985) naturalist inquiry approaches reject the postpositivist as well as the positivist assumptions about reality. Both assume reality is created or constructed by humans.

DESIGN SCIENCE

The design science approach has recently been proposed by Miller (1984), but goes back to Simon's (1969) notion that design is a tool not only for acting, but also for understanding. As with Lasswell's (1951) policy science, design sciences requires the conscious articulation of a desired state or goal. The goal posited by Miller (1984) is improved public sector performance. Miller rejects the positivist notion of value neutrality and the assumptions that there are deterministic laws governing human behavior that are beyond human control and that "the units of analysis in social systems are highly similar over time and space" (1984: 262).

In Miller's thesis the empirical reality explored by policy inquiry is largely made by humans; it is not "natural" and autonomous as the phenomena studied in the physical sciences tend to be. It is subject to incremental and qualitative change, and it is diverse at its core. It is not consistent over time and space. As a consequence, our models and specification of variables are incomplete. Things and people change, with events overtaking our articulation of policy options. Our data are inadequate or inappropriate for the questions raised and problems addressed. Moreover, human beings are not passive but rather impose their own will and meanings on events and problems. Humans and the entities they create, such as cities, institutions, programs, governments, and agencies, do not remain static. They are not passive units whose content is to be analyzed by others. They change; their social, economic and political contexts change; and as they do, comparability of our units of analysis disappear (Miller, 1984). Moreover, we cannot separate ourselves from the phenomena being studied (also see Scriven, 1984). We interact with it, and because humans are involved, reality is willfully reshaped. The resulting variations in our units of analysis make generalizations unreliable and invalid.

Design science stresses creation over observation. In Miller's judgment, neither physical nor social scientists any longer simply observe and identify patterns of behavior that can be extrapolated to the future. Rather, by their very observations and interventions, scientists increasingly alter basic structures. Since the basic structures (the patterns of relations and relationships) are altered, extrapolations to the future based on extant social science methodology are not possible. It follows that the hypotheses of design science are not generalizations or predictions about current behavior but are assertions that new levels of performance can be attained and diffused under the right conditions (Miller, 1984: 262).

NATURALISTIC INQUIRY

Lincoln and Guba (1985) present the most radical alternative to the applied science approach. They argue that there is only a constructed reality, a reality that is multiple and holistic, existing essentially in the minds of individuals. Positivism and postpositivism are rejected. Only ideographic statements specifying particular times, particular spaces, and particular contexts are possible. Value neutrality is rejected, as is the notion of causality. "All entities are in a state of multiple simultaneous shaping, so that it is impossible to distinguish causes from effects" (Lincoln and Guba, 1985: 37).

The fourteen characteristics of the naturalistic inquiry posited by Lincoln and Guba include focusing on research in natural rather than in experimental settings so the holistic reality can be apprehended; using humans rather than survey instruments as the data gathering devices; using intuitive, felt, tacit knowledge to reflect "more fairly and accurately the value patterns of the investigator"; using qualitative rather than quantitative methodologies; using purposive rather than random, representative sampling; conducting inductive rather than deductive data analyses; using grounded rather than a priori substantive theory; using emergent research designs; negotiating analysis outcomes with the subjects so their meanings and constructions of reality will be incorporated in the final report; reporting results in the case study mode rather than in scientific or technical reports; interpreting data ideographically, not nomothetically (i.e., not in lawlike generalizations); applying findings only tentatively, limiting the study, interpretations, and applications to boundaries determined by the particular study's focus; and finally, using new criteria for judging the trustworthiness of the data. These new criteria are credibility, transferability, dependability, and confirmability.

Internal validity, according to Lincoln and Guba (1985: 43), is inappropriate "because it implies an isomorphism between research outcomes and a single, tangible reality on to which inquiry can converge." External validity also is rejected by them because it assumes "absolute stability and replicability." Objectivity is rejected because values are inherent in all inquiry and the observer interacts with the observed. Within the naturalistic inquiry approach truth is established by dialectical discourse when consensus exists among participating parties.

COMMONALITIES AMONG
THE DIFFERENT APPROACHES

Though the new approaches of the 1980s to policy inquiry differ markedly from each other, as already noted, they nonetheless have much in common. Some of the commonalities include the following: (a) Values are seen as being intimately and properly involved in social science research and policy inquiry. (b) Grounded theory rising from the phenomenological tradition is a vital part of policy inquiry. (c) Qualitative analyses are considered essential to establish the context and boundaries of the inquiry. (d) The correspondence theory of truth is rejected by all new approaches described, and a consensus theory of truth is being scientific for it. (e) Among those still concerned about the scientific study of social phenomena, the model of science emphasizing prediction and control of the physical world is being replaced with a model that stresses contingency and chance. (f) There is more explicit recognition in each of the described approaches of a sense of responsibility for consciously promoting an improved democracy as well as improving a particular program.

These commonalities reflect a basic shift from the logic of policy inquiry existing in the early 1970s. The boundaries of discourse have definitely been altered. Much work, however, remains to be done before a fully satisfactory logic of policy inquiry is elaborated. A major problem, for example, exists in the shift to a consensual theory of truth. Intersubjective consensus alone is insufficient for establishing truth. There was a consensus among the Nazis that was not advantageous to the world. Linking the consensus theory to defensible goals established for society, such as developing a policy science of democracy, might help prevent gross, unethical aberrations, but care would need to be taken to ensure that a particular vision or ethic of the good society and best political system does not become the test of truth. Procedural and methodological requirements are also needed.

Postpositivist multiplism, design science, and naturalistic inquiry attempt to address the liberal epistemological contradictions embedded in the applied social science methodological approach to policy inquiry. Multiplism and naturalistic inquiry, in particular, assume that humans understand the world differently from each other, and that perceptions reflect these different understandings. Values are no longer viewed as simply public forms of private desires. Methodologies are being proposed to cope systematically with the numerous ways politics impacts meaning in policy inquiry.

The recent developments in the logic of policy inquiry suggest that considerable questioning of the viability of accepting the contradictions inherent in the liberal world view is occurring. The liberal epistemological relationship between theory and fact, reason and desire, rules and values are being challenged. The development of these revised logics of inquiry are not likely to stop questioning the liberal assumptions of our society and thought processes however.

In my judgment, multiplism and naturalistic inquiry are developing in part because a paradigm shift is occurring in our understanding of politics as well as in our understanding of how best to seek truth and usable knowledge. The operations of particular politics of meaning and the meaning of politics are connected.

Politics and policy inquiry are intertwined. Once we have replaced the positivistic foundations of the applied social science approach to policy inquiry with postpositivist multiplism or with naturalistic inquiry have we not also assumed a new type of politics? In my opinion we are moving away from a Hobbesian understanding of politics. While my crystal ball does not enable me to see precisely what we are replacing this understanding with, these new logics of inquiry seem to me to be quite compatible with developing notions of a society of individuals with shared, balanced interests rather than separable, hostile, competitive interests ala Thomas Hobbes (Hummel, 1985).

AN ALTERNATIVE
POLITICAL UNDERSTANDING

From the perspective of politics based on individuals as cobeings with shared interests, public space encompasses all humans. Freedom is constituted and protected in the public interaction of citizens addressing mutually defined problems and challenges. Freedom becomes more than a limited notion of choice related to predetermined ends or the negative restrictions placed on governmental intrusions into private space. Both freedom and caring for our cobeings (the nature of our being) require a political dialogue. This dialogue constitutes the source of democratic action and the interactive dynamic of political communication in a public space among peers (Hummel, 1985).

If the policy sciences are to be developed, and if freedom is to be promoted within and by those sciences, then power must be viewed within the framework of interactive politics and the dialogue of human cobeings with a capacity for contingent action, the capacity to begin new processes, change old ones, and create alternatives.

The assumptions of a politics of caring, of cobeing, and multiple yet shared perspectives of reality and values are compatible with postpositivist multiplism, rational ideologies, design science, and even naturalistic inquiry. They are more compatible than Hobbesian assumptions. Perhaps the fundamental shifts that we see in the various logics of policy inquiry being offered portend a more basic paradigm shift of our understanding of the nature of politics itself.

At the moment our methodological foundations for policy inquiry are moving ahead of our ontological understandings of politics and human nature. One consequence of this anomaly is that when the politics of meaning is not recognized in our evaluations and inquiries, elites or their surrogates dominate. Neither truth nor democracy is served.

REFERENCES

Attkisson, C. C. and A. Broskowski (1984) "Human Service Information Systems," pp. 20-24 in C. Windle (ed.) Program Performance Measurement: Demands, Technology, and Dangers. National Institute of Mental Health. Series BN No. 5. DHHS Pub. No. (ADM) 84-1357. Washington, DC: Government Printing Office.

Campbell, D. T. (1971) "Methods for the Experimenting Society." Presented at the meeting of the American Psychological Association, Washington, DC, September.

Campbell, D. T. (1979) "Assessing the Impact of Planned Social Change." Evaluation and Program Planning 2: 67-90.

Campbell, D. T. (1984) "Can We Be Scientific in Applied Social Science," pp. 26-48 in R. F. Conner, D. G. Altman, and C. Jackson (eds.), Evaluation Studies Review Annual 9. Newbury Park, CA: Sage.

Coleman, J. S. (1972) Policy Research in the Social Sciences. Morristown, NJ: General Learning.

Cook, T. D. (1985) "Postpositivist Critical Multiplism," pp. 21-62 in R. L. Shotland and M. M. Mark (eds.) Social Science and Social Policy. Newbury Park, CA: Sage.

Cronbach, L. J. (1982) "Prudent Aspirations for Social Inquiry," in W. Kruskal (ed.), The Social Sciences: Their Nature and Uses. Chicago: Univ. of Chicago Press.

Dror, Y. (1984) "On Becoming More of a Policy Scientist." Policy Studies Rev. 4, 1: 13-21.

Easton, D. (1953) The Political System: An Inquiry into the State of Political Science. New York: Knopf.

Elmer, V. (1984) "Performance Indicators in Housing," pp. 84-93 in C. Windle (ed.) Program Performance Measurement: Demands, Technology, and Dangers. National Institute of Mental Health, Series BN No. 5. DHHS Pub. No. (ADM) 84-1357.

Washington, DC: Government Printing Office.

Frohock, F. M. (1978) "The Structure of 'Politics.' " Amer. Pol. Sci. Rev. 72: 859-870.

Ginsberg, P. (1984) "Dysfunctional Potentials of Performance Measurement," pp. 67-72 in C. Windle (ed.) Program Performance Measurement: Demands, Technology, and Dangers. National Institute of Mental Health. Series BN No. 5. DHHS Pub. No. (ADM) 84-1357. Washington, DC: Government Printing Office.

Hart, H.L.A. (1961) The Concept of Law, Oxford: Clarendon.

Hummel, R. (1985) "Politics: The Problem of Reality as the Problem of Politics." Institute for Applied Phenomenology, Spruce Head Island, ME. (unpublished)

Kelly, R. M. (1980) "Ideology, Effectiveness, and Public Sector Productivity: with Illustrations from the Field of Higher Education." J. of Social Issues 36: 76-95.

Kelly, R. M. (1986) "Trends in the Logic of Policy Inquiry: A Comparison of Approaches and a Commentary. Policy Studies Rev. (February) 5, 3 .

Kimmel, W. A. (1984) "State Mental Health Program Performance Measurement: Selected Impressions from Three States," pp. 108-116 in C. Windle (ed.), Program Performance Measurement: Demands, Technology, and Dangers. Institute of Mental Health. Series BN No. 5. DHHS Pub. No. (ADM) 84-1357. Washington, DC: Government Printing Office.

Lasswell, H. D. (1951) "The Policy Orientation," pp. 3-15 in D. Lerner and H. D. Lasswell (eds.) The Policy Sciences. CA: Stanford Univ. Press.

Lincoln, Y. S. and E. G. Guba (1985) Naturalistic Inquiry. Newbury Park, CA: Sage.

Lipsey, M. W., S. Crosse, J. Dunkle, J. Pollard, and G. Stobart (1985) "Evaluation: The State of the Art and the Sorry State of the Science," pp. 7-28 in D. S. Cordray (ed.) New Directions in Program Evaluation: Utilizing Prior Research in Evaluation Planning 27. San Francisco: Jossey-Bass.

Majchrzak, A. (1984) Methods for Policy Research. Newbury Park, CA: Sage.

McAuliffe, W. E. (1984) "Measuring the Quality of Medical Care: Process Versus Outcome." pp. 25-36 in C. Windle (ed.) Program Performance Measurement: Demands, Technology, and Dangers. National Institute of Mental Health. Series BN No. 5. DHHS Pub. No. (ADM) 84-1357. Washington, DC: Government Printing Office.

McCleary, R. (1984) "Worker Artifacts as a Source of Spurious Statistics." Evaluation and Program Planning 7: 23-24.

Miller, T. C. (1984) "Conclusion: A Design Science Perspective," pp. 261-279 in T. Miller (ed.) Public Sector Performance. Baltimore, MD: Johns Hopkins Univ. Press.

Paris, D. C. and J. F. Reynolds (1983) The Logic of Policy Inquiry. New York: Longman.

Rorty, R. (1982) "Pragmatism, Relativism, and Irrationalism," pp. 160-75 in Consequences of Pragmatism Minneapolis: Univ. of Minnesota Press.

Scriven, M. (1984) "Evaluation Ideologies," pp. 49-80 in R. F. Conner, D. G. Altman, and C. Jackson (eds.) Evaluation Studies Review Annual 9. Newbury Park, CA: Sage.

Sechrest, L. (1985) "Social Science and Social Policy: Will Our Numbers Ever Be Good Enough?" pp. 63-95 in R. L. Shotland and M. M. Mark (eds.) Social Science and Social Policy. Newbury Park, CA: Sage.

Simon, H. A. (1969) The Sciences of the Artificial. Cambridge: MIT Press.

Smith, M. L. (1984) "Distorted Indicators in Special Education." Evaluation and Program Planning 7: 13-14.

Stoddard, S. (1984) "Developing Performance Standards and Measures in Vocational Rehabilitation," (pp. 25-36) in C. Windle (ed.) Program Performance Measurement:

Demands, Technology, and Dangers. National Institute of Mental Health. Series BN No. 5. DHHS Pub. No. (ADM) 84-1357. Washington, DC: Government Printing Office.

Unger, R. (1975) Knowledge and Politics. New York: Free Press.

Windle, C. and H. Keppler-Seid (1984) "Introduction: A Model for Implementing Performance Measurement," in C. Windle (ed.) Program Performance Measurement: Demands, Technology, and Dangers. National Institute of Mental Health. Series BN No. 5. DHHS Pub. No. (ADM) 84-1357. Washington, DC: Government Printing Office.

Zedlewski, E. W. (1984) "Social Performance in an Engineering Framework: The LEAA Experience." in C. Windle (ed.) Program Performance Measurement: Demands, Technology, and Dangers. National Institute of Mental Health. Series BN No. 5. DHHS Pub. No. (ADM) 84-1357). Washington, DC: Government Printing Office.

NAME INDEX

SUBJECT INDEX

ABOUT THE AUTHORS

Angela Browne is a Lecturer in the School of Social Welfare and School of Public Policy at the University of California at Berkeley.

Eleanor Chelimsky is Director of the U. S. General Accounting Office's Program Evaluation and Methodology Division. She came to the GAO from the MITRE Corporation. She is a former Fulbright Scholar, past president of the Evaluation Research Society, and was the recipient of the Evaluation Research Society's 1982 Myrdal Award for Government.

Peter DeLeon is a Professor in the Graduate School of Public Affairs at the University of Colorado at Denver. He teaches policy courses in Columbia's Graduate Program in Public Policy and Administration and is the author of several books and articles on the policy process.

Egon G. Guba is a Professor of Education at Indiana University. His major interests lie in the area of developing naturalistic methodology as well as in the theory of evolution. He is coauthor of a recently published book, *Naturalistic Inquiry* (Sage, 1985).

Helen M. Ingram is a Professor of Political Science at the University of Arizona. Her areas of expertise include water and natural resource policy. She is the current president of the Policy Studies Organization and is the treasurer of the American Political Science Association. Dr. Ingram is the author of many books on public policy, especially water policy. Among her publications is the coauthored book *Saving Water in a Desert City*, and (with Dean Mann), *Why Policies Succeed or Fail.*

Rita Mae Kelly is Professor of Justice Studies at Arizona State University. Her latest book is *Promoting Productivity in the Public Sector: Strategies, Problems, and Prospects* (MacMillan, 1986). She currently is editing a symposium on pay equity for the *Policy Studies Review* and working on a book entitled *Gender, Subjective Culture, and Ideology: a Study of Delegates at the 1984 Republican and Democratic Conventions.*

Yvonna S. Lincoln is Associate Professor of Education at Vanderbilt University. She holds the baccalaureate degree in history and sociology from Michigan State University (1967), the master's degree in history from the University of Illinois (1970), and the doctorate in higher education, organizational theory, and program evaluation from Indiana University (1977). She has served on the faculty of Stephens College and taught at Indiana University and the University of Kansas.

Dennis J. Palumbo is Professor of Justice Studies at Arizona State University. His most recent book is *Public Policy in America: Government in Action.* He currently is working on a book titled *The Process of Policy Innovation.* He is editor of the *Policy Studies Review.*

Michael Quinn Patton is a social scientist at the University of Minnesota. He is the author of four evaluation books from Sage: *Utilization-Focused Evaluation* (1986); *Practical Evaluation* (1982); *Qualitative Evaluation Methods* (1980); and *Creative Evaluation* (1981). He is extensively involved in conducting training and speaking on evaluation. He was the 1984 recipient of the Myrdal Award from the Evaluation Research Society for "outstanding contributions to evaluation practice and use."

Lawrence A. Scaff (Ph.D., University of California at Berkeley, 1971) is Associate Professor of Political Science at the University of Arizona. He has published work in the field of political and social theory. He has been a visiting scholar at the University of Dusseldorf and the University of Freiburg, where he held a Fulbright Fellowship.

Susan J. Tolchin is on the faculty at George Washington University as Professor of Public Administration. A nationally recognized expert in American government and politics, she has written many articles and books, including: *Dismantling America—The Rush to Deregulate* (Houghton Mifflin, 1983), Oxford University paperbound edition, 1985; *Clout—Womanpower and Politics* (Coward, McCann & Geohegan, 1974); and *To The Victor—Political Patronage from the Clubhouse to the White House* (Random House, 1971). Her works have been widely cited in newspapers and journals, as well as in two Supreme Court decisions. She is currently at work on a book on the politics of foreign investment in the United States.

Aaron Wildavsky is a Professor of Political Science and Public Policy at the University of California at Berkeley.

Carol H. Weiss is a sociologist on the faculty of the Harvard Graduate School of Education. She wrote two books on evaluation research in the 1970s, *Evaluation Research* and *Evaluation Action Programs*, as well as a score of journal articles. Since that time she has studied ways in which decision makers use (or fail to use) research and evaluation reports, and has published many articles and two books, *Using Social Research in Public Policy Making* and *Social Science Research* and *Decision-Making*. Most recently she has studied the channels through which findings from research and evaluation travel, including the mass media (*Reporting of Social Science in the Media*, forthcoming), and Congress-focused issue networks.

NOTES

NOTES

NOTES

DATE DUE

SEP 1 9 REC'D			